8 RULES OF LOVE

8 RULES OF LOVE

How to Find it, Keep it, and Let it Go

JAY SHETTY

Thorsons

Thorsons
An imprint of HarperCollins*Publishers*
1 London Bridge Street
London SE1 9GF

www.harpercollins.co.uk

HarperCollins*Publishers*
Macken House, 39/40 Mayor Street Upper
Dublin 1, D01 C9W8, Ireland

First published in the US by Simon & Schuster 2023
This UK edition published by Thorsons 2023

1 3 5 7 9 10 8 6 4 2

© Jay R. Shetty 2023

Jay R. Shetty asserts the moral right to be
identified as the author of this work

A catalogue record of this book is
available from the British Library

ISBN 978-0-00-860294-9

SELF - HELP / RELATIONSHIPS

Printed and bound in India by Thomson Press India Ltd.

This book is produced from independently certified FSC® paper
to ensure responsible forest management.

For more information visit: www.harpercollins.co.uk/green

To my mum, for teaching me
how to love endlessly

To my sister, for teaching me
how to love unconditionally

To my wife, for teaching me
how to love actually

Contents

Introduction   1

PART 1: SOLITUDE

Rule 1: Let Yourself Be Alone   15
Rule 2: Don't Ignore Your Karma   38

Love Letter to Yourself   70
Meditation for Solitude   72

PART 2: COMPATIBILITY

Rule 3: Define Love Before You Think It,   77
      Feel It, or Say It
Rule 4: Your Partner Is Your Guru   100
Rule 5: Purpose Comes First   125

Love Letter to Your Partner   161
Meditation for Compatibility   163

PART 3: HEALING

Rule 6: Win or Lose Together   167
Rule 7: You Don't Break in a Breakup   199

Love Letter to Help You Heal   241
Meditation to Heal Through Love   243

PART 4: CONNECTION

Rule 8: Love Again and Again   247

Love Letter to The World   267
Meditation to Connect   269

Acknowledgments   271
Author's Note   273
Notes   275
Next Steps   295
Index   297

Introduction

"What is the difference between like and love?" asks a student. The teacher responds, "When you like a flower, you pluck it. When you love a flower, you water it daily." This frequently cited dialogue illustrates one of my favorite ideas about love. We are attracted to beauty—we long for it—and want it for our own. This is the flower that we pluck and enjoy. But attraction, like a cut flower, eventually withers, and we discard it. When attraction develops into love, it requires more care. When we want to keep a flower alive, we don't cut it and put it in a vase. We give it sunlight, soil, and water. And it's only when you care for a flower over time, doing your best to keep it alive, that you fully experience its beauty—the freshness, the color,

LIKE   **LOVE**

the scent, the bloom. You notice the delicate detail on each petal. You watch it respond to the seasons. You find joy and satisfaction when a new bud appears and feel a thrill when it blossoms.

We are drawn to love as we are drawn to a flower—first by its beauty and allure—but the only way we can keep it alive is through consistent care and attention. Love is a daily effort. I want to develop the habit of love with you in this book. I'll introduce you to practices, mindsets, and tools that will help you love in a way that brings daily rewards, season after season.

It has been said that the greatest pursuit of human life is to love and to be loved. We believe in love—it's in our nature to be drawn to love stories, to long for one of our own, and to hope that true love is possible. But many of us also know what it feels like to be a flower that's been cut and stuck in water, only to wilt and lose our bloom. Maybe you've felt that way, or maybe you've cut and discarded a few flowers in your time. Or maybe you haven't found love yet and are still looking. These disappointments might come in different forms: Believing you were in love, then feeling misled. Thinking it was love, only to find it was lust. Being certain it was love, but discovering it was a lie. Expecting love to last, but watching it fade. Maybe we fear commitment, or choose people who do, or set our standards too high and don't give people a chance. Maybe an ex is still on our minds, or maybe we've just had a run of bad luck. Instead of falling for false promises or unfulfilling partners, instead of feeling defeated or hopeless, instead of getting your heart broken, I want you to experience the expansive love that you hope exists.

|||||||

Romantic love is at once familiar and complex. It has been seen and described in infinite ways across time and cultures. Psychologist Tim Lomas, a lecturer in the Human Flourishing Program at Harvard University, analyzed fifty languages and identified fourteen unique kinds of love. The ancient Greeks said there were seven basic types: *Eros*, which is sexual or passionate love; *Philia*, or friendship; *Storge*, or familial love; *Agape*, which is universal love; *Ludus*, which is casual or noncommittal love; *Pragma*, which is based on duty or other interests; and *Philautia*, which is self-love. An analysis of Chinese literature from five hundred to three thousand years old reveals many forms of love, from passionate and obsessive love to devoted love, to casual love. In the Tamil language, there are more than fifty words for various kinds and nuances of love, such as *love as grace, love within a fulfilling relationship*, and *a melting inside due to a feeling of love*. In Japanese, the term *koi no yokan* describes the sensation of meeting someone new and feeling that you are destined to fall in love with them, and *kokuhaku* describes a declaration of loving commitment. In India's Boro language, *onsra* describes the knowledge that a relationship will fade.

Our own culture describes love in numerous ways. If we look at the Billboard Top 50 Love Songs of All Time, we are told that love is a secondhand emotion (Tina Turner), love is a roller coaster (Ohio Players), love is a hangover (Diana Ross), love is a crazy little thing (Queen), love's got Beyoncé looking so crazy right now, and Leona Lewis keeps bleeding love. Movies idealize love, but we rarely find out what happens after happily ever after. With so many perspectives and portraits and parables of love surrounding us every day, I want this book to help you create your own definition of love and develop the skills to practice and enjoy that love every day.

||||||||

When I was twenty-one years old, I skipped my college graduation to join an ashram in a village near Mumbai. I spent three years there as a Hindu monk, meditating, studying ancient scriptures, and volunteering alongside my fellow monks.

The oldest Hindu scriptures we studied are called the Vedas. They were written on palm leaves in Sanskrit more than five thousand years ago. Most of the palm leaves no longer exist, but the texts have survived. Some of them are even online. Their presence and relevance in the modern world always amaze and inspire me. I've been studying the Vedas for sixteen years now, and for the three years I lived as a monk I studied them deeply. When I saw the practical and accessible wisdom hidden within them, I started sharing these messages and insights with people around the world through podcasts, books, and videos. A big part of my work today is coaching individuals and couples and training others to do the same. This work has allowed me to certify more than two thousand coaches, all of whom use a curriculum I developed that is rooted in Vedic principles.

I've used wisdom from the Vedas to form the concepts in this book. I turned to the Vedas because these ancient scribes speak of love in ways I hadn't heard before. What they say is simple and accessible—an old lens that offers a new perspective. The Vedas introduced me to the fundamental ideas that love has stages, that love is a process, and that we all desire to love and be loved. As I worked with individuals and couples on their relationships and transitions into and out of love, I saw that the validity of these concepts stands the test of real-life settings. Then, in comments on my videos and responses to my podcast, I saw and heard people struggling with the same recurring patterns in their relationships, many of them issues that I had successfully addressed with my clients using Vedic concepts. I wrote this book so that anyone can access these concepts and discuss them with friends, family, and partners. I drew from the guidance of the Vedas, from what has worked with my clients, from my own travels, and from what I learned with my fellow monks. I love the intersection of modern science and ancient wisdom. The ideas here are supported by both, though we are repurposing Vedic concepts in ways they haven't been used before, applying spiritual concepts to earthly relationships.

The Practice of Love

Nobody sits us down and teaches us how to love. Love is all around us, but it can be hard to learn from friends and family who themselves are just winging it. Some are looking for love. Some are giddy in love and full of hope. Some might be ghosting each other or leading each other on. Some are together but not in love. Some are breaking up because they just can't figure out how to make it work. And some seem content in their loving relationships. Everyone's got advice for us: *Love is all you need. When you meet your soul mate, you'll know. You can change them. Relationships should feel easy. Opposites attract.* But it's hard to know what advice to follow and where to start. We can't expect to get love right when we've never been educated on how to give or receive it. How to manage our emotions in connection to someone else's. How to understand others. How to build and nurture a relationship where both people thrive.

Most of the advice on love is caught up in how to find Mr. or Ms. Right. We think there's a perfect person out there for us, a soul mate, the One, and dating apps reinforce that belief. That's wonderful when it happens, but it doesn't happen to everyone, and it doesn't always stay so perfect. This book is different because it's not about finding the perfect person or relationship and leaving the rest to chance. I want to help you intentionally build love instead of wishing, wanting, and waiting for it to arrive fully formed. I want to help you deal with the challenges and imperfections we encounter on the journey to love. I want you to create a love that grows every day, expanding and evolving rather than achieved and complete. We can't know where and when we'll find love, but we can prepare for it and practice what we've learned when we find it.

The Vedas describe four stages of life, and these are the classrooms in which we'll learn the rules of love so that we can recognize and make the most of it when it comes our way. Instead of presenting love as an ethereal concept, they describe it as a series of steps, stages, and experiences that chart a clear path forward. After we learn the lessons of one level, we move to the next. If we struggle or move on from a stage before we've completed it, we simply return to the lesson we need— life pushes us back in the direction of this work. The four classrooms are: *Brahmacharya ashram, Grhastha ashram, Vanaprastha ashram,* and *Sannyasa ashram.*

If you look up *ashram* in a dictionary, you'll find that it means "hermitage." The meanings of Sanskrit words often get stripped down in their English definitions, but in practice they have more depth. I define ashram as a school of learning, growth, and support. A sanctuary for self-development, somewhat like the ashram in which I spent my years as a monk. We are meant to be learning at every stage of life.

FOUR ASHRAMS

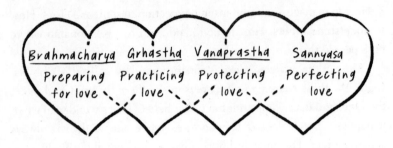

Think about life as a series of classrooms or ashrams in which we learn various lessons.

Each ashram brings us to a different level of love.

The First Ashram: PREPARING FOR LOVE

In the first ashram, *Brahmacharya,* we prepare for love. We don't get in a car and start to drive without studying for a learner's permit and practicing the core skills in a safe space. When we take a new job, we might prepare by learning a new computer program, talking to people we'll be working with about what might be expected of us, or reviewing whatever skills we might need. And we prepare for love by learning how to love ourselves in solitude. Alone, we learn to understand ourselves, to heal our own pain, and to care for ourselves. We acquire skills like compassion, empathy, and patience (Rule 1). This prepares us to share love because we'll need these qualities when we love someone else. We will also examine our past relationships to avoid making the same mistakes in relationships going forward (Rule 2).

The Second Ashram: PRACTICING LOVE

The second ashram, *Grhastha,* is when we extend our love to others while still loving ourselves. The three chapters in this stage explain how to understand, appreciate, and cooperate with another mind, another set of values and preferences.

We tend to oversimplify love, thinking of it as just chemistry and compatibility. Romance and attraction are indeed the initial connection points, but I define the deepest love as when you like someone's personality, respect their values, and help them toward their goals in a long-term, committed relationship. You may feel this way about your friends, and I hope you do, but I am talking about maintaining these qualities when you live with someone, see them every single day, and are at their side for their greatest joys, biggest disappointments, and all the mundanity and intensity of daily life.

In *Grhastha* we will examine how to know if you're in love (Rule 3), how to learn and grow with your partner (Rule 4), and how to set priorities and manage personal time and space within your relationship (Rule 5).

The Third Ashram: PROTECTING LOVE

Vanaprastha, the third ashram, is a healing place where we retreat to seek peace. We find ourselves here either after a breakup, a loss, or when family life has downshifted to require less of our attention. After learning to give love to others in *Grhastha*, and giving so much, this is an interlude where we reflect on the experience of loving others, discover what might block our ability to love, and work on forgiveness and healing. In *Vanaprastha* we learn how to resolve conflict so we can protect our love (Rule 6). We also protect ourselves and our ability to love by learning when to break up, and how to deal with it if we do (Rule 7).

The Fourth Ashram: PERFECTING LOVE

The fourth ashram, *Sannyasa*, is the epitome of love—when we're extending our love to every person and every moment of our life. In this stage our love becomes boundless. We realize we can experience love at any time with anyone. We learn how to love again and again (Rule 8). We strive for this perfection, but we never achieve it.

||||||||

Many of us pass through these four ashrams without learning the lessons they present. In the first ashram, we resist being alone and miss out on the growth that solitude offers. In the second, we avoid lessons that come from the challenges that accompany any relationship. In the third, we don't take responsibility for our healing. And the fourth—loving everyone—is something we never even consider because we have no idea it's possible.

This book follows the order of these ashrams, which essentially follow the cycle of relationships—from preparing for love, to practicing love, to protecting love, to perfecting love. Thinking about these four ashrams, I narrowed them down to the eight rules we need to learn and qualities we need to develop to move from one ashram to the next: two rules to prepare for love, three rules to practice love, two rules to protect love, and one rule to strive toward perfect love. Eight timeless, universal rules. These rules are cumulative—they build on one another. I intend for you to approach them in this order, but they're meant to serve us at any age and stage of a relationship. Some of them are counterintuitive. I talk about solitude as the beginning of love. I tell you that you must put your purpose before your partner's. I explain that your partner is your guru. These are new approaches to love that will guide you in how to improve your chances at finding love, what to look for on your first date, what to do if you have a "type," how to present yourself, when to say "I love you," when to make a commitment, how to handle conflict, how to manage a household, and when to call it quits.

Each of these rules helps you develop a mindset for love, whether you are single, in a relationship, or breaking up. You can practice solitude in a relationship. You can reframe your approach to conflict no matter what your situation. These rules come into play in all life scenarios.

This book isn't a collection of manipulative techniques. I won't give you pickup lines to grab people's attention. I won't tell you how to make yourself into the person they want you to be or how to make them into who you want them to be. This is about embracing your preferences and proclivities, so you don't waste time on people who aren't good for you. It's about learning how to display your values, not how to advertise yourself. It's about letting go of any anger, greed, ego, self-doubt, and confusion that clouds your heart and interferes with your ability to love. Along the way, I will give you techniques to help you work through loneliness, let go of expectations, nurture intimacy, and heal from heartbreak.

|||||||

When I decided to ask Radhi to marry me, I set out to arrange the best, most romantic proposal of all time. I asked a friend about engagement rings and bought her a classic diamond ring. Then, on a beautiful spring evening in 2014, I suggested to her that we meet near London Bridge to take a walk down the bank of the Thames (we were living in London at the time). I told her we were going to a nice place for dinner, knowing she would dress appropriately for the night I had planned. Just as we passed an idyllic spot with one of the best views in the city, a man suddenly appeared and gave her a huge bouquet. As she was marveling over the flowers, an a cappella group burst out of nowhere and joined the bouquet-bearing man to sing the Bruno Mars song "Marry You." I got down on one knee and proposed to her. She cried; I cried too. After she said yes, a vegan meal was delivered, and we sat down to eat at a table I had set up on the bank of the Thames. She thought that was the end of the fanfare, and we got up to head home, but as we rounded a corner, there was a white horse-drawn carriage. We climbed aboard, and it carried us through the city, passing all the major sights. She was shouting out, "I'm engaged!" and passersby cheered for us. Finally, we went to share our good news with her parents.

But on the way there, red spots appeared all over Radhi's face. By the time we arrived at her parents', she was covered in hives, and their first words to us weren't "Congratulations!" but "What's wrong with your face?" That was the day we discovered she's allergic to horses.

I thought I had choreographed the perfect proposal, but as time passed it occurred to me that all my ideas had come straight from Disney movies and viral proposal videos. Does Radhi actually enjoy a cappella music? Sure, but she isn't into grand gestures. Does she have an attachment to the Thames or to riding through London? Not really. Clearly, being near horses and covered in hives isn't her dream date. And it turns out diamonds aren't her gemstone of choice. What does Radhi really care about? She loves food, and while I'd arranged for a vegan restaurant to deliver food to us at the river, it arrived cold and bland. The one detail she would have appreciated the most was the one I planned the least, and its execution was the worst. Also, Radhi adores her family, and if I'd been considering that, I might have planned for them to jump out of the bushes to surprise us instead of the singers. She would have loved that.

We had fun, and I lucked out—Radhi said yes and never complained about any of it—but my proposal wasn't particularly personal. Throughout my life, I'd seen love presented through over-the-top romantic gestures, and I thought that was the only way to show how I felt. The hives were a gentle hint that I didn't know what I was doing; that I should think about the person standing in front of me instead of the images of fairy-tale love that constantly bombard us.

For my whole life I'd been surrounded by stories that told me how love should play out. We all are. And most of us unconsciously gravitate—in love and all things—to a conventional path. In heterosexual relationships, men still do most of the proposing. On the wedding site The Knot, 97 percent of proposal stories are of grooms-to-be popping the question. Eighty percent of brides receive a diamond engagement ring. According to a survey in *Brides* magazine, more than 80 percent of brides wear white, and 76 percent of women take their husband's last name. The nuclear family is still the most common family structure in the US, with only one in five Americans living in a household with two or more adult generations under one roof—roughly the same percentage as in 1950. Seventy-two percent of Americans live in or near the city where they grew up. And even though the number of people who say they'd *like* a nonexclusive partnership has risen, only about 4 to 5 percent of Americans are actually in a consensual non-monogamous relationship.

The storybook version of love I displayed for Radhi wasn't the love that would sustain our relationship. Fairy tales, films, songs, and myths don't tell us how to practice love every day. That requires learning what love means for the two of us as individuals and unlearning what we thought it meant. That's why I'm sharing my imperfect story. I don't know everything, and I don't have everything figured out. Radhi has taught me so much about love, and I continue to learn with her. I'm sharing all this book's advice with you knowing how much I could have used it myself and will use it in the future. Love is not about staging the perfect proposal or creating a perfect relationship. It's about learning to navigate the imperfections that are intrinsic to ourselves, our partners, and life itself. I hope this book helps you do just that.

PART 1

Solitude: Learning to Love Yourself

|||||||||||||||||||||||||||||||||||||||||||||||

In the first ashram, *Brahmacharya*, we prepare for love by learning how to be alone and learning from our past relationships how to improve our next one. Alone, we learn to love ourselves, to understand ourselves, to heal our own pain, and to care for ourselves. We experience *atma prema*, self-love.

Let Yourself Be Alone

*I wish I could show you, when you are lonely or in dark-
ness, the astonishing light of your own being.*

—HAFIZ

We can all agree that no one wants to be lonely. In fact, many people would rather stay in an unhappy relationship than be single. If you type the phrase "Will I ever . . ." into a search engine, it predicts that the next words you will enter are "find love," because "Will I ever find love" is the most popular question people ask about their futures.

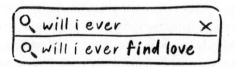

This question reveals our insecurity, our fear, our anxiety around loneliness, and these very feelings prevent us from finding love. Researchers at the University of Toronto found through a series of studies that when we're afraid of being single, we're more likely to settle for less satisfying relationships. Specifically, we're more likely to become dependent on our partners and less likely to break up with them, even when the relationship doesn't meet our needs.

Being in a relationship seems like the obvious cure for loneliness. Aren't we lonely because we're alone? But the fear of loneliness interferes with our ability to make good decisions about relationships. My client Leo had been dating Isla for nearly a year when her job took her from Philadelphia to Austin.

"You should do what's best for you," she told him. "I want to be clear. I'm not sure where our relationship is going." He was unsure at first, but a month after she left, he moved to Austin.

"Most of my friends were in relationships. I basically felt single without Isla, and I didn't want to be lonely, so I decided to join her." Instead of thinking about the pros and cons of moving—What were his job prospects? What was he leaving behind in Philadelphia? Who did he know in Austin? Did he like it there? Would this step benefit his relationship?—Leo was primarily focused on avoiding loneliness.

A month after he moved, Isla ended the relationship. Leo moved in order to avoid loneliness, but he ended up working remotely from a town where he knew nobody and found himself lonelier than ever.

Do we want to choose or stay in a relationship based on insecurity and desperation or based on contentment and joy? Loneliness makes us rush into relationships; it keeps us in the wrong relationships; and it urges us to accept less than we deserve.

We must use the time when we are single or take time alone when we are in a couple to understand ourselves, our pleasures, and our values. When we learn to love ourselves, we develop compassion, empathy, and patience. Then we can use those qualities to love someone else. In this way, being alone—not *lonely*, but comfortable and confident in situations where we make our own choices, follow our own lead, and reflect on our own experience—is the first step in preparing ourselves to love others.

Fear of Loneliness

It's no wonder we dread being alone. All our lives, we've been primed to fear it. The kid who played by themself in the playground? They were called a loner. The one who had a birthday party, when the cool kids didn't show up? They felt unpopular. Not being able to find a plus one for the wedding makes us feel like losers. The terrifying prospect of having to sit alone during lunch is such a common theme in high school movies that Steven Glasberg, a throwaway cameo in *Superbad*, has made it into the Urban Dictionary as "that kid who sits alone at lunch every day, eating his dessert." It was drummed into us that we had to have a prom date, to fill our yearbooks with signatures, to be surrounded by a squad of friends. Being alone meant being lonely. Loneliness has been cast as the enemy of joy, growth, and love. We imagine ourselves stranded on an island, lost, confused, and helpless, like Tom Hanks in *Cast Away* with nobody but a volleyball named Wilson to talk to. Loneliness is the last resort. A place no one wants to visit, let alone live.

When I spent three years as a monk, I spent more time alone than in the rest of my life put together. Though there were many monks at the ashram, much of our time was spent in silence and solitude, and we certainly didn't have romantic relationships. The emotional isolation allowed me to develop and practice skills that are harder to access among the pleasures and pressures of a relationship. For instance, the first time I went on a meditation retreat I was appalled when I saw that I wasn't supposed to bring my MP3 player. Music was my life then, and I couldn't imagine what I would do during breaks if I couldn't listen. But on that retreat, I discovered that I loved silence. I found that I didn't need anything to entertain myself. I wasn't distracted by conversation, flirtation, or expectations. There was no music or device to fiddle with to fill my mind. And I was the most engaged and present that I'd ever been.

If you haven't learned the lessons of an ashram, life will keep pushing you back to that phase of life in one way or another. Many of the key lessons of *Brahmacharya* are learned in solitude. Let's begin by assessing how much time you spend alone and how it makes you feel. This baseline audit is important whether you're in a relationship or not to see if you are using your time in solitude to understand yourself and ready yourself for love.

TRY THIS:

SOLO AUDIT

1. First, spend one week keeping track of all the time you spend alone. This means without a companion. Don't spend the time with the TV on or scrolling mindlessly through your phone. I want you to track active solo pastimes, such as reading, walking, meditating, exercising, or pursuing an interest like cooking, going to museums, collecting, building, or creating. No, you can't count the time when you're asleep. For this part of the exercise, you don't have to go out of your way to be alone. At this point we just want to observe what your habits are.

Next to the time you spent alone, write down what you did and whether doing it without a companion bothered you. You might enjoy doing dishes alone, or you might find it a painful reminder that you cooked for one. You might like to walk alone, or it might make you feel lonely. Think about why you were comfortable or uncomfortable. When do you feel comfortable alone? The point of this exercise is to help you take stock of how you spend your solo time before we develop your practice of being alone.

TIME	ACTIVITY	COMFORTABLE/ UNCOMFORTABLE	WHY?

2. Now that you've assessed your baseline solitude, start doing one new activity alone every week, and I want you to deliberately choose how to spend that time. Pick an activity that you've rarely or never done by yourself before.

See a movie, performance, or sports event

Go to a museum

Make a reservation for dinner for one

Go to a restaurant without touching your phone

Go for a hike

Celebrate your birthday

Enjoy a major holiday

Go to a party on your own

Engage in a one-time volunteer opportunity

Take a MasterClass

Try this every week for the next month. During the activity, pay attention to how you react to a new situation. Observe any intrusive thoughts that make it hard for you to be alone. Use the questions below to reflect.

How long does it take to feel comfortable?

How different would it be if you were with another person?

Are you better able to enjoy yourself alone?

Do you wish there were another person here?

Is it hard to know what to do with yourself?

Would your opinion about the activity be influenced by a companion's reaction?

(Depending on the activity) are you tempted to distract yourself or engage your mind with your phone, the TV, or podcasts?

What do you love about the experience?

What are the pros and cons of being by yourself?

If you can't go to dinner on your own without feeling uncomfortable, what would it take to make it more comfortable? You might discover that you like to bring a book or work assignment with you because it makes you feel engaged or productive. Having a brief, friendly conversation with the waiter might be all you need to start your solo dinner on the right foot.

If you see a movie on your own and miss sharing the experience with someone, find a new way of expressing yourself to yourself. Write a blog post, an online review, or a journal entry about the movie. The same is true if you take a class. Did you learn from it? What did you like? What would you have changed? Record a voice note telling yourself how you felt about the experience. It's nice to exchange opinions with someone about a movie, class, or lecture, but when you attend by yourself, you practice developing your ideas and opinions without the influence of someone else's taste.

If you are unaccustomed to hiking alone, set a fun, low-pressure goal for yourself. It might be a physical goal, like making your best time on the hike, or it might be to find something that captured your attention and bring it home with you. You might set out with the goal of taking a photo you love (that you can keep for yourself or post to social media).

The purpose of the solo audit is to get more comfortable in your own skin. You're getting to know your preferences without leaning on someone else's priorities and goals. You're learning how to have a conversation with yourself.

Solitude Is the Antidote to Loneliness

Paul Tillich said, "Language has created the word 'loneliness' to express the pain of being alone. And it has created the word 'solitude' to express the glory of being alone."

The difference between loneliness and solitude is the lens through which we see our time alone, and how we use that time. The lens of loneliness makes us insecure and prone to bad decisions. The lens of solitude makes us open and curious. As such, solitude is the foundation on which we build our love.

Solitude is not a failure to love. It is the beginning of love. During the time we spend without a sidekick, we move through the world differently, more alert to ourselves and the world. In one study, researchers gave more than five hundred visitors to an art museum a special glove that reported their movement patterns along with physiological data such as their heart rates. The data showed that when people were not distracted by chatting with companions, they actually had a stronger emotional response to the art. As the researchers wrote, those who were alone were able to "enter the exhibition with 'all of their senses open and alert' to a greater degree."

The participants also filled out a survey before and after their visit. Ultimately, those who came to the exhibition with a group reported their experience as less thought-provoking and emotionally stimulating than those who went alone. Of course, there's nothing wrong with chatting and letting the art slide past, but think of the inspiration those museum visitors missed out on. Then apply that to life in general. When we surround ourselves with other people, we're not just missing out on the finer details of an art exhibition. We're missing out on the chance to reflect and understand ourselves better.

In fact, studies show that if we never allow ourselves solitude, it's just plain harder for us to learn. In *Flow: The Psychology of Optimal Experience*, Mihaly Csikszentmihalyi writes, "Our current research with talented teenagers shows that many fail to develop their skills not because they have cognitive deficits, but because they cannot stand being alone." His research found that young people were less likely to develop creative skills like playing an instrument or writing because the most effective practice of these abilities is often done while alone. Like those talented teenagers, when we avoid solitude, we struggle to develop our skills.

The Path from Loneliness to Solitude

By itself, solitude doesn't give us the skills we need for relationships. You can't just decide you're going to use solitude to understand yourself and make it so. But if we use it to get to know ourselves, there are many ways in which it prepares us for love. Remember, in a healthy relationship, you manage the intersection of two lives best if you know your own personality, values, and goals already. So, as we make our way out of loneliness and into a productive use of solitude, we will explore our personality, values, and goals. There are three stages on the way from loneliness to solitude: presence, discomfort, and confidence.

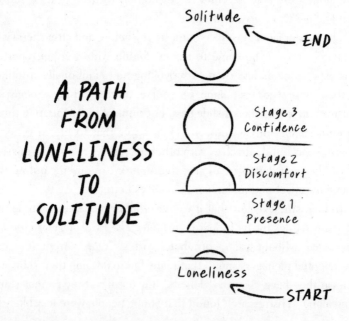

A PATH FROM LONELINESS TO SOLITUDE

Solitude

END

Stage 3
Confidence

Stage 2
Discomfort

Stage 1
Presence

Loneliness

START

Presence

The first step to making use of your solitude is being present with yourself. Even when we're not with other people, we're often busy, distracted, and distanced from our own lives. When we pay attention to how we feel and what choices we're making, we learn what we prioritize in life—our values. Those values steer how we make decisions. Being present and seeing your values gives you a sense of who you are, and you get to decide if that's the person you want to be. You spend more time with yourself than anyone else in your lifetime. Take the time to appreciate your strengths and admit the areas where you need work. Then, when you enter a relationship with someone else, you'll already have a sense of what you're bringing to the table and where you could improve. We don't think about the importance of bringing self-knowledge to a relationship, but being self-aware means you can temper your weaknesses and play to your strengths.

TRY THIS:

GET TO KNOW YOUR VALUES

Look at the choices you make in different areas of your life. Are they tied to your values or are they habits you might like to change? I've given you options to describe your attitude toward each element below, but if none of them sound like they describe you, write down what does. The more specifically you know yourself, the more you can fine-tune what you love about yourself and improve the areas where you'd like to change.

$\longrightarrow$

TIME CHOICES

Social media: I like documenting my life for my friends / Social media is not my thing; I like to be in the here and now

Weekends/Travel: I want to see the world / When I have free time, I just want or need to relax

Date night: I like to stay home and cook / I love a night out on the town

TV: I watch something every night / I curate my shows carefully and only stick with what I love

Punctuality: I'm always on time / I'm often late

Planning: I keep a calendar and stick to my plans / I don't like to be locked into commitments

HABITS

Organization: I keep everything tidy, bills paid / I wish I were more organized than I am

Exercise: I like to be active or do it for health / I find it hard to motivate

Food: I eat healthily, or do as best I can / Life is short—I eat what tastes good

Sleep: I like to sleep in if possible / I'm an early riser

MONEY

Discretionary spending: My focus is saving for the future / I spend it when I've got it

Vacations: I enjoy extravagant trips / I travel on a budget

Home, clothing, car: I keep it simple / I like the finer things

Purchases: I buy things spontaneously / My purchases are carefully contemplated

SOCIAL INTERACTION

Friends: I like spending time with lots of people / I prefer one-on-one time or to be alone (if it's the latter, you've come to the right rule!)

Family: I see my family as often as I can / I only see my family when I have to

Conversation: I like to discuss all kinds of topics in detail / I'm a person of few words

Once you know your values, you can make sure your partner respects them. If you don't respect each other's values, it's harder to understand each other's choices and decisions, which then can lead to confusion and conflict. If you don't have the same values, you don't have to fight about them or defend them, but you need to know your own so you can respect yourself, and know theirs so you can respect them—and vice versa.

Discomfort

If you're not in the habit of spending time by yourself, it may feel awkward and uncomfortable at first. It can be hard to be alone with your thoughts. You might feel like you're not achieving anything or you don't know what to do with yourself. You might feel like there's no obvious benefit to it.

To get used to the feeling of being alone, we must challenge ourselves, first in the small ways I described in the Solo Audit, but also in larger, more immersive ways.

TRY THIS:

MAKE USE OF YOUR TIME ALONE

What's something new you want to try out? Here are three different ways you can spend time alone and use it to get to know yourself better. Choose the option below that most attracts you—because part of this is learning your own preferences—or come up with your own.

1. Commit to a new skill that will take weeks, months, or longer to develop. Take the singing lessons you've always wanted, learn to roller skate, or join the quarantine throngs and finally learn how to bake sourdough. What drew you to this skill? What made you wait until now to pursue it? How does the new skill affect your confidence and self-worth? Does it fit with your image of who you are and who you want to be? It's okay to work with an instructor, such as a music teacher if you take up a new instrument. The point is to create the opportunity to reflect in solitude on what the new activity teaches you about yourself.

2. Travel alone. Learn about yourself as you plot out a weekend trip that you'll take alone. You'll learn very quickly how independent you are. This is a great activity to do *especially* if you're scared of being alone.

Are you:

    Indecisive/decisive
    Light packer/heavy packer

$\longrightarrow$

Mellow/active

Content/bored

Neat/messy

Organized/spontaneous

Do you have conversations in your head or is your internal experience quiet?

Are you decisive or do you question your choices?

Do you feel self-conscious or confident?

What aspects of travel most appeal to you?

Where would you like to go next?

3. Take on a job you've never done before. This is hard to manage if you work full-time, but if you can swing it, try a new form of work. Volunteer at a library; sign up to drive for a rideshare service; wait tables; babysit; teach. To be clear—many of these options involve interacting with other people, but the point is that you choose it alone, you embark on it alone, and you reflect on the experience alone.

What aspects of yourself are consistent no matter what you do?

What do you discover about yourself?

Is this a job that you've been curious about, or is it the extra money that matters most?

Do you like to interact with people or to work independently?

Do you prefer to be given clear instructions or to find your own way?

Are you more likely to ask permission or forgiveness?

Does work invigorate or exhaust you?

Would you like to expand this new opportunity in your life?

Knowing more about ourselves and what we enjoy helps us feel comfortable in solitude. We'll be more willing to spend time pursuing our interests without needing the safety net of a companion. The activities you choose and what you learn about yourself from those activities will expand your self-awareness and help you make the most of the time you spend alone.

Confidence

Once we are comfortable in solitude, we can work on our confidence. Oxford Languages dictionary defines *confidence* as a feeling of self-assurance arising from one's appreciation of one's own abilities or qualities. Confidence is important in a relationship because it helps us talk to the person we like without seeking their approval or hinging our self-esteem on their reaction. When we aren't looking for them to validate our tastes and choices, we can appreciate their kind words without being misled or distracted by them.

Sometimes a lack of confidence makes us think we're not lovable. You are lovable, I promise. But having me say it doesn't help you feel it. We build confidence by making time for the things that matter to us. If there are aspects of ourselves that we don't like, we should do something to change them. We have a choice: we can either change our mindset or change what we don't like. We need to get in the habit of assessing ourselves and making efforts to improve our own lives.

When most people set goals, they do so around external achievements. They want to be financially free or to buy a home. But the goals we'll develop in the exercise below center on growth, not achievement. Knowing our goals helps us prepare for love. Then, when they come up in conversation with a potential partner, you can explain why they're important to you. The other person might be supportive, dismissive, or neutral. If they don't take notice, you can flag it for them, saying, "This is actually an important goal of mine, and here's why." You'll want a partner who respects not only your goals, but *why* they are your goals.

In a relationship, remember that until you act on your goals, your partner won't know that they are truly important to you. Sometimes you have to start executing to have full buy-in. But in either case, if we don't know what our own goals are, we have no way of knowing how well they intersect with another person's.

TRY THIS:

IDENTIFY YOUR BIGGEST GROWTH AREA

Let's take a 360-degree view of your life looking at these five areas: Self, Financial, Mental/Emotional, Health, and Relationships. Choose the answer that comes closest to defining your relationship with these areas of your life. When you have completed the questionnaire, look at where you are, and think about where you want to be. Which is the area where you most want to grow?

1. Personality
   a. I don't like myself.
   b. I like myself when others like me.
   c. I appreciate myself despite my flaws and work to improve myself.

   ☐ OKAY WITH WHERE I AM   ☐ WANT TO CHANGE

2. Emotional Health
   a. I often feel anxious and unsettled.
   b. I put aside my emotions to get stuff done.
   c. I understand my emotions and try to work through them.

   ☐ OKAY WITH WHERE I AM   ☐ WANT TO CHANGE

→

3. Physical Health

   a. I disregard my body, or I don't like it.

   b. I actively work on my body because it's important to me to look good or better.

   c. I take care of myself and feel grateful to my body

   ☐ OKAY WITH WHERE I AM   ☐ WANT TO CHANGE

4. Relationships

   a. I'm insecure about some of my relationships.

   b. I rely on my relationships for joy.

   c. I invest in my relationships to help them grow.

   ☐ OK WITH WHERE I AM   ☐ WANT TO CHANGE

5. Money

   a. Thinking about money makes me feel worried and anxious.

   b. Thinking about money makes me feel excited and ambitious. I envy people who have more money than I do.

   c. Thinking about money makes me feel content. If anything, I want more to give more.

   ☐ OK WITH WHERE I AM   ☐ WANT TO CHANGE

Say the biggest growth area you've identified is financial. You overspend and it's always been a problem. Taking action in this area is something to focus on when you spend time with yourself. I could write an entire book on developing and achieving your goals, but a good way to start is to develop a growth plan using the three Cs of transformation:

THE THREE C'S OF TRANSFORMATION

1. *Coaching.* We live in a world where experts and information are easily accessible online. Start by looking for widely available resources to help you with this issue. Find a book, podcast, course, friend, professional, TED Talk, MasterClass, or online video to help you. You'll find that most of these resources will help you break your goal into achievable smaller steps, bringing a challenge that once seemed insurmountable into focus.

2. *Consistency.* Use the information you've gathered to make a plan for how to address the issue in an ongoing way. Set a goal for the year's end. This goal should be tied to action items, not an achievement. That is, your goal shouldn't be "Make a million dollars." It should be committing to ongoing efforts that will help you grow in this area.

3. *Community.* Look for a community that might help support your efforts. There are online and local support groups for everything under the sun. Find one where there is a mix of people who are in the same position you are in, people who are in the process of making changes, and people who have some measure of success in transforming their lives in the way that you wish to. Decide whether you prefer a community that is motivational, informational, or a mix of the two. Who knows? You might meet your future partner there.

Research shows that not only does high self-esteem create a more satisfying work life and better physical and psychological health, but it also predicts better and more satisfying romantic relationships. You may be wondering, *Couldn't it be the other way around? Wouldn't having a great relationship boost my self-esteem?* It's plausible, but the research says otherwise. In fact, when people with high self-esteem had a relationship that went on the rocks, their self-esteem was unaffected. They did not view the level of happiness in their relationship as a direct reflection of their self-worth.

The Rewards of Solitude

Once you're spending productive time in solitude, you begin to know your own personality, values, and goals. During this process, you develop qualities that prepare you for love at every stage of a relationship in several ways.

One Mind

We develop the ability to see and know ourselves without the influence of another mind. Frida Kahlo said, "I paint self-portraits because I am so often alone." What is a self-portrait but a study of oneself—an attempt to visually portray self-awareness? Solitude allows us to understand our own complexity. We become students of ourselves.

In her first apartment, my friend Mari and her roommate had an occasional problem with huge flying water bugs. "I absolutely could not handle it," Mari confesses. "Luckily, my roommate Yvonne was a champion water bug slayer. If I came home to one, I just went out to get a drink and wait for Yvonne." But then Yvonne went away for the weekend, and on Friday—the first day of her solo weekend—Mari came home to find a water bug in her room. *On her pillow.* "I called Yvonne in a panic. She told me to whack it. But I just couldn't. So I sat there and stared at the water bug for a long time. I thought about how unfair it was that I should hate it so much when I love butterflies. And then I opened the window and used a broom to gently usher it out into the world." This was a small moment, with a small creature, but Mari learned something about herself that she never would have if she continued to let Yvonne handle the problem for her. When we're alone we fully rely on ourselves, figure out what we care about, and learn who we are. We learn to navigate challenges on our own. We can, of course, welcome help if it comes along, but we don't expect or depend on it.

As those of you who read my first book, *Think Like a Monk*, may remember, one of the texts I refer to most frequently is the Bhagavad Gita. Part of the Mahabharata, which was written nearly three thousand years ago, the Bhagavad Gita is a dialogue between a warrior, Arjuna, and the god Krishna on the eve of a battle. This may not sound like it has much to offer modern humanity, but the Bhagavad Gita is the closest thing the Vedas have to a self-help book. In it, Krishna says, "The senses are so strong and impetuous, O Arjuna, that they forcibly carry away the mind even of a man of discrimination who is endeavoring to control them." In other words, if we're not careful, we can be attracted to something superficial or inauthentic. We have to train ourselves not to instantly like and trust the most attractive person in the room without remembering that we don't know this person or understand them.

Solitude helps us master the senses—the mind—because in solitude we're only dealing with one mind. One set of thoughts. These days, our senses are constantly overstimulated, not just by people but by all the unfiltered information that bombards us. Everything competes for our attention, and amid the noise we have no chance to identify what's important. They say love is blind because when we are overwhelmed by sensory stimulation we can't see clearly. The senses attract us to the newest, nicest, shiniest thing, without giving us a chance to reflect before we make decisions.

Our senses don't make the best decisions. The Bhagavad Gita says, "As a strong wind sweeps away a boat on the water, even one of the roaming senses on which the mind focuses can carry away a man's intelligence." There is nothing wrong with attraction, but we are easily carried away by what looks appealing, feels good, or sounds right. In solitude we learn to create space between sensory stimulation and decision-making.

If we are constantly looking for love or constantly focused on our partner, we'll be distracted from the vital work of understanding our-selves. If we don't understand ourselves, we risk taking on the tastes and values of our partner. Their vision becomes our vision. We might choose to sign on to someone's vision because we admire it—some-one might be a skilled cook whose tutelage we gratefully accept—but we don't want to mold ourselves to someone else simply because we don't know ourselves. I've had too many clients who don't realize until twenty years into a relationship that they've lost touch with themselves because they've outsourced who they are. We can integrate our partner's tastes with confidence and autonomy if we bring our own to the table.

Through choices we make in solitude, we set our own standard for how we want to live and love and be loved. With the space to write our narrative from our own point of view, we gradually overcome the influ-ence of movies, books, our parents' or caregiver's model, or a partner's wishes. We clarify our vision of love. **Solitude helps you recognize that there is a *you* before, a *you* during, and a *you* after every relation-ship, forging your own way even when you have company and love.**

Then, when our narrative intersects someone else's, we don't make choices based on infatuation or follow someone else's vision of love or passively let things play out without knowing what we want. Instead, we gradually express the standard we've developed to see how it fits with theirs. And when we're in solitude again, we reflect and evolve.

Self-Control and Patience

Two of the key skills we learn in solitude are self-control and patience. They're connected, because the more we improve our self-control, the more patient we can be. Without these two skills we become prone to following our senses and whatever attracts us.

Self-control is the time and space you create between the moment when you're attracted to something and the moment you react to it. Buddhist teacher Rigdzin Shikpo writes, "Desire is something we pro-ject outward onto another person or object. We think it exists exter-nally, within the object of our desire. But desire actually lies in our own body and mind, which is why we relate to it through the feelings it produces." When we can separate our own feeling of desire from the person we desire, we begin to feel less controlled by it, and we can take a step back and evaluate it from a more detached and less urgent place. Instead of letting your senses lead the way, the gap that you create gives you the restraint to make sure the reaction is aligned with who you want to be. That ability to restrain yourself—to create the space—is enhanced by self-knowledge.

Solitude gives us time and space between attraction and reaction. We ask ourselves: Is this truly healthy for me? Will this nourish me? Is this good for me in the long term? We develop the self-control to pause and ask ourselves these questions, and the patience to take our time answering them. We learn the difference between what feels good and what feels nourishing. Often if something is healthy for us, it seems hard before but great after. The clearest example of this is exercise, but it extends into more complex decisions, like giving up a Saturday to help a friend move or breaking off a relationship that you know isn't working. And that which is unhealthy for us seems great before but doesn't pan out well. Think about how great the idea of eating a big piece of chocolate cake seems before you do it, but ultimately it's not good for you. The same is true for more consequential decisions, like bringing a date to a wedding because you don't want to be alone even though you know it will give them the wrong idea.

A Whole Self

We've been trained to look for our "better half" or someone to "complete us." Does that make us the worse half? Does it mean we're incomplete without a partner? Even if those phrases are said lightheartedly, they set us up for dependency on someone else that can never truly be fulfilled. We look to our partner, essentially saying, "I'm bored, entertain me. I'm tired, energize me. I'm angry, make me laugh. I'm frustrated, comfort me. I'm unhappy, cheer me up." We treat our partners like human Advil, looking to them for instant relief.

We're not entirely wrong to expect this. Partners actually do coregulate each other—changes in your body prompt changes in their body, and vice versa. Neuroscientist Lisa Feldman Barrett writes, "When you're with someone you care about, your breathing can synchronize, as can the beating of your hearts." This connection starts when you're a baby—your body learns to synchronize its own rhythms by first synchronizing to your caregiver's rhythms—and it continues into adulthood. But, as Barrett points out, "The best thing for your nervous system is another human. The worst thing for your nervous system is another human." Synching with other people can log us in to their bad vibes as well as their good ones. This is why we need to self-regulate, comforting ourselves, calming ourselves down, or pepping ourselves up. If we're always turning toward others to help us tune how we feel, we'll stay more like that infant who is incapable of self-soothing and self-supporting. When you're sad, if you're lucky your partner will know how to make you feel better. People can and will help us, and that feels good, but it may not be what we need. If someone reassures us that everything will be okay, it's nice to hear and nice to have their love and support, but what we might really need is alone time to figure out how we can improve our situation.

In solitude we practice giving ourselves what we need before we expect it from someone else. Are you kind to yourself? Are you honest with yourself? Are you emotionally available to yourself? Are you supportive of your own efforts? You don't have to answer these questions right now. The more time you spend in solitude, the better you'll know how to answer them. People determine how to treat us in large part by observing how we treat ourselves. The way you speak about yourself affects how people will speak with you. The way you allow yourself to be spoken to reinforces what people think you deserve.

A relationship with someone else won't cure your relationship with yourself. Therapy and friendships and a partner might help us understand and address the sources of our sadness, but many people still feel like their partner doesn't understand them. Our culture often encourages us to put the responsibility to unpack our feelings on someone else. We expect them to understand our emotions even if we don't. Other people can help you, but if you're not trying to understand yourself, nobody else can do it for you. We've all had the friend who says, "You're right, you're right, you're right," but you can tell they're not going to take your advice. They need to do the work themselves.

Hoping a partner will solve your problems is like trying to get someone to write your term paper for you. You need to take the class, learn the material, and write the paper yourself, or you won't have learned anything. You might think, "Great, where is this class that will teach me how to lead a meaningful life? Sign me up!"

But you're already taking the class. This is what solitude is for. When you come to a relationship as a whole person, without looking for someone to complete you or to be your better half, you can truly connect and love. You know how you like to spend your time, what's important to you, and how you'd like to grow. You have the self-control to wait for someone you can be happy with and the patience to appreciate someone you're already with. You realize that you can bring value to someone else's life. With this foundation, you're ready to give love without neediness or fear.

Of course, relationships do heal us through connection, but you are giving yourself a head start by making the most of the time you spend in solitude. **You want to go on a journey with someone, not to make them your journey.**

This stage of life is designed to help us learn how to love ourselves. But if you don't learn the lessons of the first ashram of love, then you won't know how lovable you are and what you have to offer. This is an everyday practice of preparing ourselves to be in a relationship while staying true to who we are. It is one of the hardest rules in this book, and the most important.

Any step toward knowing yourself in solitude will help you love others because in addition to knowing what you bring to the table, the very *process* of learning to understand and love yourself helps you understand the effort required to love someone else. The work it took to understand ourselves teaches us that even when we're with someone we care about, it will still be hard to understand them. Perhaps the most important lesson solitude offers is helping us understand our own imperfection. This prepares us to love someone else, in all their beauty and imperfection.

Don't Ignore Your Karma

*Do not be led by others, awaken your own mind, amass
your own experience, and decide for yourself your own
path.*

—ATHARVA VEDA

When Jonny and Emmett met at an industry retreat, Emmett
sensed an instant connection. "It felt like the most natural thing
in the world," he said. "After a few dates we were spending every weekend together. He told me he loved me." But after three months together,
Jonny broke up with him. "This is the third time someone has told me
he can't 'give me what I want.' But all I want is a serious relationship!
I just have bad relationship karma," Emmett told me. He was right, in
a sense, but karma doesn't mean what Emmett or most people think.
Karma is the law of cause and effect. Every action produces a reaction.
In other words, your current decisions, good and bad, determine your
future experience. People think karma means that if you do something
bad, bad things will happen to you, like someone breaks up with you
because you broke up with someone else. But that's not how it works.
Karma is more about the mindset in which we make a decision. If we
make a choice or take action with or without proper understanding, we
receive a reaction based on that choice. If you hide that you're going to
a party from your partner, and then you run into their best friend at the
party, and that person tells your partner they saw you, and your partner
is upset—that's karma in action. You made a choice, and you have to
live with the consequences of that choice. Punishment and reward

are not karma's purpose. Rather, karma is trying to teach you—in this case transparency and honesty. I don't want you to attribute every good or bad thing in your life or the world to karma. That's not productive. Karma is more useful as a tool than as an explanation. It enables you to use your past experiences to make the best choices now.

The Karma Cycle

Karma begins with an impression. From the time we are born, choices are made for us. We're surrounded by information and experiences that shape us: our environment, our parents, our friends, our schooling and religious instruction. We don't pick these influences, but we observe and absorb their messages. *Samskara* is the Sanskrit word for impression, and when we are young, we collect *samskaras*. The impressions that we carry from these experiences influence our thinking, behaviors, and responses. As an impression grows stronger, it starts to shape our decisions. If you grew up putting milk in your cereal bowl, then adding the cereal, that becomes your norm. Then you move out and get a roommate who tells you you're doing it wrong, that it makes much more sense to put the cereal in before you add the milk. Now you have a choice. Will you stick with the impression that you absorbed as a child, or will you try a new way? As we get older, we gain the intelligence to curate our impressions by choosing what we watch and who we listen to. We also have the opportunity to revisit, edit, and unlearn past impressions.

In youth, choices are made for you.

These become impressions.

As an adult, you use these impressions to make your own choices.

Those choices generate an effect, a consequence, or a reaction.

If you're happy with the consequence, you probably won't change your impression.

But if you don't like the consequence, you can revisit the impression and decide whether it steered you wrong. If it did, you can break the cycle by forming a new impression, which then steers you to a new choice, from which you get a new reaction.

THE KARMIC CYCLE

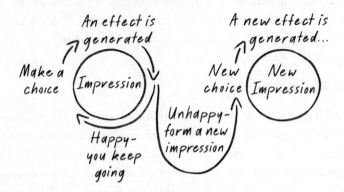

This is the cycle of karma.

We are meant to learn from our karma, to use it to inform our decision-making, but that isn't easy. Life is busy and we think that what we learned is just the way things are. But when it comes to love and cereal, our *samskaras* can lead us astray.

Karma and Relationships

I had a client whose ex-boyfriend left an impression on her. He was extremely ambitious, trying to get a foothold in a new career. She liked his drive but was unhappy that he was never available. Then she met a man who was extremely attentive. At the end of their first date, he asked her out again, and from then on, he couldn't have been more available—texting her, making plans, and checking in to see how her day was going. This was exactly what she'd been looking for! Within a few weeks, they started spending almost all their time together. But after a few months, she realized what was really going on. He wasn't just attentive, he was obsessive. The attention he was giving her was based on insecurity, not love. He was possessive and scared that she would leave him. My client had made a choice based on an impression, but her focus was too narrow. Her karma taught her that her impression was too reactive. She didn't need or want to be someone's entire focus. She just wanted him to be present when he was with her. In the course of these two relationships, my client used her karma to refine what she was looking for in a mate.

The impressions we form in our youth tell us what love should look like and feel like. They suggest what's attractive and what's dorky, how we should treat others and be treated, what profession they should have, and who should pay for dinner. But if we don't understand how our impressions were formed and how we make choices, then we keep repeating the same karma. The same impressions lead to the same choices. We love others in response to the way we've been loved by others. But if we can put our impressions in context, so we see and understand their origins, then we have the perspective and opportunity to form a new impression. For instance, if I understand that I guilt-trip my partner because my mother guilt-tripped me, then that recognition inspires me to break the cycle. Understanding our impressions is the first step to freeing ourselves from the *samskaras* planted by a childhood over which we had no control.

The choices that we make based on a new impression are conscious. We can see if we like the results better. If our parents had a volatile, passionate relationship, we might form an impression that this is what love is supposed to look like. But if—and sometimes we realize this when we're young—we are quite clear that we don't like the outcome of that volatility, then we create a new impression and decide that the love we seek is exactly *not* what our parents modeled. Then we might make it a priority to avoid drama. This new impression may create its own challenges—we may play it too safe, or we may be so focused on what we *don't* want that we forget to think about what we *do* want. But we have opened our minds and freed ourselves from our first *samskara*, and now we have the opportunity to create new impressions through trial and error.

Karma is a mirror, showing us where our choices have led us. We pick the wrong people and repeat mistakes in relationships because of the *samskaras* we bring with us from the past. Instead of unconsciously allowing the past to guide us, I want us to learn from our past to make decisions. We need to identify these *samskaras* in order to manage their influence. We do this for two reasons: First, when we learn from the past, we heal it. And second, this process helps us stop making the same mistakes.

Unearthing Our Samskaras

Our expectations and desires around relationships are shaped by our earliest experiences of love. Think about where you first absorbed ideas of what love should look and feel like. The strongest influences are most likely the love you witnessed between your parents or guardians; the love you did and didn't receive from them; the first romance movies you watched; and the first serious relationships you had. In our search for love, we subconsciously try to repeat or repair our past experiences. We imitate or reject. But we often give these early influences undue weight. They affect our choices, for better and worse. They interfere with our judgment more than we realize.

Let's begin with a visualization. We are trying to let go of who we are and to reconnect with a subconscious part of our selves, and visualization is the best way I know to travel to another time and place.

TRY THIS:

YOUNGER-SELF MEDITATION

Try to unearth the impressions left by your past and under-stand how they are influencing your idea of love. This isn't about finding fault in others or putting them on a pedestal. It's simply about isolating the emotional patterns that influenced you in your early years.

←

You can think of this meditation as an archaeological dig. There are artifacts to be found—some buried treasures, some half-exposed, some worthless. They show the richness and damage of years past and have much to teach us about life.

Tap into unresolved, unfulfilled desires by visiting yourself at age thirteen or fourteen. Give your younger self all the words, wisdom, and hugs they need. Embrace your younger self. What did your younger self need to hear that you were never told?

You're beautiful.
You're courageous.
Believe in yourself.
You'll be okay.
You're not stupid.

What would your younger self say in response?

Thank you for coming back to tell me this.
Don't be so stressed.
You should take up singing again.

After you have had this conversation with your younger self, give that version of you an embrace, and thank them for this insight.

When I guide people through this meditation, most of them find that they had some sort of insecurity in their youth, and that child is still within them, still struggling with that self-doubt. However, one man told me after the meditation that his younger self looked at him and said, "Come on, man. Get over it. Just pick yourself up and move on." It felt to me like his younger self was saying, "Tough it out. We're strong. We can handle anything." His ego was protecting his vulnerability. Even if we feel there's nothing to heal, sometimes the wounds are so deep, we can't see them anymore. We take a stoic approach, we tell ourselves we're fine, but we don't recognize that we must take stock. Cut to a year later, when this man messaged me out of the blue to say, "I realize I need to become more compassionate with the people I love and myself. It's just not how I'm wired. I don't feel like I have time to dwell on other people's thoughts and emotions."

I answered, "You don't take the time to dwell on your own emotions." It had taken him a year, but he was finally ready.

The younger-self meditation helps us identify the gifts and gaps that have clung to us since childhood, but this is only the first step toward letting go of bad impressions and taking control of the choices we make in relationships. To go deeper we'll examine three influences on our *samskaras*: our parents, the media, and our first experiences of love.

Parental Gifts and Gaps

In the *New York Times'* "Modern Love" column, writer Coco Mellors describes falling for a neighbor who makes it clear to her that he doesn't want to be in a relationship. She knows she is lying to him when she says she doesn't want anything serious either and admits that "though I didn't know it at the time, I was repeating a familiar pattern. I grew up chasing my father's love, a man who, like my neighbor, could be affectionate or absent depending on the day."

Matha Pitha Guru Deivam is a Sanskrit phrase much repeated in Hinduism. It means "mother, father, teacher, God." Your mother is your first guru. She teaches you about love. She teaches you about care not through instruction but through her interactions with you. And father is right there next to her, of course. It's a basic Freudian principle that the early relationships we have with our parents and caregivers establish relationship dynamics that, like Mellors, we're compelled to replicate as adults. When we're young, we completely rely on our parents, and we figure out ways to attract their attention, to inspire their affection, and to feel their love. The love they give us shapes how we engage in love. *Matha Pitha Guru Deivam* is a simple concept with far-reaching implications.

In their book, *A General Theory of Love*, Thomas Lewis, Fari Amini, and Richard Lannon, who were all all professors of psychiatry at the University of California, San Francisco, write, "We play out our unconscious knowledge in every unthinking move we make in the dance of loving. If a child has the right parents, he learns the right principles—that love means protection, caretaking, loyalty, sacrifice. He comes to know it not because he is told, but because his brain automatically narrows crowded confusion into a few regular prototypes. If he has emotionally unhealthy parents, a child unwittingly memorizes the lesson of their troubled relationship: that love is suffocation, that anger is terrifying, that dependence is humiliating, or one of a million other crippling variations." But I believe that even the child with the "right" parents faces their own challenges when it comes to finding love. If a child grows up seeing love as protection, caretaking, loyalty, and sacrifice, that's what they identify as love. Unless our childhood experiences were traumatic, and often even if they were, we tend to view them as normal. Then, when we are loved by someone who shows it differently—for example, through joy, time, and abundance—it may take us longer to notice and appreciate those qualities as genuine expressions of love. If your parents loved you, you might become a good and kind person. Or you might hold those you meet to an impossible standard of love. Unless we do this work of examining our *samskaras*, we're often unaware of these impressions. We just assume the way we think and feel is the reasonable response. In this way, the gifts our parents give us can create as many pitfalls as the gaps. **If there is a gap in how our parents raised us, we look to others to fill it. And if there is a gift in how our parents raised us, we look to others to give us the same.**

My mother's love for me was a gift—it enabled me to give love to others. But my parents never went to my rugby matches. Because of that gap, I first looked for validation from my peers. I wanted my

PARENTAL GIFTS & GAPS

We seek partners who fill in gaps in how our parents raised us.

Gift

We seek partners who give the same gifts we were given as children.

Gap

friends at school to think I was strong and tough because I was eager for some kind of support that I didn't get at home. By the time I became a monk, I still hadn't found a way to satisfy my longing for validation. But during my studies at the ashram, I looked in the karma mirror and realized that even when I did get the validation I yearned for, I was never satisfied. Even when I received authentic, positive feedback from others, I was never satisfied. And I think this is often true—that it's hard for others to truly understand what we go through to get a good result. **We first seek validation from those closest to us. Then, unsatisfied, we look for it from everyone. And finally, we find it in ourselves.** It was the gap that my parents created that eventually taught me this lesson. I had to be happy with myself.

Parental gifts and gaps play out in various ways in our relationships. My parents always gave me gifts that made me feel special on my birthday, whereas Radhi's family's gift to her was quality time. These are cherished aspects of each of our childhoods, but on my birthday, Radhi might give me quality time when I am expecting a gift. The more aware we are of our expectations and where they came from, the more we can communicate our needs and adapt to our partners. We all respond differently to the gifts and gaps we faced. If you saw your parents argue, you might grow up to be argumentative or defensive. Or you might heal yourself from it and make a conscious effort not to treat others that way. Or you might help others work through their conflicts. If your parents create a volatile household, you might try to keep the peace at all times and hide your true feelings. Karma lets us choose how to respond, and the options can be subtle and varied. This isn't about being right or wrong. We are looking for where we have used our karma in ways that have benefited our relationships and where we are still making unconscious choices. If your father was a jerk, you might date a bunch of jerks until you finally wise up and settle down with a nice guy. This is learning the lesson of karma.

Many of us feel like we didn't get the right upbringing. This could be anything from not having our basic needs taken care of to not having opportunities that would have helped us get a better footing in life. Even if our parents believe in us, encourage our strengths, assure us that our disappointments aren't the end of the world, and consistently scaffold our confidence in other ways, they can't hand us a perfectly developed psyche in a neatly wrapped package. And many parents themselves struggle with self-confidence, self-esteem, self-improvement, self-love, self-care. It's hard for them to pass these qualities on to their kids when they have their own challenges.

It might sound like we're doomed, but I promise you we are not. We're just focusing too much on what our parents should have done or wishing they'd behaved differently rather than figuring out what we ourselves can do. No matter how imperfect a situation we were born into, we can learn from our karma and use it to guide us into and through the relationship we want.

TRY THIS:

IDENTIFY PARENTAL GIFTS AND GAPS

MEMORIES

Write down three of your best memories from your childhood.
Write down three of your worst memories from your childhood.
Identify a challenging time in your childhood. Did your parents help you through it? How? How did it affect you?

Your answers may not be black or white. A loving response might have soothed you or it might have fostered a dependent relationship. A harsh response might have damaged your self-esteem or built your resilience. What matters isn't whether your parents were the best parents in the world, it's a question of how their treatment of you played out in your development.

EXPECTATIONS

What expectations did your parents have of you? Did these expectations motivate you? Put pressure on you? How do they affect your relationships?

If your parents expected you to achieve a certain level of success or to be in a relationship with a certain kind of person, you might either be unnecessarily attached to that outcome, or you may have reacted against it. How are those forces still at play in your life? I had a friend whose parents drilled it into her that she should marry someone ambitious, but her last boyfriend broke up with her because, as he put it, "I don't want to be your business partner. I want to be your boyfriend." She had to let go of what her parents wanted for her and rethink her ideas of what a true partner should be.

MODELING

What elements of a relationship did your parents model that you liked/disliked?

So often in relationships we reject or repeat what our parents did. If they argued, you may avoid conflict. If they had a certain power dynamic, you may expect the same in your relationship or avoid it at all costs.

EMOTIONAL SUPPORT

What kind of love and emotional support do you wish your parents had given you? What did you miss out on?

Once you become aware of a gift or gap that you're bringing to relationships, you can start to address it.

1. *Recognize.* The first step is to recognize where and when that impression steers you wrong. Does it come up on social media? With a particular group of people? When you try to celebrate with your partner? When you travel?
2. *Remind yourself.* The reminder is a note to yourself about how you want to be or don't want to be. Set a reminder that will catch you in the moment when you're at risk for acting in a way you'd rather not. Do you have a challenge ahead where you'll expect a kind of support that your partner doesn't usually give? Are you jealous when you see your partner interacting in groups? Does a certain kind of behavior always trigger your anger? Before the moment happens, find a way to remind yourself that you want to change in that moment, time, and space. It might be as simple as putting a Post-it Note on your

bathroom mirror or writing a note to yourself in your journal or asking your partner to remind you of what you're working on.

3. *Repeat.* Make your reminder into a mantra, a phrase that you repeat to yourself over and over. When you do this, it's more likely to come to your mind in the moment when you need it. It might be "Love is free of guilt" or "Anger is not the answer" or "Ask before you assume."

4. *Reduce.* Before a reaction or expectation goes away, you'll find yourself indulging it less. Make your partner aware so they know that you're working on reducing it.

5. *Remove.* Finally, over time, with attention and repetition, you'll break the habit of the expectation.

Whether our parents neglected or fulfilled us in ways large and small, when we first leave the nest, we are hardwired to look outward, to others, for validation and satisfaction instead of inward, to ourselves. We gravitate toward partners who may fill our voids, but we may also fail to open our minds and hearts to people who might suit us better.

Looking in the karma mirror helps us stop chasing others who might fulfill emotional needs from our childhoods and start fulfilling them ourselves. At the same time, the more you become aware of these influences in your own life, the more you'll be able to see how a partner's parents impact them. This gives you greater understanding and patience with yourself and your partner.

Movie Magic

Our parents aren't the only *samskaras* in our approach to love. From the time we're children, movies, TV, music, and other media sell us a romanticized ideal of love. Snow White sings "Someday my prince will come," and we are promised that the person of our dreams will show up, we'll quickly recognize them as our destiny, and they will sweep us off our feet and carry us into the sunset.

In *Forrest Gump*, Tom Hanks as the titular character walks onto a bus for his first day of school, and when Jenny invites him to sit next to her, he narrates, "I had never seen anything so beautiful in my life. She was like an angel." The love story takes off from there. Romances want us to believe in love at first sight. But in his book *Face Value*, professor Alexander Todorov shows that first impressions are likely to be wrong. "We think that people who look happy are more trustworthy, and we think that people who look tired are less intelligent, though these impressions have no link to reality. We assign positive qualities to faces that we consider 'typical,'" and "although there is no 'average' human face, [we] like faces that are closer to [our] own definition of a typical face.'" In spite of the unreliability of first impressions, a group of psychologists at the University of Pennsylvania combed through data from more than ten thousand people who had tried speed dating and found that most of them decided whether they were attracted to someone within just three seconds.

Studies show that first impressions like this are easily influenced by factors we may not even register. In one study, psychologists from Yale University had participants briefly hold either a cup of warm or iced coffee. They were then given a packet containing information about a person they didn't know and were asked to assess that person. The people who had held the warm coffee described the individuals they read about as being substantially warmer in personality than those who had held the iced coffee. (So the next time you arrange a first date, you might want to take them for a nice hot cocoa instead of an ice cream sundae.)

When it comes to meeting people, the *context effect* refers to how the atmosphere in which we encounter them can impact our impression of them. Think of running into someone in the lobby of a theater after you've just watched a romantic comedy—you're cued to think of their potential as a love match more than if you ran into them after watching the documentary *Slugs: Nature's Little Scamps*. Or imagine meeting someone at a wedding—which is like having just watched a hundred romantic comedies. You might be more likely to see that person as having marriage potential than if you met them at a bar.

Cinematic images of love set the standard for how love should occur, and often they make us feel like we're not achieving the level of romance that we should. In *500 Days of Summer*, Tom, who writes greeting cards, shows his boss a Valentine's Day card and says, "If somebody gave me this card, Mr. Vance, I would eat it. It's these cards, and the movies and the pop songs, they're to blame for all the lies and the heartache, everything."

Hollywood is hardly the only culprit. The Bollywood movies that I watched as a child did a number on me. I dreamed of that romantic happily ever after that Bollywood always touted. You would think that I outgrew these notions when I served as a monk, but as I described in the Introduction, when I wanted to ask Radhi to marry me, my images of engagements came from this *samskara*. Hence the riverbank, a cappella, horse-drawn extravaganza. Radhi and I worked out, thank God, but her allergic reaction to the horse reminded me that I should think about the person in front of me instead of succumbing to the media influences surrounding me.

Similarly, when I wanted to buy her an engagement ring, I asked a friend how to pick one. He told me to get the nicest ring I could, spending about two to three months' salary on it, so I did. I didn't ask him how he came up with that figure. If I had, he probably would have said, "Oh, it's what someone told me when I was getting engaged." Only years later did I find out that before World War II only 10 percent of engagement rings were set with diamonds. Then the diamond industry contrived to make them the official jewel of marriage and love. Almost fifty years later, having achieved that, they set out to define how much a man should spend on a ring. In 1977, an ad for De Beers jewelers showed the silhouettes of a couple on a beach. The shadow of a man slips a diamond ring on the shadow of the woman's finger, and the gold-banded ring is the only color in the ad. They kiss, and the voice-over says, "The diamond engagement ring. How else could two months' salary last forever?" It was jewelers who told the world exactly how much a man should spend on an engagement ring! How's that for a conflict of interest? That ad was released before my friend was even born. And yet it influenced him, me, and millions of others, spreading the belief that if you love someone, you should spend a big chunk of change on a diamond.

There are fewer rom-coms being produced these days, but when we examine our ideas of love, we have to look back to the ideas that were planted when we were young, before we were watching critically, before we had any experience against which to judge them. When Lily James played Cinderella in the 2015 movie, the Swarovski crystal-studded glass slipper didn't actually fit on her foot. "No maiden in the land fits the shoe," she told the *Washington Post*. "So the prince is going to die alone." **The promise of a happily ever after turns out to be an obstacle to happily ever after.**

TRY THIS:

MEDIA LOVE

Think of the first time you heard a love song or saw a movie that shaped or changed how you feel about love. What characteristics of love did it present? Do you believe in them? Have you achieved them in your past relationships?

> You had me at hello—*Jerry Maguire*
>
> I wish I knew how to quit you—*Brokeback Mountain*
>
> To me, you are perfect—*Love Actually*
>
> As you wish—*The Princess Bride*
>
> You want the moon? Just say the word, and I'll throw a lasso around it and pull it down—*It's a Wonderful Life*
>
> I'm also just a girl, standing in front of a boy, asking him to love her—*Notting Hill*

When we understand the *samskaras* that media have planted about love stories, then we don't require Hollywood perfection in our own relationships. We're willing to try a love that starts slowly or plays out differently.

First Loves

Our ideas of love are also shaped by our early romances. In 2015, the artist Rora Blue invited people to anonymously post messages to their first loves. Over a million people responded with notes like, "You ruined me, but I still write you love notes on paper plates and napkins" and "You'll always be etched into my bones" and "I loved losing myself in you, but it's been forever and I still can't find myself" and "If I keep my eyes closed he looks just like you." There's a biological reason first loves create *samskaras*. A key area of our brain—the prefrontal cortex—doesn't develop fully until we're about twenty-five years old. As brain expert Daniel Amen describes it, the prefrontal cortex helps us to think before we speak and act, and to learn from our mistakes. Young people "think" with their feelings. Without a fully developed prefrontal cortex filter, much of our mental life runs through our amygdala—a brain center associated with emotional processes like fear and anxiety. As we age, our passion is tempered by reason and self-control, and we don't feel with the same wild abandon. Those of us who felt the passion of young love may remember it as more intense than anything in adult life, even if it wasn't ideal or even healthy.

The first time you enter a relationship out of pure infatuation, the person might break your heart. If you don't accept the lesson and enter your next relationship again out of infatuation, then the second time, you might find yourself bored and acting out of character. The third time, the person might steal your money. Karma will bring you the same lesson through a different person again and again until you change. And sometimes it will bring you the same lessons with your partner over and over again. Vedic teachings say that there are three levels of intelligence. In the first level, when someone tells you the fire will burn you, you listen and learn and never touch fire. In the second level, you experience it for yourself. You touch fire, it burns you, and you learn not to touch fire again. In the third level, you keep burning yourself, but you never learn. If we don't heed our karma, we're stuck in the third level of intelligence, and we bear the scars. We forget that what we experienced in the past holds information about how we'll feel if we do it again. Often, when we believe that we have bad luck in relationships, the real problem is that we keep ignoring the data and refusing the karmic lesson. In other words—if you don't learn anything, you repeat the same mistake. Karma encourages you to reflect on the choice, the reason you made it, and what you should do differently next time.

Let's look deeply at some of the "types" we date and what karmic lessons they have to offer.

The Rebel. In the movie *I Know What You Did Last Summer*, Julie says to Ray, "I hate this, I really hate this. You're gonna go and you're gonna fall for some head-shaven, black-wearin', tattoo-covered, body-piercing philosophy student."

Ray answers, "That sounds attractive."

This character is found over and over again in literature and movies—from Rochester in *Jane Eyre* and Heathcliff in *Wuthering Heights* to Edward in *Twilight*.

Being attracted to someone who bucks the system isn't necessarily a mistake. But if you keep hoping adventure and mystery will give way to loyalty and responsibility, it's time to learn from your choices. Why are you attracted to this person? Are they offering you the relationship you want? If you're ready to move into a deeper commitment, then

FIVE TYPES WE FALL FOR

Rebel   Chase   Project

F-boy   Opulent One

you'll need to choose someone based on the qualities they have to offer instead of just their rebellious allure.

The Chase. Sometimes we're drawn to someone who is emotionally, even physically unavailable. They keep moving, but sometimes pause just long enough to keep us hoping. We are enchanted by them, so we convince ourselves that they will stop in their tracks and suddenly give us their time and attention. We're sure that once they finally focus on us, they'll fall in love with us. So we commit ourselves to tracking them. Where are they? How are they spending their time when they could be with us? When will they call? How can we make ourselves visible and available without seeming desperate? When we are caught up in the chase, we are not getting to know a person, discovering compatibilities, learning about each other, and growing together. All of our romantic energy is invested, but there is no return.

In her book *Why Him? Why Her?* anthropologist Helen Fisher, the chief scientific advisor for Match.com, explains that playing hard to get creates a phenomenon she calls "frustration attraction." She writes, "Barriers intensify feelings of romantic love . . . probably because the brain pathways associated with pleasure, energy, focus and motivation keep working when a reward is delayed." However, she adds that researchers have looked at the eventual result of playing hard to get and found no evidence that it helps establish a long-term relationship. No matter which side of hard-to-get you're on, if you are not spending time together, you're not building a relationship.

If you're drawn to the thrill of the chase, be aware of what you're choosing. If you start a relationship with a musician who is constantly on the road, then you can't expect them to give up their career and spend all their time with you. When someone is unavailable, they will generally stay that way. Are you drawn to them because you are looking for someone who is as busy as you are? Or did you grow up with an unavailable parent, so that is the only level of love you think you deserve? To use your karma well, you must be conscious of who you're choosing, why, and whether they fit what you want in your life, as you began to explore in Rule 1.

The Project. Sometimes a partner needs saving. You are compelled to take care of them, giving them attention, help, and stability. This may play to your nurturing side. In the short term it makes you feel competent and in control. They need you, and you feel like you can help them live a better life. But in the long term if they aren't transforming, you feel drained and resentful because you've become that person's caregiver. You're not equals. And you're investing far more in the relationship than they are.

Dominating a relationship bolsters our ego and makes us feel important. It doesn't require us to question ourselves or to follow our partner's suggestions. But ultimately it interferes with the long-term connection we're trying to form. We're attracted to the dynamic rather than the person. If you love the role of guiding, leading, and giving advice, you can find that elsewhere in your life.

TRY THIS:

RELATIONSHIP ROLES

Here are some questions to help you examine what role you played in your most recent relationship or expect to have in a new relationship. Is it what you want? You'll play all the roles I describe below, but you want to move toward being supporters of each other while consciously allowing for moments of being fixers and dependent.

TYPE 1: FIXER

Did you find yourself constantly trying to solve, nurture, help, or make the other person better? Were you trying to carry them, trying to make their goals happen for them?

TYPE 2: DEPENDENT

Did you feel like you relied on your partner too much? Did you go to them with all your issues and expect them to find solutions?

TYPE 3: SUPPORTER

Did you like their personality, respect their values, and want to help them toward their goals?

Did you respect how they spent their time and kept their space, or did you always want them to change it?

The fixer has a parental mentality. You feel that it's your responsibility to take care of the other person, nurture them. Their happiness is your priority. This mentality can be useful, but it can also go overboard. When you parent your partner, it makes them behave like a child.

The dependent has a childlike mentality. You rely on your partner. You want them to figure it all out, and you get upset when they can't solve everything for you. Sometimes we settle into this mentality when we have a domineering partner. It can feel comforting to have someone else take the lead. But we lose out when we don't follow our own path and shape our own lives.

The supporter is their partner's champion. You're not a parent, you're not a child, you're side by side with your partner. You're trying to take responsibility; you're trying to develop patience; you're trying to help the other person grow, but you're not trying to micromanage. This is the Goldilocks "just right" mentality.

For a quiz to help figure out the relationship role that you play, please visit www.RelationshipRoles.com.

It's natural to move in and out of all three of these roles throughout our relationships. Sometimes we take the lead. Sometimes we're more comfortable following. What we're trying

←

to avoid is dating a type with whom we are stuck in the same dynamic all the time.

Being a full-time fixer means your partner isn't taking their own journey. We don't have the right to take it for them. It's not our role to fix something that may not even be broken. Being fragile full-time means you lack confidence and seek validation from others. You feel broken and want someone to fix you. Being with someone who supports this side of you interferes with you taking responsibility for your own growth, joy, and success.

The supporter is an ideal to strive for. Both partners communicate as equals. Your partner is always teaching you, but you are always teaching them. And when you both understand that you're both teaching and learning at the same time, that's when you create a partnership. (More on this in Rule 3.)

The F-boy or F-girl. When we date someone who sleeps around, they are clearly communicating that they aren't interested in an exclusive commitment. If that's what you're looking for, consider whether it's worth staying in it for great sex. Sex can distract us from making good choices about who to be with and whether to stay with them, and one of the biggest causes of that distraction is the hormone oxytocin. According to neuroscientist and psychiatrist Daniel Amen, oxytocin is related to feelings of being in love, and the release of oxytocin can support and even accelerate bonding and trust.

Generally, men have lower levels of oxytocin than women, but sex causes men's oxytocin levels to spike more than 500 percent. New York University neuroscientist Robert Froemke says that oxytocin acts like a volume dial, "turning up and amplifying brain activity related to whatever someone is already experiencing." During and after sex, we feel more in love, but it's not actually love. We feel closer chemically even though we're not closer emotionally. Additionally, the hormone actually has a temporary blocking effect on negative memories, so all of those "little things" that were bothering you or that argument you had beforehand—which might have been a major warning sign—could fade after sex.

When I interviewed husband-and-wife relationship experts John and Julie Gottman on my podcast, John said that oxytocin can be the "hormone of bad judgment." He says, "You keep thinking it's going to be okay because that hormone makes you feel safe and secure and you don't see the red flags the person is sending saying, 'I'm not trustworthy.'"

If someone makes it clear that they aren't interested in committing, there can still be a fun connection, but know that you aren't likely to learn much from them.

The Opulent One. The Bhagavad Gita talks about six opulences: knowledge, fame, money, beauty, strength, and renunciation. Sometimes we are attracted to someone who has a single opulence, and this is enough to prematurely convince us we're in love. In Beyoncé's song "Halo," the light surrounding someone convinces her they're "everything [she] need[s] and more," yet someone's "halo" isn't necessarily an accurate indicator of who they are. In psychology, the *halo effect* is a type of cognitive bias where we form an inaccurate impression of someone or something based on a single trait or characteristic. For instance, if someone is attractive, we're more likely to assign other positive attributes to them, like intelligence, wit, or kindness. This particular halo effect is called the *attractiveness stereotype*. One study showed that teachers graded attractive students more favorably when the class was in person, but not when the class was online and the teachers couldn't see the students. Other studies showed that servers deemed to be more attractive made higher tips. When we see a good-looking person, we might make unconscious assumptions that they're wealthier, or more ambitious, or more likable, and so on, and this can influence our attraction to them.

The Bhagavad Gita says that the six opulences show us the fallibility of desire. We want attention but a million likes won't make us feel loved. We want beauty, but we try to make youth (which is not the only kind of beauty) last forever. We want money, but it won't buy happiness. Try googling "lottery winners" if you want proof of that. If we look for the opulences in a partner, we are being sold a temporary bill of goods. The Bhagavad Gita says that divine love of God is to know their greatness but gravitate to their sweetness. You may know all of your partner's accolades and achievements, but that doesn't define them as an individual. **Being attracted to our partners for what they have or what they've achieved is not a bad place to start, but it's not a good place to end.** Abilities and achievements don't matter so much as qualities and actions. We make the mistake of assigning qualities to people based on their abilities. We assume that a good communicator will be trustworthy. We think a writer must be thoughtful. A manager must be organized. The only way we can know what qualities a person truly has is by spending time with them and observing them. Only when we know someone intimately and deeply do we find the sweetness in them.

TRY THIS:

REFLECT AND LEARN FROM A PAST RELATIONSHIP

We tend to base success in relationships on how long they last, but their actual value lies in how much we learn and grow from them. If we understand that, we can examine the choices we've made, assess why we picked a person, figure out what went wrong, and develop a better sense of whom to pick and whether we need to change anything for next time.

1. What energy were you in when you chose to be with your ex?
    Energy of ignorance. In this energy, you might have picked someone because you were bored, because there was nobody

←

else around, or because you were lonely. Choices made in ignorance lead to depression, pain, and stress.

Energy of passion. In this energy, you picked someone
because you wanted one of the opulences. Decisions made
in passion start well but have to deepen into understanding
and respect or else they end terribly.

Energy of goodness. In this energy, you chose someone
with whom you felt connected and compatible. There was
mutual respect, and often these relationships end with some
feelings of respect still intact.

2. Why did it end? Be as honest with yourself as you can when
   you assess what went wrong in this relationship.

3. Learn from it. What can you think of that you will try to do differently next time? Can you enter your next relationship from
   an energy of goodness? Can you set aside opulences and
   look for qualities that make good partners?

You Attract What You Use to Impress

The opulences highlight a very practical way of understanding karma.
If we are attracted to someone for their ambition, that's what we get—a
person whose priority is ambition. There's nothing wrong with ambition . . . until you realize that you want someone who has lots of time
to share with you. Sometimes we feel like none of the options before
us are people we want to date. And then we have to ask ourselves, *Why
are these my options?* Why are we attracting these people, and how can
we attract the ones we want? Again, karma has the answer. If you put
something into the world, you get it back. This is karma in its most
basic form. If I use money to present myself as valuable, I'll attract
someone who believes that money is what makes me valuable.

When we present ourselves, we are signaling the dynamic we want, how we expect to be treated, what we think we deserve. I had one client who was a successful entrepreneur. He was upset because every woman he met "only wanted him for his money." But every picture he posted in his online profile showed him in a supercar or him in front of another home he'd bought. He said, "I'm not like that in person." But he shouldn't have been surprised that he was attracting a certain type of person.

If you use wealth to impress someone . . . you are committing to whatever it takes to sustain your wealth. But one day you may want to change how you spend your time. You may want to feel that your partner values you for more than your net worth.

If you use your body to impress someone . . . you are putting yourself in a position where aging is hard to accept. One day your body will change, and you may want a partner whose love will last for years.

If you use your social status to impress someone . . . you may find that someone with a higher social status is more attractive to your partner. Or something may change your status and you'll want a partner who can support you through a hard time.

If you use your intellect to impress someone . . . you may find that you don't feel an emotional connection.

If you use sex to impress someone . . . you are setting a standard for physical connection that may be hard for one or both of you to sustain if attraction fades.

When we put ourselves out in the world, whether it's on a first date, social media, or a dating profile, we are saying, "This is the version of me that I want you to like." It's important to put out the version of yourself that you want someone to be attracted to, as opposed to the version of yourself that you think someone would be attracted to. These are two different things. If you attract someone through a persona, then you're either going to have to fake being that promotable person forever, or they're eventually going to discover the real you.

One study showed that 53 percent of online daters lied in their profiles—women more than men, and more often about looks (doing things like posting an old photo so they looked younger), and men more often about financial status. Considering that men tend to rank physical attractiveness as a highly valued characteristic in a potential partner and women tend to rank financial success similarly, you can see how that might play out, at least in heterosexual relationships. Even if your self-positioning is more subtle, and you're willing to play out the role you've invented indefinitely, you will always know in your heart that you aren't loved for who you really are. You've made them fall in love with a character that you created, not you. By pretending to be someone else, you will attract strife into your life. Save yourself that time and energy.

It's natural to want to present the best version of yourself. You may be doing this through the opulences, whether by trying to slip where you went to college into conversation or taking your date to an expensive restaurant to demonstrate wealth or uploading your most seductive photos to a dating website. We can easily get caught up in judging ourselves by our net worth, or the way we show it in material possessions; our friends or followers; our physical appeal. But we all know people who have high "value" using these metrics and still have low self-worth. There is a saying that the poor man begs outside the temple while the rich man begs inside it. Or, as Russell Brand puts it, "The more that I've detached myself from the things that I thought would make me happy like money and fame and other people's opinions, the more truth is being revealed." We market ourselves to others using our opulences, but doing that won't benefit us in the long run. We want to show our real personality, values, and goals, so we are loved for what matters most to us.

The converse is also true. Be aware if opulences are what attract you to your partner and beware if they're all that attracts you. You don't want to end up with someone whom you're only attracted to physically, or whose social life captivates you, or whom you only connect with about work, or whose external success compels you. These qualities are tied to temporary situations and characteristics. They won't last, and when they are gone, so is the relationship.

When I met Radhi, I had nothing. No—that's not true. What's true is that we've been together ever since all I had to offer her was myself, and that seemed to be enough.

TRY THIS:

WHAT YOU SHOWCASE

When there's a disparity between what attracts your partner and what you love about yourself, you may struggle to live up to their vision. First, make a list of what you love about yourself. Think about the qualities you are most proud of and try to steer clear of the opulences. Are you kind, caring, hardworking, honest, creative, grateful, flexible, reliable? Now, for each of your long-term or defining relationships, make a list of the qualities you think that person saw and appreciated in you. We want to build relationships where we are loved for what we love in ourselves.

What You Want from Someone Else First Give to Yourself

Once we have a better sense of the *samskaras* we've gathered over the years, we can look at how they've influenced our choices and see if we like the results. We don't want to make the same mistakes over and over again. We want to carry the gifts from our pasts into the present, but we can't assume our partner will receive them exactly as we expect. We don't want to bring gaps to our relationships, expecting our partner to fill them. We want to fill our own gaps.

As you observe your partner or potential partner, consider what draws you to them. Is your judgment influenced by outdated criteria from your past? If your parents gave you all their attention, are you expecting that from a partner? Do the movies you saw in your youth have you expecting to be swept off your feet? Was your first love remote and unavailable, so you're stuck in a pattern of repeating that dynamic? One of my clients was getting really angry at his wife when she didn't come home from work on time. I asked him why he was having such a strong reaction, and in the course of our work he realized that his own mother never came home on time, and it had bothered his father. He had "inherited" his father's anxiety. I asked him what his wife's lateness signified for him. After some thought, he said, "It's like she doesn't care about me and doesn't want to spend time with me." I suggested that he ask his wife about it, and we talked about how instead of saying, "So how come you're always late?" in an accusatory tone, he could ask, "What have you been working on? Is it exciting or stressful?" It turned out that his wife was stressed about a project, and that she thought in three months' time she'd be able to start coming home earlier. She didn't realize that it would have eased his mind to know about this project and when it might end, but even more important was his realization that the reason for her lateness differed from his interpretation. It wasn't a perfect happily ever after, but he was able to come to terms with the situation instead of enduring his inherited anxiety. He asked for time with her over the weekend, and they figured out how to address both of their needs.

Our relationships aren't supposed to be responses to what our parents did and didn't give us or balms for the insecurities of our youth. If we look to our partners to fill an emotional gap, this puts undue pressure on our partner. We are asking them to take responsibility for our happiness. That's like saying, "I won't drive my car until my partner puts gas in it." Why wait for someone else to make you feel good? And that's why it's so deeply important that we heal ourselves, taking charge of that process instead of shifting blame and responsibility to a partner. If we're trying to fill an old void, we'll choose the wrong partner. A partner can't fill every gap. They can't unpack our emotional baggage for us. Once we fulfill our own needs, we're in a better place to see what a relationship can give us.

Meanwhile, and always, you can give yourself what you want to receive. If you want to treat yourself, you could make plans to go someplace you've never been before, or arrange a birthday celebration for yourself, or dress beautifully for an upcoming event. If you want to feel respected at work, you could decide that you're going to make a list for your own benefit of everything you contributed to a project. We think of feeling appreciated, respected, and loved as core needs in a relationship, but when we attend to these needs for ourselves in small ways every day, then we don't have to wait for our partner to deliver them through a grand gesture.

TRY THIS:

GIVE YOURSELF WHAT YOU WANT TO RECEIVE

Fill your own gaps by looking for ways to treat yourself the way you're looking for others to treat you.

I never felt appreciated by my parents.
If you want to be appreciated . . .
What do you want to be appreciated for?
What can you do every day that makes you feel appreciated?

I never felt like my parents thought I was special.
If you want to feel special . . .
What do you want to feel special for?
What can you do every day to make yourself feel special?

My parents didn't respect my feelings or opinions.
If you want to feel respected . . .
What do you want to be respected for?
What can you do every day to respect yourself?

These are hard questions, so take your time with them. Answers may not come quickly. Ponder them for a day. A week. You may gradually start to identify recurring negative thoughts that you've carried from your past. If you keep telling yourself, *I'm nobody until someone tells me I'm someone*, it will make you more prone to insecurity, stress, and pressure. If you often tell yourself that you're not good enough, you become not good enough. We need to disrupt those negative patterns by developing new thought patterns. It may feel forced or fake, but when you practice these new, positive thought patterns, you start living up to them.

Check In with Yourself

Set aside three minutes before you start your day and three minutes at the end of your day to make sure you're filling your own gaps. Attaching new habits to the beginning or end of things is natural to us and the best way to bring the behaviors and beliefs we need into our lives.

In the three minutes you've set aside in the morning, sit by yourself and pick one thing you can do for yourself today to improve your day. It might be deciding to make a lunch date with a friend you haven't seen in a while. It might be showing up at a yoga class or taking no phone calls for the first hour of the morning. To wake up and hope the day will be great is outsourcing the day. Instead, pick just one act you can perform yourself that might change your day for the better.

In the last three minutes of the day, assess how you felt about the one thing you picked. Did it help your day? Should you try it again tomorrow or choose something else?

Expanding Our Love

Our preparation for love began with two rules guiding us to solitude and self-examination. We began practices to transform loneliness to productive time in solitude. We unpacked our pasts and began to unlock our *samskaras* so that we can learn from our karma. Whether you're in a relationship, looking for one, or leaving one, these rules help you build and maintain the skills you need for love. By now, you're already better prepared for love than most people! And that opens the door for you to share your love with another person. One of the translators of the Bhagavad Gita, Eknath Easwaran, said, "Love grows by practice, there's no other way." Now, as we move into the practice of love, we will build our ability to recognize love, define it, develop it, trust it, and, if and when we are ready, to embrace love.

Write a Love Letter
to Yourself

Writing a letter to yourself can help you establish a dialogue with yourself and gain self-awareness about how you're thinking and feeling. This, in turn, will help you make choices and take the next steps in your life.

Dear Self,

We've been together since the beginning, and it's thanks to you that I get to experience this life. You are closer to me than anyone, the only one who knows all that I've seen and done. The only one who has witnessed the world through my eyes. Who knows my deepest thoughts. My darkest fears. And my biggest dreams.

We've been through a lot together—everything, in fact. The highest highs, and the lowest lows. You're with me in my greatest moments and the ones I'd like to do over. And no matter what, you've always stuck by me. We are true partners—you are the only one about whom I can say without a doubt that we will always be together.

But in spite of your loyalty, and your caring, I've sometimes ignored you. I haven't always listened when you told me what's best for me or nudged me in the direction I should go. Instead of looking to you, I looked outward, at what others were doing or saying. I distracted myself, so I couldn't hear your voice. Instead of caring for you, I sometimes pushed too hard. And yet you've never abandoned me. You've always forgiven me. And you've always welcomed me home, without judgment or criticism.

For all of that, I thank you. Thank you for being gentle with me. For being strong. For always being willing to learn and grow with me through my mistakes, and my triumphs. And for over and over reflecting back to me the best of what is inside me. Thank you for showing me what unconditional love truly means.

Love,
Me

Meditation for Solitude

This meditation is focused on self-love. When we practice love and gratitude for ourselves, we nourish the soil in which love is rooted, and from which love in its many forms will grow and blossom.

This meditation is best practiced in bed, before you go to sleep at night and when you wake up in the morning.

1. Find a comfortable position.
2. Close your eyes, if that feels good to you. If not, simply soften your focus.
3. Whether your eyes are open or closed, gently lower your gaze.
4. Take a deep breath in. And breathe out.
5. If you find that your mind is wandering, that's okay. Gently bring it back to a space of calm, balance, and stillness.

Self-Gratitude Meditation

1. Breathe normally and naturally. Take a moment to notice the pattern of your breathing.
2. Allow your focus to shift to your body. Notice where it touches the bed, and where it does not. If there's a sheet or blanket on you, notice the sensation where it touches your skin.
3. Now, bring your attention to the soles of your feet. Notice how they feel. Express gratitude to your feet for what they allow you to do. "I am grateful for your support. I am grateful for how you ground and connect me to the earth." Use whatever language feels natural and welcome to you.
4. Allow your attention to move upward to your lower legs,

your knees, and your thighs. Notice how they feel. Express gratitude to them. "Thank you for your steadiness. Thank you for helping me move around in the world."

5. Bring your focus to your arms. Notice your upper arms, elbows, forearms, and hands. Give thanks. "Thank you for all you do to help me interact with the world around me, enabling me to care for and express myself."

6. Allow your attention to shift to your face. Notice the nose that lets you smell, the mouth that enables you to eat, the eyes that let you see, and the ears that let you hear. Express your gratitude. "I'm grateful for the richness you bring to my life, allowing me to enjoy nourishing food, to hear music, to smell flowers, and to take in the beauty of nature and the world around me."

7. Now, take a moment to go inside, beneath the skin. Scan slowly downward, starting with your brain. Express gratitude to your brain for all the important functions it is able to perform. "Thank you for all you do to coordinate and monitor this miraculous organism that is me. For enabling me to process information, to think, to joke, to appreciate, to feel compassion, and to take action."

8. Lower your focus to your heart. Notice its rhythm as it beats inside your chest. Express your gratitude. "Thank you for working all day and all night, whether I appreciate you or not. Whether I acknowledge you or not."

9. Shift your attention to your lungs. Notice how your rib cage softly expands and collapses with each breath. Give thanks. "Thank you for filling me with life."

10. Allow your attention to drop to your stomach. Notice how it feels. Thank your stomach. "I am grateful for how you digest food to create the energy I need for each day."

11. Slowly, shift your focus back out to your whole body. Take a moment to express gratitude to your body, or to your mind, for whatever stands out to you in this moment.

PART 2

Compatibility:
Learning to Love Others

||||||||||||||||||||||||||||||||||||||||||||||

The second ashram, *Grhastha*, is the stage of life when we extend our love to others while still loving ourselves. This stage introduces the challenges of learning to understand, appreciate, and cooperate with another mind, another set of values, and another set of likes and dislikes on a daily basis. Here we explore the challenges of *kama/maitri*—loving others.

Define Love Before You Think It, Feel It, or Say It

My boyfriend told me he loved me, and a week later he fully ghosted me.

I told my partner I loved her. She said, "Thank you."

I was dating a girl for several weeks. When I told her I thought I was starting to fall in love with her, she said she needed more space.

We've been together for three years and we say "I love you" before bed. Same time every night. I'm not sure it means anything anymore.

We say "I love you," or wait for the right time to say it, or hope someone will say it to us, but there is no universal agreement as to what it means. For some it means "I want to spend the rest of my life with you." For some people, saying "I love you" means "I want to spend the night with you." Between those two intentions are infinite others, and some of us say it without any particular intention because, in that moment, we just feel something we interpret as love. This leaves a lot of room for confusion, miscommunication, and false expectations. Writer Samantha Taylor says, "The first time I told my now-husband I loved him, we were spending one of those long nights on the phone early in our dating relationship. Back when people actually talked on the phone. Delirious with sleepiness, I told him that I wanted to tell him I loved him but didn't want to scare him off. 'Don't worry,' he told me. 'Saying 'I love you' isn't a big deal to me. I love my mom. I love my friends. I love you, too.' Great. He loved me like his MOM. So romantic." He was telling her that his definition of "I love you" was different from hers: broad, low-pressure, and not particularly romantic. She adds, "Fortunately, he must have grown to love me in a romantic way, because we've been married for almost ten years."

We say "I love you" in so many different contexts—with family and friends and lovers—that it doesn't indicate anything but the presence of some sort of affection. And yet we have expectations based on what we assume it means to the other person. "I love you" doesn't include commitment. It doesn't promise you want to have children together. It doesn't guarantee that you'll put any effort into making a relationship work. It's a beautiful start, but not a substitute for many other meaningful conversations.

A survey showed that men are quicker to say "I love you" than women, taking an average of 88 days. A whopping 39 percent of them declare their love within the first month. Women take an average of 134 days, and 23 percent of them declare their love in month one. It's hard to imagine that the people who feel love within weeks actually live up to what their partners think that statement means.

You may feel like you know someone because you've spent time with them and you like their personality, but you may not know their dreams, their values, their priorities, the things that matter to them. You think you know their heart, but you just know their mind. Love takes time.

I'm not saying you need to understand someone fully before you fall in love. We're always learning new things about our partner. But too often we leap to love based on a very small amount of information. In any other area of your life, it's very unlikely that you make a big decision based on such a small amount of information.

Love is not black-and-white—you either love someone or you don't, and there's only one way to do it. Some people renew their vows every ten years, either to recommit to love or to express how their love has evolved. Some people have long-distance love. Some people are friends with benefits. Some people get divorced, but they find a way to parent together peacefully and comfortably. Recently, a guy came up to me at a wedding and told me he just got out of a long relationship. He said, "We love each other, but leaving each other was the best way to carry on loving each other." That's love too. To discount the many forms of love is to miss many beautiful possibilities. Understanding the nuances allows you to define and honor the love you have with the person you're with. As soon as we say "I love you," we're going to have to live up to those words, not by our definition, but by the definition of the person we love. On the flip side, when we accept someone else's love, we have to realize that they aren't using our definition of love.

Before we decide that we're in love, before we tell another person we love them, and before we determine what it means when they say those words to us, we must consider how we define love. What do we expect love to feel like? How do we know we love someone? How do we know if they love us? The only way to avoid miscommunication is to talk about love using far more than those three words. This rule will help us figure out what we mean when we say "I love you," what it may or may not mean when our partner says it, and how to find a meaning we can share.

The Four Phases of Love

When we tell each other we love each other, we rarely elaborate, unless it's to add a romantic flourish like "so much" or "to the moon and back." It's pretty black-and-white—we've either declared our love, or we haven't. We don't leave much room for variation or degrees of love. But we can take some cues in the practice of love from the Bhakti tradition, an eighth-century movement in Hinduism. Bhakti describes the journey of falling in love with the divine in stages: The first stage is *sraddha*, where we have the spark of faith that makes us take interest in the divine. Notice how even when we're talking about connecting with the divine, there's a preliminary desire. Curiosity and hope drive us to engage. This leads us to the next stage: *sadhu-sanga*, desiring to associate with spiritually advanced persons. Here we find a spiritual teacher/guide/mentor who can help us develop our practice. After that is *bhajana-kriya*, where we perform devotional acts, like attending services and praying. As our devotion gets deeper, we become free from all material attachments (*anartha-nivrtti*), achieve steadiness (*nistha*) in self-realization, and find enthusiasm (*ruci*) for serving the divine. This taste leads us to further attachment, which is called *bhava*. This is the preliminary stage of pure love of the divine. Then finally we reach pure love for the divine, *prema*. This is the supreme stage of life, where we have attained the highest form of a divine loving relationship, unbound by awe and reverence or any kind of hierarchy.

Because the Bhakti Stages of Love describe an intimate, direct relationship between a person and their god, they can apply in many ways to how we love each other. So I decided to bring the model down to earth and reinterpret it for the practice of understanding and loving another person.

When it comes to love, we expect that we'll know when we know. But our experience of love can be different at different times. The four phases of love I'm about to describe can all look like love and feel like love, and they are all part of the journey of love.

How do you know if you're in love with someone? Love isn't being called every day or having your chair pulled out for you or feeling warm and fuzzy when you see someone. Love isn't a purely romantic fairy tale, and it isn't pragmatically checking qualities off a list. Looking at these phases helps us understand love differently, define love for ourselves, and better articulate our feelings of love. At the same time, seeing the levels of love helps us understand why our partner might have a different concept of love than we do. Knowing what phase you're in helps orient you for progress to the next phase, and when you can't see yourself getting to the next phase, then you might enjoy it for a while, but know that it's not sustainable.

We might not progress in exactly this order, and the rest of this book will show you how we cycle back through the phases. This is a cycle we will repeat not just with one partner, but with pretty much everyone who plays an important role in our lives. This is the practice of love.

1. Attraction
2. Dreams
3. Struggle and Growth
4. Trust

Phase One: Attraction

In Phase One, we feel a spark of intrigue, interest, and attraction. This makes us want to figure out if someone is worth our time and effort. Researchers describe what we call love as three distinct drives in the brain—lust, attraction, and attachment. When we move from lust to attraction, we're taking the generalized desire to connect with *someone* and focusing it on a specific person. The brain chemicals involved in lust differ from those that produce attraction. Lust is governed more by testosterone and estrogen, whereas attraction includes dopamine (the reward chemical) and norepinephrine (the brain's version of adrenaline, which when combined with dopamine can generate that feeling of euphoria around the target of our attraction). Additionally, levels of the feel-good hormone serotonin actually drop in this phase, which contributes to our feelings of anxiety and passion in the early stages of attraction. We have an exciting surge of hope and belief that someone could be the right person for us. We feel intrigue and interest. We swipe right. Love often starts with this thrilling hint of possibility. It means: you intrigue me. I want more. Chemistry like this feels amazing, but we should be careful not to think that chemistry is the only way love begins or that it is the entirety of love. Time helps you understand whether what you're feeling is truly love. Think about what it's like when you place an order for a chair on a website. It looks good online. It fits beautifully into a room pictured on your favorite home store site. But when it arrives, it isn't comfortable to sit on. In attraction, we observe people for how they appear, but we don't understand what it's like to have a relationship with them.

I used to know this guy who came up to me every month and told me he had fallen in love with another girl—someone he'd bumped into or met on Instagram. For a week, he'd be completely infatuated. And then a few weeks later it would be someone else. In the attraction phase we have glimpses of love that show us its beauty.

Lingering in the attraction phase is pleasurable. With new people, we've carefully exposed what we want them to see—our best features. There are few arguments, expectations, and disappointments. We can sustain the fantasy of a perfect match. But it takes a deeper connection to go beyond Phase One.

Science supports the idea that having deeper connections bodes well for relationships. Professor Matthias Mehl at the University of Arizona in Tucson and his team studied whether the conversations we have affect our well-being. Specifically, they were looking at the difference between small talk and having deep, meaningful discussions. They had seventy-nine participants wear recorders for four days while they went about their daily lives. The devices were designed to record snippets of ambient sound, netting about three hundred recordings per participant over the four days. The researchers then listened to the recordings and noted when the participants were alone or talking with others, and when their conversation was superficial ("What do you have there? Popcorn? Yummy!") or deep ("She fell in love with your dad? So, did they get divorced soon after?"). The researchers also assessed participants' well-being through a series of statements such as "I see myself as someone who is happy, satisfied with life." They found that higher rates of well-being were associated more with people who had deep conversations than those who made more small talk.

Going deep isn't a technique. It can only be a genuine experience that leads to a true connection. But we can examine our own willingness to open up and be vulnerable with people as we build trust with them. Social scientists say that vulnerability leads to *reciprocal, escalating self-disclosure.* What this means is that over time, a couple begins to reveal vulnerabilities to each other—that's the self-disclosure. Sharing parts of yourself doesn't mean baring your whole soul all at once. Sometimes, when we are caught up in the moment, we're tempted to do that. But if we gradually unveil our personalities, values, and goals, we start to see if there is a connection. Letting yourself be vulnerable with this intention keeps you feeling protected—like you aren't exposed too much too fast to a person you can't trust. If it all goes well, you reveal increasingly intimate facets of yourself at a pace where you feel comfortable—that's where the escalating comes in. And the disclosure is a gift that you give back and forth to each other—that's reciprocal. It is with reciprocal escalating self-disclosure that we start to truly know a person.

The Three-Date Rule. In my experience working with clients, three dates usually provide enough time to determine if you and another person would be a good match. These three dates don't have to be your first three dates, and you don't have to do them one after another. You can spread them out. Sometimes it's nice to just see a movie!

In these dates you'll focus on three areas: whether you like their personality, whether you respect their values, and whether you would like to help them achieve their goals. For simplicity's sake, I'm going to suggest focusing on these qualities sequentially, one per date, but you'll probably be uncovering some aspect of each dimension during each date. First, we start with personality because it's the easiest thing to spot, understand, and connect with. In their personality, you'll see how their past has shaped them. Second, you'll explore their values, which define who they are today. And third, you'll try to recognize their goals, which encapsulate what they want in the future.

Date One. Do you have fun together? Do you enjoy each other's company? Does conversation flow? What makes you comfortable and what makes you uncomfortable? The first date is to find out if you really enjoy each other's personalities. To do so, you need to shift between small talk and deep talk. The topics we gravitate toward, favorite movies or vacation plans, don't help us know people deeply. Instead, you can start to ask questions that inspire both of you to reveal more personal details, including your quirks and imperfections. Remember—we share vulnerabilities gradually, as we get to know and trust each other, so on this date your focus is to see if you enjoy and appreciate their personality. Try to learn something new about them or see a side of them you haven't seen.

Here are some light questions you can ask on Date One. You'll see that they are questions about taste and preferences. They tread in areas where most people are comfortable, but they create the possibility to show real passions. When you ask someone what the best meal they ever had was, the question isn't just about food. It opens up a bigger conversation about where and when they had the food and what made it special. If you ask what they wish they knew more about, you find out about their curiosities and unfulfilled interests. If you hit on a strong interest, like taste in movies or books, you can dig deeper into why they like what they like and find out how introspective they are. Even if you think you know your partner well, the answers might surprise you.

What's something you love to do?
Do you have a favorite place?
Is there a book or movie you've read or seen more than once?
What is occupying your thoughts most at the moment?
What's something you wish you knew more about?
What's the best meal you've ever had?

This isn't an interview. Every conversation has two sides, and one aspect of your partner's personality these questions will reveal is whether they're curious about you. Do they ask for your own responses to these questions and dig deeper when they turn the conversation to you?

TRY THIS:

PREPARE FOR DATE ONE

Take the questions I suggested you ask your date and write out your own answers to them.

What's something you love to do?
Do you have a favorite place?
Is there a book or movie you've read or seen more than once?
What is occupying your thoughts most at the moment?
What's something you wish you knew more about?
What's the best meal you've ever had?

Once you have your answers, ask yourself what they might tell a person about you. Do these questions bring up some of your strong interests? Do they give you a chance to reveal important aspects of your personality? If not, are there other questions that would? Add those questions to the list you bring to your next date.

Date Two. Your "Date Two" could come after any number of dates spent dancing or going to museums or talking casually over dinner. But knowing that you enjoy the same movies or like the same cuisine doesn't really tell you if your values are compatible.

Gently encourage your date to share meaningful stories and details about their life. Take turns with these questions, and make sure, again, that it's not an interview. In fact, if they hesitate over a question, you might say, "I know it's a hard question, I'll go first." Your answers can reveal your own values. If the question is who's the most fascinating person you've ever met, don't just give a name. Say what interested you about the person, what you learned from them, or what you would ask them if you could meet them again. If you're telling a story about something you've done that's out of character, then tell them what is *in* character for you, why you hold that value, and what made you diverge from it.

If they're not immediately open, that's okay. Escalating self-disclosure is a slow build. Sometimes when we're ready to share, we think it's the right time for them to open up as well. But people do this at their own pace, in their own time. Ask questions and listen carefully to the response to gauge if the person is hesitant. Give them openings to change the subject, asking, "Is this too heavy a topic?" or "Would you rather not go here right now?"

Not only do we want to avoid grilling our date, we also don't want to overshare. Taking up all the oxygen in the room with unsolicited, deeply personal stories will only make the person feel overwhelmed. Your ability to be vulnerable and open will help them be vulnerable and to share what feels comfortable at this stage.

Here are some uncommon questions you can try out on Date Two that will help you learn what they find interesting, how they deal with challenges, what they value, how they tolerate risk, and how they make decisions.

> *Who's the most fascinating person you've ever met?*
> *What's the most out-of-character thing you've ever done or would like to do?*
> *Have you ever had a big plot twist in your life?*
> *If you won the lottery, what would you spend the money on?*
> *What's the most spontaneous thing you've ever done?*
> *What is a tough thing you dealt with in your past?*
> *What makes you proud?*
> *What would you do if you had enough money to not need a job?*

Notice how all these questions approach deeper issues without pressure or intensity. You're not asking the worst moment of someone's life or what their darkest secret is. These questions are framed to learn about the other person, but in a playful way. Don't treat your opinions as if they're better than your partner's. They're just different viewpoints that emerge from different backgrounds, different experiences, different upbringings.

Date Three. Date Three should occur when it feels natural to share some of your ideas for the future. Just as you don't need to share the same values, you don't need to have the same goals. One of you might have your whole life mapped out and the other might still be exploring what gives their life meaning. On Date Three you can try out some deeper questions, such as the ones listed below.

> *Do you have a dream you'd like to fulfill one day—a job, a trip, an accomplishment?*
> *What would you like to change about your life?*
> *If you could meet anyone, who would it be?*
> *Is there a single moment or experience that changed your life?*
> *Is there someone you consider to be your greatest teacher?*

Using the information you glean on these three dates, you can determine if you like a person's personality, respect their values, and want to help them pursue their goals. Notice the verbs I chose here. You don't have to have the same personality so long as you enjoy each other. You don't have to share their values so long as you respect them. Their goals don't even have to be things you want or enjoy. But are you interested in having these aspects of who they are and who they want to be as part of your day-to-day life, and coming to pass near or alongside you? Certain goals, like robbing a bank, should be deal-breakers. It might be that you like them so much that you'd be excited to help them with anything, within reason, that they want to pursue. Or if their goal is to eradicate homelessness in Los Angeles, such a noble goal might in itself make them more attractive.

Attraction leads to dreams. When our attraction to a person continues over time, we start to fantasize about the relationship that could develop. What adventures we could have with this person. What our life together would look like. We find ourselves in Phase Two.

Phase Two: Dreams

In the second phase of love, many of us move fast. Our attraction to this person tells us that they might match our dreams. But our dreams can cloud our vision of the other person—and our own needs. In this phase, we strive to dismantle false expectations and focus on designing, building, and nurturing a strong relationship, based on realistic expectations rather than intoxicating dreams.

False Expectations. In this phase of love we often have in mind a checklist of the qualities our partner should have. Sometimes these are very specific and/or tied to the opulences: successful, owns a home, likes to watch basketball, is a certain age or a certain level of fitness, is ready to get married in the next year. Psychologist Lisa Firestone says these unrealistic expectations are exaggerated by technology. "Online dating sites can promote the overwhelming notion that there are endless choices in the world, leaving some of us to get stuck in a cycle of perpetual searching or what one [team of researchers] called 'relationshopping.' We may unintentionally find ourselves seeking perfection or one person who can fill every imaginable criterion we've created in our mind (or on our profile)." This list-making can turn dreams into requirements. Any potential partner will come with a past, challenges, and possibly trauma, just as you do. You simply won't find someone who ticks every box on your checklist.

It's okay for different people to fill the different needs on your checklist. Research shows that the happiest people have *multiple* close relationships, so, whether we're coupled or single, we shouldn't look to any one person to meet all of our needs. John Cacioppo, a neuroscientist who researched love and affection, told the *New York Times*, "One of the secrets to a good relationship is being attracted to someone out of choice rather than out of need."

We might also hope that our partner wants the same things in life that we do—the same standard of living, the same family structure, the same likes and dislikes, the same friends, the same notions of how money should be saved and spent, the same plans for the future in terms of how hard we will work, how successful we will be, where we will live, how we will handle unexpected challenges, and how frequently we will make changes. Even if we don't say this, or even think it, we subconsciously believe that we must share the same values and goals to be in love. When one person wants to spend Sunday with their family and the other wants to play golf, or he wants to meet her friends but she's not ready, they can rashly take it as a sign that they're not meant to be. Or, later in a relationship, if they don't want to move when we do, we might take it to mean that they don't love us. And if they don't want to get married when we do, we think it's the end.

It's also not uncommon in this phase to expect our partners to read our minds, to understand us as soon as we speak, and to agree with us. We expect them to channel our emotions and desires, to select the gift we crave, to intuit how we want to celebrate our birthday, what we want for dinner tonight, how much attention we want, how much space we need.

But creating something together is better than wanting the same thing. **How you handle your differences is more important than finding your similarities.**

In Phase Two we ground our dreams in reality by establishing rhythms and routines that create the space to nurture the relationship slowly and carefully.

Rhythms and Routines. Instead of chasing the dream of what it might be to live happily ever after with this person, spend time getting to know them, building your connection. **Dreams are an illusion. Reality is far more interesting.** In corporate settings, where systems are strong, I urge leaders to incorporate sentiment in order to soften the rigidity of organization and process. And in relationships, where sentiment is strong, I embed systems to help bring structure and order to the emotional landscape.

Rhythms and routines help us maintain a steady pace that lets us get to know each other gradually and genuinely. We acknowledge that we are both looking for a long-term relationship and hoping this is it. When we establish rhythms and routines together, instead of trying to meet false expectations, our relationship is grounded in how much time we'll spend together and how we'll spend it. We don't have to wonder when the person we're interested in will call us next. We don't play games like waiting a certain number of days before returning their call.

We also start to set healthy boundaries while observing how our partner responds to them. Boundaries can be physical—some people choose to take their time becoming sexually intimate—and they can also relate to time and emotions. A small survey conducted by High-Touch Communications Inc. found that after work hours, most people expected friends, family, and romantic partners to respond to a text within five minutes. But when it came to work hours, they gave friends and family an hour, but *still* expected a romantic partner to respond within five minutes! (I've learned to give Radhi around five days. With a reminder!)

Clinical psychologist Seth Meyers advises new couples to exercise caution. In *Psychology Today*, he writes that lots of physical interaction right away heightens emotions and can color how you see the other person. Looking at them through rose-colored glasses could make you overlook red flags that would be more apparent or concerning if you weren't under the influence of the bonding chemicals we release as a result of physical contact—especially sex. Plus, you're forcing emotional intimacy with someone you barely know, and as Meyers points out, '[I]f you don't really know the person eliciting those intense emotional reactions, you may put yourself at risk. If the person is kind and good and wants the same things as you, there is no problem; if the person doesn't have the same relationship goals as you, you may end up feeling lonely and betrayed." He recommends that for at least the first month, you see one another no more than once a week, and if things are going well, then you can slowly dial up the frequency of your dates. "When you encounter a new potential friend, for example, you probably don't rush to see that friend several times per week after you first meet," Meyers writes. "Why should the guidelines for starting a romantic relationship be so different?"

The time and space we spend apart enhances the time we spend together. We want to find a balance among time together, time alone, time with our own friends, and time with collective friends. In a week, you might decide to spend one night alone, three nights together, two nights with friends that you both know, and one night with your own friends.

This gives you time together, time to decompress, time to experience other people's energy together, and time to decompress in a different way with your own friends. When you do this, you should tell your partner why it's important to you to structure your time this way. Merely saying "I need alone time" leaves them wondering what they've done wrong, while saying "I need alone time because I'm stressed out" gives them a chance to be supportive and understanding. The schedule outlined below is just a sample, but it gives you an idea of how to think about your own schedule.

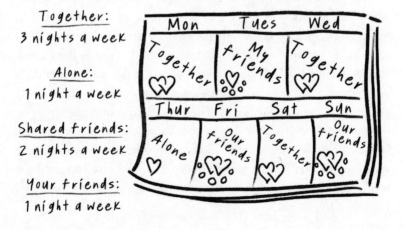

SOCIAL CALENDAR FOR THE WEEK

Together:
3 nights a week

Alone:
1 night a week

Shared friends:
2 nights a week

Your friends:
1 night a week

Mon	Tues	Wed
Together ♡	My friends ♡	Together ♡

Thur	Fri	Sat	Sun
Alone ♡	Our friends ♡	Together ♡	Our friends ♡

TRY THIS:

SET A SCHEDULE

Together, work out how often you talk, message, and see each other. Find an easy rhythm and healthy ratio that works for both of you. Decide how you want to divvy up your free time. Not every week has to be the same, but when you have a sense of how you're going to spend your time, you don't feel that you're in competition with other interests.

Nights by yourself
Nights together
Nights with mutual friends or family
Nights with your own friends

Instead of setting rhythms and routines, we often worry or wonder where the relationship is going or complain to our friends about it. We're afraid to have conversations with a partner because we don't want to put pressure on them or to be perceived as needy. But conversations about what feels right to both of you at this point are entirely appropriate. When you have these conversations, the other person may not respond the way you hoped. Their pace and commitment may be different from yours. This doesn't mean the relationship is doomed. It means you can proceed with more clarity. And if these topics scare someone off, you haven't made a mistake. You've saved yourself the weeks and months you might otherwise have spent waiting for the relationship to play out.

Instead of:	Do this:
Wondering why they never call	Set a time to connect rather than leaving it up to hope or chance
Thinking they're too busy for you	Discuss how busy/available you are in the upcoming week
Thinking they're moving too quickly	Tell them you'd like to move at a slower pace, but it doesn't mean you're not interested
Thinking they're moving too slowly	Tell them you want to make sure you've got the same aspirations
Worrying because they haven't introduced you to their family or friends	Learn about their closest relationships by asking questions and finding out who is important to them and why
Wondering if they're seeing other people	Ask them if they want to be exclusive and hear them out

In these conversations you may not always like what you learn. If the person doesn't react or respond in the way you wanted, it doesn't mean this relationship won't work. It means you can move forward in one direction or another with clarity.

Phase Three: Struggle and Growth

We are meant to fall in love, be in love, and stay in love. But we can't do any of that if we expect every day to be Valentine's Day. Trouble is inevitable. It comes when, as a couple, we inevitably discover the various ways in which we aren't aligned. In Phase Three we confront those differences and disappointments and figure out if we want to put in the effort that resolving—or living with—them requires.

When I was a monk, as you might imagine, we did a lot of self-reflection, and at one point my teacher asked a group of us to rate how much we were struggling with our minds on a scale of one to ten. Our work was intense, and we all gave ourselves pretty high struggle ratings. Then he said, "Well, imagine if there were two minds trying to get along." Two different people from different households with their own beliefs, values, expectations, and dreams—there is no way this experiment can run smoothly. Love means that you value your partner enough to confront difficult areas.

Relationships are masterfully designed to annoy us. It's easier on your own, when there's nobody around to question you or bear witness to your flaws, but that's not why you're in a relationship. Bringing awareness to your relationship is uncomfortable. Many couples bump up against an opportunity for realization and feel it as a burden. We expect love to flow naturally, but this is extremely rare, and often it means that we're not taking on the tougher issues. We need to make mistakes, identify what we need to change, and work on doing better. This is where we grow as individuals and together.

Many of these challenges are simple and domestic. For example, in my house growing up, we ate dinner, had dessert, hung out and talked for a while, then cleaned up. In Radhi's house they ate dinner, cleaned up, had dessert, and only when everything was all done would they relax into conversation. When we first started entertaining as a couple, after dinner Radhi would clean up on her own, and I felt guilty that I wasn't helping. I always said that I'd clean a bit later, and I meant it. But she was locked into the ritual from her upbringing, and I was locked into mine. Someone might say they'll clean up later and their partner might believe they're just being lazy, but more often differences like this originate in backgrounds, cultures, and habits.

The small hurdles are issues like: she snores; he's always late; they would rather watch TV when I want to go to a museum; I can't stand her best friend; he wants to spend every holiday at his parents' home; they have three cats and I'm allergic. And there may be bigger hurdles like: he has massive student debt; she has a temper that scares me; we have a long-distance relationship and neither of us wants to move; she doesn't want to have children and I do.

Disagreements large and small may challenge your confidence in your bond. You may feel: *I thought I loved you, but . . .*

In that situation, there are three routes you can take. Two of them lead to important realizations. You can leave the relationship, in which case you realize this person doesn't suit your priorities. You can work through the issue together and grow, in which case you realize you're feeling positive enough about your bond to evolve together. Or you can stay together without changing anything, in which case you don't realize anything. I advise you not to make the third choice.

This phase is very important when it comes to defining love. Because you either realize that something is a deal-breaker for you, or that you are willing to go through the growth that facing the issue involves. And if it's the latter, you will come through the experience with a stronger, more resilient love. We will discuss relationship challenges like these in more depth in Rules 5 and 6.

Phase Four: Trust

After we've overcome a challenge together, we grow. We learn to tolerate, adjust, and adapt. The growth that we do together builds into trust. Evaluating the breadth and depth of your trust for someone is a way of understanding and defining your love in the fourth and highest phase. Sometimes, we assume trust is binary: either we trust someone, or we don't. But trust increases gradually through actions, thoughts, and words. We shouldn't trust someone instantly just because they're kind to us. We give them our trust because little by little, day after day, we have shared more of ourselves and seen what they do with our honesty. All of the earlier phases build on one another to get us here.

Trust begins with ourselves. We need to be trustworthy. This means aligning what we think, say, and do. When we think something, we express it, and then we carry through with the idea. This means we can trust ourselves. So, if I feel like I need a night to myself, I communicate that to my partner. And then I take the time. I feel the benefit of the gift I've given myself, and I trust myself to take good care of myself. My partner sees me following through on my ideas, observes the results, and recognizes my trustworthiness. Then I do the same for my partner. I follow through on my promises to them. I show them that I am trustworthy and in doing so inspire them to respond with an equal level of trust.

We trust people more when they make us feel safe, when they make healthy decisions, and when we feel like they conduct their life based on values that we agree with. To evaluate the depth and breadth of your trust for your partner, consider these three aspects: physical trust, mental trust, and emotional trust.

Physical trust is when you feel safe and cared for in their presence. They want to be with you, they're present and attentive, and being around them feels good.

Mental trust is when you trust their mind, their ideas, their thoughtfulness. You may not agree with every decision they make, but you trust the way they make decisions.

Emotional trust is when you trust their values and who they are as a human. Do they treat you well? Are they supportive? Do you trust how they behave not just with you but with the other people in their life, from close friends to a waiter?

It's okay if you don't have absolute trust for your partner across this spectrum, and they can make mistakes that challenge your trust. When you identify weak spots, consider how significant the weakness is. How does it affect you? If you don't trust them in areas that are important to you, you can give your partner grace and maintain trust by sharing honestly around the issues. It's impossible to have trust if there is dishonesty, secrets, or gaslighting. Trust builds very slowly and needs to be nurtured and sustained. Think of it as growing by percentage points. Each time someone thinks, says, and does the same thing, trust grows by one percentage point. In the beginning, you trust them to speak the truth—about whom they're with, what they're doing, and what they think. Each time they do, trust grows another point. Then, as we ask them to understand our emotions and they listen, the points add up. When we share our faults, trust grows further. But trust fluctuates. If they fail to understand us or they mislead us or they betray us, our level of trust sinks and needs to be rebuilt. When we overcome a challenge together, trust grows again. We begin to trust them with our plans and dreams. And finally, we trust them enough to share our trauma with them.

When our trust is high, we feel a love that is physically and emotionally safe and secure. Our partner becomes the person we turn to with good news and bad news, knowing that they'll be on our side and by our side, helping us to weather challenges and celebrate successes.

TRY THIS:

DAILY TRUST

One of my favorite ways to show trust every day is to notice and recognize when someone follows through on a promise. Often, we reward people with thanks and gratitude when they surprise us with a nice gesture. Your partner prepares a delicious dinner that you didn't expect, and you heap on the gratitude. We do the same when they do something that they rarely do. But trust comes with quiet reliability. What about the partner who makes dinner for us regularly? We should show our appreciation for the efforts that they make daily. The more you reward it, the more they'll repeat it. And we build their trust in us the same way, by showing up.

←

This week, make an effort to thank your partner for the effort and energy they consistently bring to your partnership. Be specific. Instead of saying, "Thanks for listening," you can say, "I know I always come home and unload my emotions from work on you. I really appreciate how you listen and give me helpful advice."

Love brings us through all of these phases over and over again. We never stop deepening our faith in each other. We endlessly find our attraction renewed. We work to remove impurities. Love means that we're happy to go through this cycle together.

Now the dreams that you had in Phase Two are real. They may be different; they're probably better than anything you dared to dream. Instead of fantasizing in your head, you can try out new dreams together.

TRY THIS:

BUILD REALISTIC DREAMS TOGETHER

Establish a monthly check-in. Commit an hour every month to talking about your relationship. This gives you an opportunity to reaffirm what's working and redirect what's not working.

Identify a highlight. What are you grateful for? This helps you both know what's going well.

←

Identify a challenge. What are you struggling with? This helps you see what needs work.

Find something to work toward together this coming month. It could be a date night, a birthday celebration, a trip, a plan to redo a room in the home. You can look through a website to research a vacation you want to take. This way you're building your dreams together. Together, you're working on how you want your relationship to look and feel.

To experience all that relationships have to offer means facing the challenges and rewards of every stage of love. Sometimes people jump from relationship to relationship because they're trying to avoid the challenges that love requires. You could date someone new every three months and have a lot of fun. But there is no growth in the cycle of just flirting, hooking up, and ditching. It is this ongoing growth and understanding that helps us sustain the fun of love, the connection of love, the trust of love, the reward of love. If we never commit, we'll never get to love.

Once in a place of trust and commitment, you and your partner reveal yourselves to each other, and share more of yourselves than you allow anyone else to see. This exchange puts you in a unique position. We don't usually think of relationships in terms of learning and teaching, but that is exactly what we will explore in the next chapter: how to learn from and teach our partner.

Your Partner Is Your Guru

*Love does not consist of gazing at each other, but in look-
ing outward together in the same direction.*

—ANTOINE DE SAINT-EXUPÉRY

There is an old Zen story about a young man who, looking for a
teacher, decided to visit two ashrams. At the first, he approached
the guru there, bowed, and said, "I am looking for a guru. Do you think
you can teach me?"

The guru smiled. "Of course. I think you would be a wonderful
student, and I would be delighted to share my wisdom with you."

Then the young man visited the second ashram, approached the
guru there, and bowed. "I am looking for a guru. Do you think you can
teach me?"

The guru bowed back to him but shook his head. "Really, I know
very little," he said, "but if you'd like to come back later, perhaps we
can sit together and watch the sunset."

The young man smiled and nodded, then chose the second guru.

When I introduced the Vedic life stages, I mentioned that each of
them is referred to as an ashram. Ashrams are often associated with
a revered teacher—a guru. Since ancient times, people have traveled
from all over the world to learn from spiritual teachers such as Ramakrishna or Neem Karoli Baba, or to Dharamsala to learn from the
Dalai Lama in his temple there. A guru is beyond a teacher, guide, or
coach. They are like the captain of a ship who helps you cross the tur-
bulent ocean of life with deep compassion and friendship.

In the ashram, the teachers sat at the back of the classroom and listened to the students. They asked for feedback after they taught their classes. We weren't assigned our gurus; we chose them—a single teacher to take us on as their student and protégé—and they chose us. In school, before I went to the ashram, I struggled with authority. Maybe it was the fault of my ego, but I felt judged and criticized by my teachers. In contrast, the teachers I met as a monk were full of compassion, empathy, and humility.

Early in my monkhood, I was in London with my guru, Radhanath Swami. We were staying in quarters close to the temple, and I was seeing to his meals and other needs. Nonetheless, every day the first thing he did when he saw me was to kneel down before me, touching his head to the ground. He was nearly seventy years old, and I was only twenty-two, the new kid on the block, but he was paying respect to the soul or spiritual force within me. He would never say, "You're my disciple, so do this." He never played the guru card. And I would never say, "You're my guru, you should be figuring this out for me." I never played the student card. Each of us approached the other with awe and reverence. A committed romantic relationship highlights this awe and respect in a different way because there isn't one guru and one student. You are both gurus and students for each other.

We don't usually think about our partners as teachers or guides. But none of us can see ourselves or the world clearly on our own. We know from our reflections in solitude that each of us sees the world and each other through a different telescope with a limited range. Psychology researcher Jeremy Dean at University College London says that typically we form our concept of how others see us based on how we see ourselves, which is inherently flawed. From the view inside our heads, we are the center of our own world and everything we experience is in some way related to us; psychologists call this *egocentric bias*. That's not narcissism; it's just what comes from viewing the world through a single lens. Others see us differently, through *their* perceptions. Granted, our partners have their own biases, but learning to see ourselves through their eyes both expands and fine-tunes our own perception of ourselves. Your partner is like a mirror held in front of you.

This mirror isn't meant to make you feel bad and shouldn't have that effect. When you can't hide from someone, this makes you more transparent and aware of what you need to work on. There is no judgment or force, but support and encouragement while you work on yourself.

Your partner should be someone you want to learn with and learn from and learn through, and vice versa. We learn with someone when we try something new together and reflect on it afterward. We learn from someone when they have expertise they share with us or use to guide us. Learning through someone is the hardest. In living with another person's mind, heart, and energy, we grow through observing their behavior toward us. We need to have the attention and patience to process their behavior and figure out the lesson it's teaching us. This is particularly hard if they're annoying us. We assume it's their fault instead of realizing that their actions—and our reactions—are educating us about ourselves. At the same time, we offer lessons to our partner through our behavior and actions toward them. This shared journey is the heart of the *Grhastha* ashram, the second stage of life.

As a guru, we think about how our actions impact our partner. **A guru offers guidance without judgment, wisdom without ego, love without expectation.** Being a guru for your partner doesn't mean imparting wisdom to them (that sounds unpleasant, at best), but it does require patience, understanding, curiosity, creativity, and self-control.

You can't grow these qualities in a vacuum. Your partner is the best person to help you learn them. Although monks' relationships with one another aren't romantic, living in a communal space meant we couldn't hide much from one another. Everyone knew if you kept yourself clean. Everyone knew the quality of your meditation. Long-term relationships are similar, but each person is even more exposed than we monks were. Your partner knows everything about you, the good and the bad.

Anyone you encounter might have something to teach you, but not everyone is your guru. Our best friends, closest family, and fellow monks (for those of us who have them) can't help us learn these lessons because they can't see us as completely as the people we love romantically. A close colleague might appreciate my successes more than my wife but never have met my family. A friend might be better company at a soccer game, but I don't want to go home to him every night. A roommate, like the monks, will certainly see most of the good and bad, but might not be invested enough to help me work through my challenges. My friends and family might have varying levels of respect for my spiritual practice, but Radhi is the one who knows if I actually meditated this morning! She sees me more often and in more contexts than anyone else. Nobody is better positioned to help me become better.

When I was fortunate enough to have a breakthrough in my career about a year into our marriage, Radhi didn't seem to care very much. She didn't celebrate it. She had agreed to move with me to New York because she believed in me, but there I was having this great moment, and when she didn't seem impressed, I started wondering, *Why doesn't my wife respect me?* I was sure she loved me. We met when I had nothing. She had other options. She told me she loved me in many ways. But my material success wasn't having the effect on her that I expected. And then I thought about how earlier that same year, when we were four months from going broke, I had told her I'd figure it out. Her response was, "I trust you." I realized I didn't want or need her to love me for my achievements. I didn't need her to validate me. It's easy to respect success. She was offering me something greater: her unconditional support and faith in me. That meant more than her celebrating my external success ever could.

Radhi's disregard for material success helped me develop the quality of loving myself for my values. She taught me this without meaning to. She never said, "I love you for your values." I grappled with this all on my own. This is how we are each other's gurus without training, trying, or even realizing we are doing it. Radhi didn't even realize I'd learned the lesson until, years later, I told her. I was so lucky that she fell in love with me when we had nothing. If I had already had a certain level of recognition, I definitely would have made the mistake of wanting a wife who would appreciate my success more.

Relationships Are for Growth

If we choose a partner we can grow with, then they are always teaching us.

Researchers Arthur and Elaine Aron developed "self-expansion theory," which states that relationships—especially the one with our partner—enable us to live a bigger, richer life by expanding our sense of self. Self-expansion theory says we're motivated to partner with someone who brings to the relationship things we don't already have, such as different skills (You know how to unclog a drain!), personality traits (You're the life of the party!), and perspectives (You grew up overseas!). Our partner expands our sense of who *we* are because they expand the resources to which we have access.

The most common complaints I hear people make about their partners are, in essence, that they don't do what they want them to do ("She doesn't do her share of the household chores," "He's rude to my parents," "They never give me compliments," "He forgets my birthday"). But if you think your partner should do what you want when you want, I want to change how you look at your partner. That's not a relationship, that's ownership. Ownership is born of control. We definitely don't want that dynamic with our partner. A good partnership is transactional. Transactions are part of getting along with another person. We figure out schedules, we coordinate responsibilities, we balance our lives. But a great relationship needs more than transactions. It needs growth. Love is not just compliance or trade. Love is working through it together. We touched on this in the last rule, when we looked at the third stage of love—disappointment and revelation. In this chapter we'll talk about how you learn from each other most by overcoming challenges together.

Life becomes more enjoyable when you know each other, watch each other grow, and grow together. We say we want to grow old together, but we forget to give significance to the growing part. The guru/student dynamic is what makes you feel like you're connected to your partner. You have to put effort into a relationship in order to get something out of it—but it's not a vending machine. You can't put in effort and expect an immediate, guaranteed reward. What you invest will have to be heartfelt and true, and what you receive will be illuminating.

TRY THIS:

ASSESS WHETHER YOUR PARTNER IS SOMEONE YOU CAN LEARN AND GROW WITH

Even when we're just getting to know someone, we can spot signs that they're more than a fun companion—that they would be a good partner to grow with. If you ask yourself these questions, you'll be surprised at how much you already know about your partner's capacity to learn with you.

For each question, rate whether your partner does it always, sometimes, or never.

1. *Do they like learning about themselves?* If someone isn't curious about learning about themselves, they may struggle to learn about you. If someone has a passion for growing, they'll help you grow. Do they like to try new things? Are they self-aware? Are they open to therapy or coaching or other ways of self-development? Do they like having conversations about how they make decisions or choices?

☐ ALWAYS   ☐ SOMETIMES   ☐ NEVER

2. *Do they understand their own emotions?* Is your partner good at understanding and expressing their emotions? Do they talk about their day on a superficial level only, or do they share emotions in a real way? When they tell a story, is their emotional state part of it?

☐ ALWAYS   ☐ SOMETIMES   ☐ NEVER

$\longrightarrow$

←

3. *Do they try to understand you? Are they curious about you?* Self-awareness often but not always leads to curiosity about others. Do they use their emotional skills to better understand you? If they haven't gotten to a place where they can expand their radius of care and love, it means they are still in *Brahmacharya*. They are still a student of themselves and not ready to learn with you.

☐ ALWAYS ☐ SOMETIMES ☐ NEVER

4. *Can they entertain themselves?* It's easier to learn with another person if they love solitude. It means they have their own journey and their own path, which allows you to travel your own path beside them.

☐ ALWAYS ☐ SOMETIMES ☐ NEVER

5. *Are they open to finding new ways of solving problems?* For example, if they're having trouble with a colleague, do they talk to you or a friend about it? Are they willing to talk to the colleague, to propose a compromise, or to shift gears by asking the person out to lunch? Learning and growing means having the determination and flexibility to address issues from new angles. That inclination is transferrable to a relationship.

☐ ALWAYS ☐ SOMETIMES ☐ NEVER

6. *Do they support others in their growth?* Look to see if they make the effort to support a friend, a sibling, or a mentee. Is helping others a part of their life? This shows you that they can extend their radius of love and care as is necessary in *Grhastha*.

☐ ALWAYS ☐ SOMETIMES ☐ NEVER

→

7. *Do they inspire you to be better and more?* A partner can make you feel ambitious, not to impress them but because they believe in your abilities and give you the confidence to follow your interests and inclinations.

☐ ALWAYS   ☐ SOMETIMES   ☐ NEVER

Your answers to this assessment don't make or break your relationship. Look at the questions to which you responded "never" or "sometimes." This tells you the areas where you need to take the lead. If your partner never spends time in solitude, understand that this is something you'll have to either accept or encourage them to start in ways that appeal to them. You might come up with activities that will help them spend time reflecting. (See the TRY THIS exercises in Rule 1.) Or they might have low self-awareness that will impact your relationship. If they don't try to understand you, you have to gently educate them about how you work, saying things like, "When I'm tired after work, I have a shorter fuse. Let's save figuring out our finances for the weekend."

When we enroll in a class or rent an Airbnb, we research it before we commit. Exercises like this are research into our relationship. A partner who doesn't check all these boxes could still develop into someone with whom you want to learn and grow, if you're open to teaching each other.

Become a Better Guru

In *The Guru and Disciple Book*, Kripamoya das talks about how traditional spiritual gurus and their students help one another. He lists fourteen qualities of the guru that were first described by the medieval philosopher Vedanta Desika. I've included the Sanskrit descriptions and Kripamoya das's translations of some of these qualities below to show how the qualities of the teacher and the student that I describe are grounded in scripture.

Do Not Lead, Serve

One of the guru qualities that Kripamoya das lists is *dambha asuyadhi muktam*, which means "exhibits no inauspicious characteristics such as egoism or jealousy." Remember how my guru, Radhanath Swami, bowed down on the floor in front of me? A guru doesn't lord his position over his student or try to control them. Zen master Shunryu Suzuki was set to visit the Cambridge Buddhist Association, in Massachusetts, arriving on a Wednesday evening. The day before, several members started cleaning the house in preparation for the visit. They were cleaning the meditation room when the doorbell rang—it was Suzuki Roshi, arriving a day early. When he saw what they were doing, he smiled, tied up the sleeves of his robes, and joined in the cleaning. The next day he found a ladder and started scrubbing the windows.

A guru doesn't hesitate to play any position if it helps their student. There is no ego involved. The guru is honored and grateful to support another. A real guru doesn't want power but empowers their partner.

The guru is not trying to command, demand, or force their partner to do anything or be a certain way. Instead of saying, "You should do this," the guru says, "I'd love to share this idea with you" or "Have you ever thought of it this way?"

In the ashram, if a monk didn't wake up on time, their guru wouldn't yell, "What's wrong with you? Why didn't you show up at morning meditation?" Rather they might say, "Did you sleep well? Is there any way I can help you?" The guru is focused on the behavior's cause, not its consequence.

In the Marvel movie *Doctor Strange*, surgeon Stephen Strange is a self-important narcissist. Then an accident severely damages his hands, leaving him unable to perform surgery. Desperate to regain his abilities, he travels to Nepal in search of a teacher called the Ancient One. When Strange arrives, he sees an older man with glasses and a long goatee, sitting reading a book. "Thank you, Ancient One, for seeing me," he says. The woman pouring Strange's tea stands up. "You're very welcome," she says. His education has begun.

The Ancient One shows him a chakra chart, and he dismisses it, saying he's seen it in gift shops. Then, after forcing Strange to experience alternate dimensions, the Ancient One asks, "Have you ever seen *that* before in a gift shop?"

Strange, in awe, says, "Teach me."

The Ancient One just says no.

Our guru powers aren't so vast, and our lessons may not be so succinct, but the point is that when your partner sees you aren't trying to control or assert authority over them, you bolster their trust and confidence.

Set a Good Example

Another guru quality that Kripamoya das lists is *sthira dhiyam*, meaning that the mind remains firmly fixed, even in difficult situations. This means the guru should try to behave in an exemplary way. Radhi wanted me to go to the gym and to eat right, but she didn't nag me about it. Rather, she guided me to a healthier lifestyle by living it herself. She doesn't cut corners in her own practice, and I wouldn't have switched my habits if she hadn't been so consistent in her own commitment. The guru doesn't model good habits because they're trying to preach or instruct or brag, but because it makes them joyful and happy. I have a client who complained that his wife spent too much money on bags and shoes. But when I asked him about his own spending, he admitted that he had just bought a fancy new car. She'd have to buy hundreds of shoes and bags to come close to the cost of that car. So he was imposing standards on her that he wasn't adhering to himself. If he was worried about their finances, he could suggest that they both start monitoring their spending habits, but he couldn't impose his values on her spending without reining in his own. The guru will never ask the student to do something that they're not comfortable doing themselves. They lead by example. St. Francis said, "It is no use walking anywhere to preach unless our walking is our preaching." When you lead by example, you come to understand how difficult it is to grow because you're doing the hard work of growth yourself. This gives you compassion and empathy toward your partner rather than judgment and expectations.

Support Their Goals, Not Yours

Dayalum is the guru's quality of having spontaneous compassion and kindness for students. I expand this to suggest that the guru should make sure they support the student's own path.

There is a story in Bhakti scripture about a stone bridge being built over the sea between India and Sri Lanka. All the animals help build the bridge. The strong monkey god, Hanuman, is chucking massive rocks and boulders into the growing structure. He notices that the squirrel, eager to do his share, is throwing little pebbles in the same direction. Hanuman sneers at the squirrel. "How is that even going to make a difference?"

Then Lord Ram, the virtuous prince overseeing the project, steps in. He says, "You are each doing the most you can according to your capacity. The rock is equal to the pebble." He points out that the pebbles help the boulders stay in place and thanks the squirrel for his efforts.

We take pride in noticing our partner's potential and urging them to fulfill it, but we don't want to impose our goals on them. Our goal is simply to help them get to the next step in their journey, not the next step in our vision of what their journey should be. If our partner wants to learn to meditate, we might find an app or a nearby center where they can begin their practice, but we don't tell them how often they should meditate or what they should expect from it. If our partner has a conflict with a family member, we might direct them to resources to help make the peace or rearrange our plans to give them the time to do it, but we're not going to plan a vacation with the relative to force the issue. The same is true for getting in shape, or work goals, or making friends in a new neighborhood. We want to help them become the best version of the person they want to be. We support their dreams. We genuinely want to see them grow. But if we're trying to get them to do something *we* think would be best for them, they're not likely to trust our insights.

When Sokei-an Shigetsu Sasaki, a Japanese monk who went on to found the Buddhist Society of America, had just started studying Zen Buddhism, he met legendary teacher Soyen Shaku, the first Zen Buddhist master to teach in the United States. Shaku had heard that Sokei-an was a wood-carver. "Carve me a Buddha," he said to the young monk. A few weeks later, Sokei-an presented Shaku with a wooden statue of the Buddha, which Shaku tossed out the window. As Sokei-an later said, it seemed an unkind action, but it wasn't. "He'd meant for me to carve the Buddha in myself." Shaku didn't want a gift from Sokei-an. He wanted Sokei-an to do something for himself. The guru does not project their goals, ambitions, and timelines onto the student. The guru lets the student show them how to be supportive in the way that they need and want. (But I also suggest you don't throw anything your partner gives you out the window.)

TRY THIS:

HELP YOUR PARTNER KNOW THEIR GOALS

Instead of telling your partner what their goals should be and how to reach them, ask them three questions.

1. What's really important to you right now?

2. What do you need to get there?

3. Is there anything I can do to help you?

In this way, you let your partner lead themselves to their answers. Understanding your partner's goals without editing them to suit yours is one of the greatest gifts you can give someone. When we hear other people's goals, we automatically put them through our filter and lens. That's too small, or too big. Your perspective is important, but we don't want to project or predict. We don't want to share our own limitations or aspirations. Make sure to listen to their reasons, what motivates them and why. You will learn from this too.

Guide Them to Learn in Their Own Way

In Kripamoya das's list, the guru is a friend and guide, always seeking their welfare as a well-wisher: *dirgha bandhum*. To be a good guru, watch and access how your partner learns and determines the best way to present whatever it is you want them to learn. If they don't like reading, suggest podcasts. If that doesn't resonate with them, see if there's a course they'd like to take. I've had clients tell me, "My partner doesn't practice meditation or mindfulness enough. I am trying to make them read your book." My question would be, "What do they enjoy? Basketball? I have an amazing interview with Kobe Bryant. Music? Jennifer Lopez and Alicia Keys have both been on the podcast." Find a way to connect your partner to your interests through their interests.

TRY THIS:

IDENTIFY YOUR PARTNER'S LEARNING STYLE

Which learning style best describes your partner?

Hearing. Your partner likes to take in new information through their ears. They like to listen to podcasts, audiobooks, or TED Talks.

Vision. Your partner likes to watch someone demonstrate a skill or to follow a diagram. Your partner learns best from YouTube or MasterClass.

Thought. Your partner likes to absorb information in their head, so they might like to read a book on a topic of interest, taking notes to put it into their own words as they go.

Motion. Your partner learns by doing. They'll want to take a workshop where they get to try out new skills as they acquire them.

Match your partner to a learning style. To do this, first ask them if they know how they best learn. If they don't know, ask them when they last learned something new and what form it came in. If you're still drawing a blank, observe what they spend their spare time doing. Do they watch documentaries? Listen to audiobooks? You can even help them find a way to test all the approaches and see which one they prefer. Then give them guidance for how to learn using the formats I suggest above for each style. You can give them a gift to inspire them, do some research for them, or experiment together. Gurus look for creative ways to share ideas for their partner rather than forcing them or pushing them.

Wanting to help our partner should not be confused with wanting to control our partner. One of the most common ways we try to control our partner is to impose our timeline on them. You may do something in a day while your partner takes a week. Your timeline is not correct. A guru moves at the time and pace of the student, without a deadline.

If I said to Radhi, "Let's talk about your goals right now," she would shut down. But if I said to her, "On Sunday, let's go to a park and write in our journals about what we want from this year, then talk about it together," she would be delighted. I try to offer her suggestions that match her rhythm. Let your student set their own pace, and when they don't reach their goals and feel sad, don't say, "I told you to do it earlier." Be patient and thoughtful as they do the work, offering your time and resources and supporting them while giving them the confidence to do it on their own. Don't do it for them, but provide encouragement and guidance in a supportive way. Through this restraint, you're developing patience and compassion. This is how, as a guru, you yourself are growing as you help your partner grow.

Don't Criticize, Judge, or Abuse

Kripamoya das describes the guru as being free from deceitful speech, always telling the truth: *satya vacam*. I take this in a slightly different direction, where I ask you to be mindful of the way you speak to your partner, so you don't mislead them or shut them down. It's not what you say, it's how you say it. Telling your partner they're sloppy won't change them. "Stop playing PlayStation" won't work. Think about the classroom where you would best learn. It is welcoming, accessible, and there is a natural flow of conversation and activity. Nobody wants a teacher who yells at the class or sends students to stand in the corner. We want students who respect teachers and teachers who respect students—a peaceful, sustainable exchange.

Researchers have identified critical feedback as one of the most common triggers that send us into a fixed mindset, which Stanford professor Carol Dweck describes in her book *Mindset* as when we see our qualities as fixed traits that can't be changed. When we're in the fixed mindset, we focus on the perception that we've been judged to be somehow incompetent rather than seeing the growth opportunity that the criticism might provide. When our partner says, "When you do the laundry, all our clothes end up wrinkled!" we hear something like, "You're inadequate and incapable." As a guru, we must pay attention to how we give feedback so it's more likely to be received in the spirit we intend. Something more like: "I really appreciate your help with the laundry. I realized that when I let the laundry sit in the dryer for a while before folding it, it ends up wrinkled. So now, if I have to run an errand or do something else, I don't start the dryer until I'm back. You might try another approach, but the main thing is, neither of us likes ironing. You think we could try that? Or do you have a better idea?" Yes, communicating this way takes a lot more words. And yes, it requires more effort to frame your feedback this way, but it's worth it because it's more likely to keep the other person engaged and responsive to your criticism.

Gurus don't use anger, harsh words, or fear to inspire their students. They realize that fear is a good motivator in the short term but over the long term it erodes trust. Criticism is lazy communication. It's not constructive, compassionate, or collaborative. Look for ways to communicate so that the other person can consume, digest, and apply your input effectively. Offer them a "love sandwich" where you deliver a piece of constructive criticism between two tasty slices of positive feedback. Give suggestions instead of criticism. For example, my client's husband was struggling with unreasonable demands from his boss. She wanted to say, "Well, you let them walk all over you!" but that would injure his ego and hurt his feelings. Instead, she reminded him that he was very talented, but only human, and suggested that he talk to his boss not in terms of what he couldn't get done, but what he could get done in the allotted time. While his boss was unsympathetic and unyielding, my client's husband thanked her for supporting him and on further discussion they decided that after he finished his project, he would start looking for another job.

Imagine you're taking a long-awaited vacation and your partner booked the Airbnb for the wrong date. Instead of berating them for their incompetence, remember all they did to plan this trip. Don't say, "You messed this up and you're going to figure it out!" Instead, offer to book a hotel for the night while they sort out the Airbnb. Remember, you are trying to nourish your partner's joy. You highlight the good, you help create a path, you amplify their potential. Instead of criticizing in public, you compliment in public and in private.

Instead of this:	Say this:
"You never do x; you're so bad at y." (criticizing what they do wrong)	"I appreciate it when you do x" (acknowledging what they do right)
"If you ever do that again I'm leaving you."	"This is how it makes me feel when you do that."
"Did you see what x's partner did for them?"	"I really appreciate when you do x for me"
"This is your fault, so you fix it."	"I know you're struggling with this; can I help you?"
"You've changed. You were never like this before."	"It's normal that we're changing and having to reset expectations."

Become a Better Student

Some of us find it easier to lead than to be led, particularly when our partners aren't skilled and patient gurus. But even in those circumstances, we have the opportunity to learn from our partner. What if they just sit around all day? Well, maybe it irks you to see your partner relax because you don't allow yourself to take a break. Your partner is unconsciously teaching you that you need to give yourself downtime.

And if our partner criticizes us or isn't inclined to help us grow, we must be the kind of student who, by our behavior and qualities, brings out the best in our guru.

My guru at the ashram said that if a teacher was a ten out of ten, then the student might only be a one out of ten because the teacher would constantly uplift them. But if the teacher was a one out of ten, the student would have to rise to be a ten out of ten in order to learn from the teacher. In other words, if you approach your studies diligently enough, with an open mind and heart, you can learn even more from a mediocre teacher than you might from a great one.

Be Open-Minded and Curious

Kripamoya das also cites fifteen qualities of the good disciple. One of them is *tattva bodha abhilasi*, meaning "has an eagerness to learn." The Buddhist term *shoshin* means "beginner's mind." We want to come to our relationship with the open willingness of a new student, no matter how long we have been together. Zen master Shunryu Suzuki said, "In the beginner's mind there are many possibilities, in the expert's mind there are few."

As a student, being open to the new means that when your partner makes suggestions, inviting you to explore new ground, you are receptive. If your guru offers you bad advice or presents it harshly, avoid the understandable temptation to dismiss it or react with anger. Instead, explore the possibility that your partner might actually have some wisdom to share, by asking them the right questions. Questions that aren't rhetorical or condescending but rather are sincere efforts to understand the idea. You might ask: "Can you help me with specific ideas?" Or: "If I wanted to take your suggestion, where would I begin?" Or: "Could you explain that to me step by step?" Or: "I would love your advice—can we discuss this when we're both in a better space?" There's an old saying, "When the student is ready, the teacher will appear." It's a symbiotic relationship.

Practice Humility

To ask the right questions, one needs intelligence but also humility. Humility doesn't mean to be meek and weak. It means being open to learning and honest with ourselves and others about our strengths and weaknesses. Kripamoya das described the student as *tyakta mana*—humble and prideless. Indeed, humility is essential for love in general because it keeps the ego—love's enemy—at bay. Ego and pride end more relationships than anything else because most misunderstandings are based on ego or pride. Ego mires us in the false belief that we're always right, that we know best, and the other person is wrong. This belief makes it impossible to learn from our partner.

If you watch Nathan Chen skating in the Olympics, you don't think, *I'm such a bad skater. I'm small and worthless.* You recognize and appreciate his grace and skill and the years of effort he put into his art. Humility is honoring other people's skills, abilities, and growth rather than dishonoring your own.

TRY THIS:

APPRECIATE YOUR PARTNER'S KNOWLEDGE

Next time you're talking with your partner, notice an expertise they have that you usually take for granted. How can you find something extraordinary in what you already know about your partner? Maybe they think before they make a decision. Maybe they always write thoughtful thank-you notes. Maybe they consistently offer you good advice when you don't know exactly how to ask for something at work. Look for skills your partner has that you've never acknowledged. When you notice one, share it with them. This appreciation is nourishment for your partner's strengths.

Be a Good Translator

Kripamoya das said that the student controls mind and speech—*danta*. Stephen Covey, author of *The 7 Habits of Highly Effective People*, might agree with that guidance. He said, "Most people don't listen with the intent to understand; they listen with the intent to reply." There are three steps to responding effectively when your partner shares an issue they have with you. First echo what they said, then say what you heard, explaining it back to them in your own words. Finally, when you're sure that you both understand the issue at hand, tell them how you feel. We tend to respond with what we feel first, using what they said to justify our feelings.

Say your partner tells you, "I was embarrassed when you didn't introduce me to your friends." They're telling you how they feel.

If you respond first with how you feel, you might say, "Well, you never include me in conversations with *your* friends." But if you tell them, "I'm hearing that you're upset with me. Why did it make you feel that way?" you give your partner an opportunity to make sure that they're explaining themselves effectively. You're showing them what they sound like, and now they can be more focused on how they speak and share what they're saying. At the same time, you're clarifying what you're trying to do in the relationship—to connect and make the other person feel understood. Your guru can take a cue from the tone you set.

TRY THIS:

INTRODUCE A NEW IDEA

Practice your communication skills by bringing up a new topic and being attentive to what your partner says, listening to the points they make and helping them uncover and articulate the feelings, needs, and wants underneath their words.

Pick an open-ended topic that you haven't discussed before, one that might inspire you both to imagine something new you might do together.

Suggested ideas:

What if we both quit our jobs and moved?

What if we traveled for a whole year?

If we can retire one day, what would we do with our time?

If we had a million dollars to give away, who would we give it to and why?

←

Questions to explore (you can each answer these questions, but your focus should be on listening to your partner's responses):

What's the first thing that comes to your mind when I ask this question?
Why does what you said appeal to you?

Then, show your partner that you heard them:

Explain to them what you heard them say their idea would be.
Discuss what preferences and priorities you think might underlie that idea.
Tell them what you learned about them in this conversation.
Talk about whether there's a viable version of what they wanted that you could bring into your lives now.

For example:

If the question were how you would spend a year of travel, perhaps your inclination would be to move to the south of France to eat *pain au chocolat* for a year, but your partner wants to plan a bike trip across the US. You can recognize their longing for physical activity. Maybe they are also expressing a desire to experience travel at a slower pace, or to spend time camping along the way. Once you've understood more about their fantasy, you could consider getting them a bike for their birthday. Or maybe you'll plan a weekend cycling trip together.

This is practice for how you can listen to your partner instead of listening to reply when you encounter more challenging, emotionally loaded topics.

Appreciate the Guru

Kripamoya das said that the student is *krita-vid-sisya*—grateful for knowledge. Notice and appreciate it when your partner is offering you help without reward or return. We don't often stop to thank them for their constant presence, their willingness to help, and the simple, small things they do. Take time to thank them and notice what they get right and do well even if it seems simple and easy. Showing gratitude like this creates a feedback loop, where they feel grateful for your appreciation and are inspired to continue in their guru-like ways.

TRY THIS:

ACKNOWLEDGE THE GURU'S SKILLS

Think about your partner's skills as a guru. What are their strengths? Have you taken the time to acknowledge them? And if you perceive some of these areas as weaknesses, is there anything you can learn about yourself from your reaction? Find the areas where your partner is your guru and thank them. You can thank them out of the blue, or the next time they show these qualities.

1. Leads through service
Your partner is willing to play any role in order to help you, even if it's not their field of expertise. Maybe they function as a manager, an accountant, an IT technician, a food delivery person. Do they help you out of compassion rather than telling you what to do?

2. Leads by example
What do they commit to and do without fail? If you can't find anything, you're probably not looking hard enough.

$\longrightarrow$

3. Helps you to your goals, not theirs

Your partner allows you to be yourself. They don't force or urge you to be different. They may not be serving or helping you, but when they don't force you to be someone you're not, that's a form of support.

4. Offers guidance without criticism, judgment, or abuse

When you've fallen short on your goals or made a mistake, your partner supports you and encourages you without pressuring you.

Students need to be acknowledged as well. You can do the same exercise for the qualities of a student.

Your Guru Is Not Your God

Alongside the openness of being a student comes perhaps the most important quality to your relationship with your guru: to maintain your sense of self. Just because you learn from them doesn't mean you shape yourself to their ideal and stop learning from anyone else. It doesn't mean you stop going to other people for different activities and insights. Your partner is your guru, not your god. They help you become better, but they aren't better than you.

It's normal to take on some characteristics of our partners. Studies have found that couples start to adopt the same mannerisms, to sound alike, and even to eat the same quantity of food. Some merging of habits is inevitable, but we want to retain our individuality within the relationship. We want to take on positive qualities of our partner without becoming them (or their assistant). You are always writing your story. When you meet someone, you start cowriting with them. The stories intertwine. In the Vedic scriptures, this is described as your karma being intertwined, but not your soul. I think of this as cowriting your karma together. Karma is the activity in your life, but your soul is your identity. You might change and grow together, mixing your karmas, mixing the energy of two families and two communities, but don't lose your identity. **Remember your own personality, values, and goals. Don't lose the thread of your own story.** Spend time in solitude. Don't cancel plans with friends and family. Pursue your own interests, not just your partner's. This is not slighting, ignoring, or betraying your partner. It's fueling your growth in ways that they can't, which means you'll have even more to offer them. And if you have no more growing left to do together, you can take time apart. That's okay.

We must break up if our partner becomes abusive toward us. A guru would never teach through abuse. Abuse only teaches you to fear your partner, to suppress your instincts, to ignore your own pain, and to feed someone else's ego. Emotional, mental, and physical abuse should be deal-breakers for everyone, and that's clear when you think about your partner as your guru. Why would your guru hurt you? How can you grow when you are hurt and scared? And if you are suffering in any of these ways but blame yourself, try asking yourself: Am I learning from this person? Are they learning from me? Is this the way I want to learn? If the answers are "no," then deciding to leave is the greatest gift you can give yourself, and there are many organizations that can help you do so safely.

The Guru's Greatest Gift

We have heard people say of couples, "They grew apart," but we never say, "They grew together." Yet, if you are not growing apart, that is most likely what you are doing—quietly but surely helping each other observe, learn, and grow in all directions. The discomfort of change is offset by the delight of shared understanding. The growth that a guru and student cultivate keeps a relationship exciting and new even as it matures and you grow more familiar with each other. In the next chapter we will talk about the most important way a guru can help a student grow: in pursuing their purpose.

Purpose Comes First

The meaning of life is to find your gift. The purpose of life is to give it away.

—DAVID VISCOTT

Dharma: The Compass

Many years ago, I asked a client and his partner to write down their priorities in order. His list said: 1. Kids. 2. You (meaning his wife). 3. Work. Her list said 1. Me. 2. Kids. 3. You (meaning her husband). He was hurt and dismayed that she put herself above everything else. But then she explained. "I put myself first because I want to give the best version of myself to you and our family." Putting oneself first sounds selfish, and it can be if you're eating all the cookies or grabbing the best seat at the table. But for any of us to bring the best version of ourselves to our relationships, we have to pursue our own purpose or spiritual calling. In Hinduism it's called our *dharma*.

Dharma is the intersection of passion, expertise, and service. Living in your dharma means that you've connected your natural talents and interests with a need that exists in the universe. Your dharma doesn't have to be your job. You're fortunate if you can earn a living following your calling, but that isn't always possible. Also, your purpose doesn't have to dominate your life. It might be a hobby, your involvement in church, being a parent, starting a company. It could be volunteering for a dog rescue in your spare time or organizing a local group to help people out of debt or blogging about budget travel. Dharma is not so much about any particular activity—it's more about *why* you do that activity, whether it's to create something, to connect people, to share what you've learned, to serve others or the world. Whatever it is, your dharma is not a casual interest. It's a passion. It defines you. When you practice it, you think, *This is who I am*. **Your dharma is a journey, not a destination.** It can take a long time to find the ways to best extract meaning, joy, and fulfillment from your pursuits. As long as a person is pursuing their purpose, they're already living it.

The Vedas describe dharma as one of the four fundamental pursuits that drive us forward in life, shaping our choices and actions:

dharma—*purpose*
artha—*work and finance*
kama—*pleasure and connection, your relationships with others*
moksha—*liberation from the material world, when you connect with the spirit*

THE FOUR PURSUITS

Notice that dharma comes first in this list, which is no accident. The Vedas were intentional about the order, even though these pursuits overlap and intersect with one another throughout our lives. We may not think of purpose as a basic need like financial security and social connection, but it is actually even more essential.

Dharma comes before *artha* because it guides how you spend your time, money, and energy. It gives meaning to the money. The same principle applies to relationships—if you have no sense of purpose, you don't bring thoughtfulness and compassion to your pursuit of pleasure. When you prioritize these four pursuits in the order the Vedas suggest, dharma clarifies your values and priorities to yourself and your partner. You pursue money with a clearer sense of how it should be spent, and you pursue love with a desire to create a meaningful life with your partner. Eventually these three pursuits lead to *moksha*, where all we do is devoted to a spiritual journey.

The Vedas aren't alone in prioritizing purpose. Researchers from the University of California, Los Angeles, and the University of North Carolina wanted to see whether hedonia—the kind of self-satisfaction that comes from opulences like fame or riches, along with personal gain and pleasure—looks different in our bodies from eudaimonia— the satisfaction that comes from having a deep sense of purpose and meaning in life. They gave participants a survey asking questions such as how often they feel happy (hedonia), and how often they feel that their life has a sense of direction and meaning (eudaimonia). The researchers found that while those with higher levels of hedonia generally experienced more positive feelings, they had weaker immune profiles, including higher inflammation and other markers that made them more prone to illness.

Anthony Burrow, a professor of human development at Cornell University, led another study that showed a strong sense of purpose can even make us immune to the likes (or lack of likes) we garner on social media. First, he and his research partner had participants fill out a series of questionnaires measuring the degree to which they felt connected to a sense of purpose in life. Then the participants were told they would be helping to test a new social networking site. First they

had to start building their profiles by posting a selfie. The researchers gave them a camera, then pretended to upload the image to the
fictional website. Then, after five minutes, they told the participants
how many likes their selfie had gotten compared with other people's
photos—above average, about the same, or below average. Finally, the
participants filled out another questionnaire that measured self-esteem.
It turned out that those with less of a sense of purpose in life experienced spikes or drops in their self-esteem based on how many likes
their selfie got, or didn't get, while those with a stronger sense of purpose were relatively unaffected. Their self-esteem held steady.

Purpose insulates and protects our self-esteem, and research has
connected high self-esteem to more satisfying relationships. As Burrow
says, "We are confronted with the ups and downs of life, but purpose
is an active ingredient that helps us stay stable." We bring that stability
to one another. It's a foundation on which we can build our life with
our partner.

There's a story attributed to the Buddha about two acrobats—a
master and his assistant. The master climbed to the top of a bamboo
pole and told his assistant to follow and stand on his shoulders. "We
will demonstrate our skill for the crowd, and they will give us some
money. You will look out for me, and I will look out for you, and that
way we will be safe." The assistant assessed the situation, then shook
her head. "No, master," she said. "You will look after yourself and I will
look after myself, and then we will show our skill. And in *that way* we
will make some money and be safe." This is why my client's wife was
onto something when she put her purpose first in her list of priorities.
A couple's approach to their dharmas should be like that of the assistant acrobat: "You go do what you need to do, while I go do what I need
to do."

People think that putting the other person first is a sign of love.
We romanticize the idea of making sacrifices and devoting ourselves
to another person, and there are beautiful ways to do so. But I've seen
people who put their own purpose aside and years down the line feel
lost or misled. They regret their choices and resent their partners for
not helping them prioritize their purpose. And with reason—I don't

condone resentment, but if your partner can bear to watch you give up your purpose, that's not love. **Your purpose has to come first for you, and your partner's purpose has to come first for them.** Then you come together with the positive energy and stability that come from pursuing your purposes.

You may wonder why I'm talking about finding your own purpose in a book about relationships. It's something you do in solitude, even within a relationship. But just as solitude helps us enter a relationship with self-knowledge, so knowing our purpose helps us sustain and grow a relationship holding on to our sense of purpose and supporting our partner's efforts to do so too.

In every relationship there are actually three relationships: your relationship with each other, your relationship with your purpose, and your partner's relationship with their purpose. We need to pay attention to all three. This seems hard, but it actually makes life easier. If you want to truly love someone and give them your best self, then you have to be your best self. Much as a depleted parent has a harder time caring for their children, a person who doesn't take care of their own purpose has a hard time supporting their partner in theirs. By looking after ourselves, we prepare to look after others. As marriage and family therapist Kathleen Dahlen deVos told HuffPost, the happiest couples are those who can move past their initial obsession with each other to prioritize their own pursuits and goals. "When couples rely solely on each other to meet all of their emotional intimacy and social needs, this 'merging' can stifle healthy personal growth or threaten to slip into co-dependency." DeVos adds that couples need to maintain their individual identity within the relationship rather than let the relationship define them.

When you are both actively pursuing your purpose, your relationship benefits in several ways. Dharma helps you live a passionate, inspired, motivated life, a life you want to share with someone. You also have the pleasure of living alongside someone who is fulfilled. There is great joy in seeing the person you love doing what they love. Furthermore, you're more aware of, and sympathetic to, the struggles they might have along the way.

When we aren't pursuing our purposes, troubles arise. Sometimes when you think there's a problem between you and your partner, the root of the dissatisfaction is that one or both partners aren't following their purpose. My client Aimee was upset that her partner, Marco, a guitarist in an up-and-coming band, was always touring. But when he cut a tour short to spend more time with her, she felt too guilty to enjoy it. She realized that if she herself had a goal to work toward, that would better solve the issue between them. When Aimee, who was a painter, started teaching lessons out of a friend's garage, she got excited to put on a group show with their best work. Marco made sure he could leave the tour to attend the opening of the show, and though she was busy during his visit, she felt proud of what she had accomplished and happy to share it with him.

Even in a household that looks ideal—where your work lives and home life check all the boxes—if either partner doesn't know their purpose or isn't actively engaged in it, that individual emptiness impacts the relationship. The partner without a purpose might become envious of the other's progress, in which case both partners miss out on the joy, energy, and contentment that two people who are fueled by their purpose bring to each other.

If one person in a couple feels lost, they might start to feel like their partner, who is comparatively busy and fulfilled, doesn't care about them. The busy partner might worry about their partner not having a life beyond the relationship. They might feel responsible for entertaining their partner and keep them busy. Ultimately, each might resent the other for how they spend their time.

In a relationship, we must be careful that neither partner loses track of what they care about, what they value, and what makes them feel true to themselves. Now we'll look first at how you can prioritize your dharma within a relationship and then at how to help your partner prioritize their dharma.

How to Prioritize Your Dharma

Sal Khan went to business school, but he didn't think he had the fortitude to be an entrepreneur. Instead, he began a lucrative career at a start-up hedge fund. Then, during a visit from family, he discovered that his twelve-year-old cousin was struggling with math. Sal offered to tutor her remotely. It was 2004, so the pair used a combination of phone calls and early messenger technology. Within a few months under his tutelage, Sal's cousin retook her math placement test and went from a remedial class to an advanced class. Soon other family members, then friends all over the country began reaching out to Sal for tutoring. Sal started recording his lessons and uploading them to YouTube, plus he created custom software for people to practice the lessons. Khan Academy was born. Sal still enjoyed his hedge fund job, but he felt most engaged and excited by the opportunity to share his lessons in the hopes they'd help others. He had found his purpose.

If you don't know where to start, I recommend following this progression:

The Pyramid of Purpose

Learn—Devote time to learning in the area of your purpose

Experiment—Take what you learned and try it out for yourself in order to discover what works for you and what doesn't

Thrive—Perform your purpose, building consistency and steadiness in what you're doing

Struggle—Face the challenges that inevitably come and use them for growth

Win—Celebrate successes, big and small

PYRAMID OF PURPOSE

Win
Struggle
Thrive
Experiment
Learn

Learn

Purpose begins with curiosity. We think starting means *doing*, but it actually begins with learning. Don't skip or avoid the learning phase. The reason we say knowledge is power is that it can help you overcome any fear of the unexpected.

TRY THIS:

LEARN ABOUT YOUR PURPOSE

We learn about our purpose by considering and exploring our interests and skills.

PASSIONS

Ask yourself questions to identify your passions.

> If you could be paid to do anything, what would it be?
> Are there hobbies you loved as a kid but don't do anymore?
> Do you have a hidden talent?
> Have you seen someone else that you consider to have your dream job?
> Is there something you'd be doing if you weren't limited by where or how you live?
> Is there something you used to be good at that you miss?
> Is there a talent you haven't been able to pursue lately?

STRENGTHS

Identify what roles you play at home or at work to identify your strengths.

→

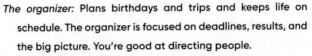

The organizer: Plans birthdays and trips and keeps life on schedule. The organizer is focused on deadlines, results, and the big picture. You're good at directing people.

The energizer: Outgoing, enthusiastic, and optimistic, the energizer gets people excited to go do what the organizer planned.

The empathizer: Emotionally intelligent, patient, a good listener, and supportive, the empathizer is intuitive about how people are feeling.

The analyzer: Detail oriented, systematic, careful, and cautious, the analyzer spots issues that could become problematic.

YOUR PURPOSE IS WHERE YOUR PASSIONS INTERSECT WITH YOUR SKILLS.

Once you've identified passions and skills, find ways to learn about them.

1. Take a class, read a book, or listen to a podcast in your area of interest. Can you get a certification that will help you develop your talent?

2. Look for groups of people who can inspire you by what they're doing or how they do it.

3. Try out something in the area of your purpose over the weekend. Observe what excites you and deepens your interests.

My favorite way to learn is to speak to people who are already doing what I want to do. When a doctor goes to a conference on a specific disease, they connect with other doctors studying that disease. They learn about advances in science. They hear about new treatments or research. The same is true in any area of passion. A mentor will help you form a vision of how you can start to pursue your purpose and what your life might look like as you continue to live in your purpose. The mentor can also give you concrete advice as first steps you can take, how you can network, and where else you can turn to learn more.

Even if you can't find people in your field, just being around others who are actively pursuing their purpose can be extremely inspiring. Ask questions; be curious. Find people who enjoy talking about how they found their way. If they're not in your community, look to the greats who tell their stories in books, on YouTube, in TED Talks, and on podcasts.

TRY THIS:

MEET WITH A MENTOR

1. FIND POTENTIAL MENTORS.

Use your existing contacts to connect with people who are experts in your field.

Reach out to them on social media.

Examine the resources you used to learn (books, TED Talks, podcasts, etc.) and follow up to see if those who might have guidance to offer are willing to give you even ten minutes to ask them questions.

$\longrightarrow$

2. ASK QUESTIONS. TAKE NOTES ON THEIR RESPONSES.

Start with logistical, tactical, and practical questions:

> **How did you get started?**
> **What did you do to improve?**
> **What techniques do you use?**
> **Do you have partners?**
> **And any other questions about how the process works.**

Don't be afraid to be specific with your questions. When you don't ask specific questions, you don't get specific answers.

You can also ask emotional and mental questions that can help give you an idea what you might love about the process and what you may struggle with.

> **What part of the process do you enjoy most?**
> **What do you hate about the process?**
> **What do you wish you'd known when you started?**

3. PROCESS.

After talking to a mentor, look at your notes. Are there people you should call? Skills you should develop? Opportunities you should pursue? Translate the information you were given into action items and put them into your calendar where relevant.

In order to learn, you have to commit time, and in order to commit time, your partner has to be on board. They have to understand the values that make you want to spend your time this way, and you want to make sure that they don't feel like you are stealing the time from them or your family (if you have one). You do this by working together to decide where the time will come from.

Pulitzer Prize–winning journalist Brigid Schulte was struggling with the conflicting demands of work and parenting. She had no time for herself, including any passion projects she hoped to take on. At one point, desperate to squeeze extra time from her schedule, she took a time-use survey where she recorded what she did all day. The results shocked her, showing that she had an extra *twenty-seven hours* in her week. This time was largely invisible to Schulte because it was in scraps of ten minutes here and twenty minutes there—or "time confetti," as she dubbed it. By jumping around from task to task throughout her days, switching focus among her to-do list and her phone and other distractions, Schulte was shredding her schedule. Once she started batching her tasks and eliminating unnecessary distractions, she found longer blocks of time, which she says are essential to learning, coming up with new ideas, and seeing things we might not see otherwise. Ultimately, she found enough time to research and write a book, *Overwhelmed*, which became a *New York Times* bestseller.

TRY THIS:

SPARE TIME WORKSHEET

You can recover lost time by documenting every minute of your day and batching tasks as Schulte did, but this exercise is a simpler approach, where we look at whether the time we're spending is in alignment with our values.

Show yourself what you truly value by devoting a consistent proportion of your free time to learning in the area of your purpose. With your partner's help, look at how you currently spend your spare time, both together and apart (this is also a great way for the two of you to get a snapshot of your values and to see if you want to make any other changes to how you spend your free time).

First, as done in the sample chart below, calculate the total hours you spend every week on the activities I've listed and any others you'd like to include. Then, in the second column, calculate how much time you're willing to **take away** from those activities and **reallocate** to learning about your purpose.

Activities I enjoy	Time I currently spend	Time I will now commit to spend
Refueling / pure leisure	4 hours/week	3 hours/week
Exercise	4 hours/week	4 hours/week (no change)
Socializing	8 hours/week	7 hours/week

$\longrightarrow$

←

Activities I enjoy	Time I currently spend	Time I will now commit to spend
Entertainment	15 hours/week	10 hours/week
Total time spent on activities that are not my purpose	31 total hours	24 total hours (I have freed up seven hours per week)
Learning about my purpose	0 hours	7 hours

Engage your partner in this process. If you don't communicate with your partner about what you're excited to pursue, they may wonder why you don't want to spend time with them. If they sign on to this plan, they'll understand and respect why you're spending your time as you do.

Experiment

Experimenting is putting your learning into practice to find out what works for you and what doesn't. You conduct mini-tests of what you've been pursuing. If you took a communication class that told you to look people in the eye when you talk, now you make a concerted effort to follow that advice. If you want to teach, you could try offering a seminar, helping out another teacher, or starting a blog. If you want to sell a craft, you could start posting on Etsy. If you want to offer a service, you could test it out by doing it for free for your friends. Apprenticing, shadowing, interning, and volunteering are all ways of dipping your toe in the waters of something you think might be your purpose. This period of experimentation is meant to take the pressure off—no judgment, no criticism, and no guilt from yourself or your partner. You don't have to be perfect. Mistakes can give you valuable information about both your skill level and your field of interest.

In this phase, you can invite your partner to come with you as you experiment. A lot of couples may try to take a class together, read the same book, or watch a documentary at the same time. This is great if you share interests, but if they can't come or aren't interested, don't be disheartened. This is your purpose, not theirs.

We often pressure our partners to be as enthusiastic as we are about our passion. Or we wonder if they're right for us because when we talk about our passion, they don't have much to add to the conversation. Our partner doesn't have to share our passions. Even if they do, that doesn't guarantee success in a relationship. Remind yourself why you are with them and remember that being alike isn't necessary for a happy relationship.

Besides, it's often better for each of you to do your own learning. Then you can move at your own pace and bring what you've found to your partner. This way your partner is still part of the process, and they don't feel mystified or alienated as you proceed. You want your partner to feel loved and connected as you find ways to learn and develop your purpose. Just be sure to let them know when you'll be experimenting so that they can decide how they want to schedule the time—perhaps they'll be experimenting too.

Learning and experimenting could be a five-month journey or a five-year journey. Remember, no matter where you are on the pyramid of purpose, you are already in pursuit of purpose. There is no finish line to cross before you're living your purpose.

Thrive

Learn and experiment until you hit a level of expertise where you know what you love and what you don't love about your purpose, what works and what doesn't. Then you go for it. Learning doesn't yield results, and the results from experimenting are random. Now you are making those efforts serve you. You take steps to perform your purpose, building consistency and steadiness. This might mean accepting a new job. It might mean launching a small business. It might mean rescuing a dog or volunteering as a teaching assistant. This new effort takes time, but you establish a routine and set measurable goals. You wanted to jump into *doing* at the start, but your performance will only be as strong as the learning and experimenting you did beforehand. If the results aren't satisfactory, then you go back to learning and experimenting. If nobody is visiting your Etsy shop, you make efforts to learn how to market it. If you feel like you could be a better teaching assistant, ask the lead teacher to mentor you. When you can produce measurable, replicable results and you start to get noticed, it builds confidence and motivates you to keep pushing forward.

In order to thrive, you have to ramp up your efforts, and pursuing your purpose may start to consume more of your time and energy. It's vital that you share what you're doing and what you need from your partner in this phase. Remember, you are taking care of your own needs so you can give to the people you love.

Struggle

I know what you're thinking. *Is struggle really necessary?* I hate to break it to you, but there is bound to be some struggle at all the levels of the pyramid. You may learn that following a certain path is prohibitively expensive, or that nobody is responding to the way you chose to share your passion, or that you need to work on your skills far longer and harder than you anticipated. You might encounter unexpected hiccups. You might fail and have to start all over again. We can't avoid struggle, but the deeper we understand it, the more we can use it to grow.

When you struggle, explain to your partner what you're going through. If someone knows why you're tired, distracted, or upset, they'll be better able to support you in the ways we talked about in Rule 4.

Be careful not to label every challenge as struggle. There's always something to struggle over, but don't allow it to become your whole reality. When you keep a balanced view of struggle, you can learn and grow through it without letting it get the best of you.

When you are going through a challenging phase, it's also important to remind your partner that it's not their fault. You can be open about what you need but clarify to your partner that this is your burden, not theirs. In fact, if you're stuck and uninspired regarding your own purpose, it might be an ideal opportunity to direct your free time and energy toward your partner's pursuits (later in this rule I'll tell you how). This clear-eyed approach allows you to discover new ways to nurture your own, independent purpose. You might help your partner build their online presence and realize that your calling is to be an online marketer. Or you might get involved in the design end of a partner's work and decide to study graphic design. Just remember: Nobody is satisfied through another person's dharma. If one pretends to share the other's dharma, they won't be able to use their true gifts. Dreams don't have to be big; they just have to be yours.

Win

Lewis Hamilton is Formula One racing's winningest driver, with 103 wins and 182 podium finishes between 2007 and 2021.

Each Formula One race lasts roughly two hours, and there are twenty-three races per season. That means that over fifteen years, he spent about 683 hours racing; that doesn't count qualifying, or practice time. To be a top driver, in season, Hamilton also does roughly five to six hours of physical training per day. Over fifteen years, that's about 13,300 hours spent working out. Now, let's say that when Hamilton wins a race, he spends about ten minutes on the podium. That means that over fifteen years, for all those hours spent training and racing—and not even including practice, Hamilton spent about .1 percent of

FOCUS ON THE PROCESS

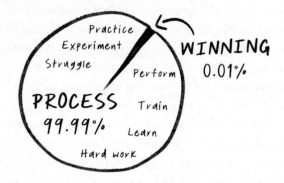

his time in the winner's spotlight. (Don't trust my math? If you must know, I based this on *41,000 minutes racing + 800,000 minutes training + 1,030 minutes on the podium.*)

Standing on the top of the podium is a rare pleasure. You're at the peak, and you're being recognized for it. This is the level we all want to live in. We want to sit on top of the mountain, having done all the hard work, and be acknowledged and recognized for what we've achieved. We want to just stay there.

The most important thing to remember about winning is that it's a by-product of the first four levels. You only get to win if you've gone through all four of the other levels first. So if you live for the award show, the followers, and the fame, you're going to be disappointed to discover that winning is rare and only accounts for a tiny fraction of the time you spend in your purpose. You have to love the lower parts. Life is not spent at the pinnacle. Those mountaintop events are only a tenth of 1 percent of the experience. Winners are still learning, experimenting, performing, and struggling. It's all part of the journey, and it's all valuable.

TRY THIS:

SET GOALS TOGETHER*

Once a year, set aside time to talk to your partner about your purpose and goals. You have to maintain your goals the same way you maintain a home. Every year you clean the gutters, change the batteries in the smoke alarms, and take care of repairs. In a relationship you check in on your purpose and how you both feel you're fulfilling it. You can have a dream together and a personal dream. Your goal might be to learn to paint, while your partner's goal might be to learn web design. Your goal together might be to learn to dance.

What are you trying to achieve? Are you working to acquire a skill that serves your purpose? Are you looking for a job that is closer to your purpose? Are you trying to find more time for your purpose?

What do you want from your partner? How can they help you fulfill your purpose? Do you need emotional support? Do you want them to help you fulfill other responsibilities, so you have more time for their purpose?

---

* Before you sit down with your partner to do this exercise, think about how you plan to present it. If you say to your partner, "Jay Shetty said we should answer these questions about our purpose every year. Let's do it now," you probably won't get great results. Same goes if you lay it on them like an evangelical preacher. Don't rush to your partner to implement a new frequency or form of communication. First, digest these ideas on your own. Start quietly supporting your partner's purpose rather than announcing your plans to do so. Observe the effect it has on you, your partner, and your relationship. Share what you notice with your partner in a communication style that you know works for them.

What does your partner want from you? Do you believe in their purpose? What ways can you think of to help them pursue it?

When you maintain your home, there are also issues you have to address more frequently than once a year. You pay the bills monthly, change a lightbulb when it goes out, or fix a leak. If a challenge comes up for you or your partner, make sure you discuss it together.

Help Your Partner Prioritize Their Purpose

Helping each other fulfill your purposes is so central to the success of a relationship that in the traditional Vedic wedding ceremony it's the final vow: *"Together we will persevere in the path of dharma (righteousness), through this vehicle of householder life."* This doesn't mean you take over their dharma. It means you make room for it.

Often in a household, it feels like there is only room for one partner's purpose. Studies show that men's salaries go up after they have children while women's salaries go down. An article in the *New York Times* says that even when you control for hours, salaries, and other factors, "the disparity is not because mothers actually become less productive employees and fathers work harder when they become parents—but because employers expect them to." In reality, as the *Times* reports, "71 percent of mothers with children at home work, according to the Bureau of Labor Statistics, and women are the sole or primary breadwinner in 40 percent of households with children, according to data from the Pew Research Center." Employer bias is the only reason for the discrepancy. It's a problem, but all the more reason to make sure that if anyone in your relationship is a woman, she doesn't leave her purpose behind.

The process of climbing the pyramid of purpose illuminates how we can help our partners. We see them on a parallel climb and use the lessons we're learning to give us patience and ideas for them.

Help Them Learn

People often don't know where to begin. Watch for when they light up, when they spring to life in a conversation. Observe what brings them joy and what their strengths are, then use what you see to encourage and affirm them. These insights help your partner accelerate their learning and experimenting. Remember to be a good guru. Don't be pushy or get mad at them if they don't follow your advice. They have to come to it in their own time and at their own pace. You can't force them. You can only be there for them as they figure it out. You aren't trying to get them to the next step in your journey but to the next step in their journey.

If your partner has interests but hasn't shaped them into a purpose, encourage them to explore without judging their path. We aren't born knowing our purpose or ready to pursue it. Help your partner to follow up on something they're curious about. You can book a trip to a museum or find books or TED Talks to help them explore what they're especially curious about. Take a look at your commitments and priorities, and make sure your partner has the freedom to pursue their curiosity instead of, for example, expecting that they'll spend their spare time with you.

When I met Radhi, it was clear that she loved food, and I encouraged her to explore that interest wherever it might lead her. People always told her, "You should open a restaurant," but I didn't impose my goals on her. I tried to support her growth by simply telling her to devote time toward learning and experimenting. I felt glad for us as a couple and for her alone to make whatever sacrifices it might take for her to pursue her interests. When we first arrived in New York, she started as an apprentice under an Ayurvedic chef. She went from there to teaching yoga, to getting her Ayurvedic qualification, to helping a restaurant build its menu. I didn't pressure her to choose a career goal or ask when her quest would end. When our partner is looking for their purpose, we support from the sidelines. We provide advice when asked but let them make their own decisions. We don't accuse them of being unproductive—we praise them when they make progress.

Don't say this:	Do say this:
"What's taking so long?"	"How can I help you?"
"You need to make a decision now!"	"Let's set a deadline together that feels realistic for our home and life."
"Look at Person X. They're doing so well."	"Have you thought about who inspires you and might be a good mentor?"

While your partner is learning, don't try to be their mentor. A mentor is skilled in the area where one wants to learn. The mentor has applicable experience and knowledge to guide them to ways they can thrive in their purpose, along with the willingness to help. Your partner is your partner in love. You are each other's guru—learning about yourselves and each other. But you don't have to be mentors or business partners. Instead, help them think of ways to connect with mentors and come up with questions to ask when they have a chance.

Help Them Experiment

A friend of mine was interested in doing stand-up comedy. He was just getting started, and there was no way a club would have booked him at that stage in his career, so one night his wife transformed their small, urban garden into a stand-up club. She put out folding chairs for the guests, strung lights between the trees, and served popcorn. He came out and did a stand-up set for ten friends. This was a fun and inspired way for my friend's wife to support her partner's experimentation. You can help your partner by creating opportunities for them to practice their passion and strengths. Maybe you have a friend in a related industry whom they can shadow. Maybe you have a connection who could help them develop their skills. Be an audience, help gather an audience, or help them with the aspects that are not within their skill set.

Give Them Time and Space

Inspired as Sal Khan was when he launched Khan Academy, he had bills to pay. His wife was just completing medical school, and they had escalating rent and a growing family. It seemed ridiculous to even consider quitting his safe hedge fund job to go all-in on a nonprofit. But a friend kept calling to tell him that his purpose was not to be a hedge fund investor, but to help the world the way he'd helped his cousin. When Sal approached his wife about the idea, she was supportive, but concerned about their financial situation. Eventually she recognized that Sal was having trouble focusing on anything other than the academy. They decided to dig into the money they were saving for a down payment on a house, and Sal quit his job. "It was incredibly stressful," Sal says. "I was waking up in the middle of the night in cold sweats." Finally, an investor came through. It was a major turning point for Sal, and today Khan Academy is one of the largest online learning platforms in the world. This is an extreme example, and I'm not recommending that anyone necessarily quit their day job. This would still be a success story if Sal had stayed at the hedge fund while tutoring or left it to found a company with moderate success. The point is that his wife supported him when he took a calculated risk.

Sometimes it's hard to watch your partner direct their time and passion elsewhere. You may feel that your partner is fulfilled by their purpose, not you. "I think I should be more important than my partner's purpose" is the complaint I hear most often about purpose in a relationship. We want more of the attention our partner is giving to their purpose. But if someone gives us their time because we demand it, we don't get the best of them. Instead of pulling them away from their purpose, you can join them in their journey, whether they are learning and experimenting or putting their purpose into action. Also, remember that you won't feel competitive or envious of the time they spend on their purpose if you're satisfied in your own. As Albert Einstein said, "If you want to live a happy life, tie it to a goal, not to people or things." Don't stop them, limit them, or make them feel bad about pursing their purpose.

Be Patient When They Struggle

We might grow frustrated when our partner struggles with their dharma, particularly if we don't agree with their choices and strategies along the way. If they want to quit, or constantly change their approach, or plunge recklessly forward, we have to be a good guru. When they share an idea with us that we don't like, we listen. We take time to feel gratitude for their honesty. We don't have to like it, or accept it, or think it makes them the world's best strategist. But we allow them to share. We pay attention. We observe carefully. We seek to understand instead of projecting our own desires and limitations onto them. If our partner doesn't think we'll understand, they won't open up or tell us the truth. Sometimes we are brusquer and more judgmental with our partners than anyone else in our lives. Treat your partner with at least the same respect you would give a friend or colleague and offer them mindful responses that help them grow their purpose. Helping your partner find their way isn't always easy. Sometimes it creates new tensions in the relationship. They might feel pitied or pressured. But those new tensions are better than the old ones—because being depressed and confused and not knowing your dharma is worse than knowing it and struggling to make it work.

When they don't make the progress that we think they should, we might try to manage or control them. We become frustrated when they don't take that meeting we set up for them or they don't attend an event where they might build their network. Sometimes we are triggered because their behavior reminds us of something we worry about in our own life. We might fear that we aren't succeeding in our career or purpose, and we're projecting our own fear onto our partner. The first step we should take is to check our own purpose. Are we fully engaged in it? Do we feel momentum? Focusing on it might relieve the worries you have about your partner.

But other concerns might be coming into play. We might be going through the motions of giving our partner space while feeling scared that they're never going to deliver. Or we might be worried when we look at how they're doing in comparison to other people. All these triggers compel us to criticize and judge, which interferes with our partner's ability to grow. You don't have to hide your concern. In fact, you should share it. But share it with support and love, without imposing your standards or expectations on them. They may not be interested in or motivated enough to take action in this moment, and that's okay.

Two of the ways we tend to share our concern are problematic for different reasons. Sometimes we try to force our partner forward. If your partner is miserable and wants to quit their job, you might freak out and say, "You can't do that! You know perfectly well that we can't afford it!" When we do this, we are using fear and guilt to motivate them. Or we might swing in the opposite direction, saying what we think is the right thing to say without really meaning it. In this case we sometimes use hyper-motivational language like: "You're a superstar! You can do anything you want! You can make this happen tomorrow." But if you don't believe this, it rings false.

Force is pressure. It blocks the space your partner might use to tell you that they want to move forward but aren't sure how. They can't be vulnerable and talk honestly with you. Contrived motivation expands the space artificially. Your partner might quit their job and stop working for a year, and when you ask why they'll say, "Well, you said I could do whatever I want." Both of these methods—force and false motivation—interfere with your partner's ability to address the situation with you realistically. A gentle, positive nudge is much more powerful than a fear-based argument or motivational push. A nudge says, "I appreciate that you're trying your best—here's something else you can try."

This nudge comes more naturally when you remove judgment and criticism from the dialogue, because now there is space for open, honest, vulnerable conversation. In this space, make sure your partner knows you're aware of what they're going through. Be patient with them. Recognize and appreciate their worthy efforts, no matter what the results have been. The tone of this conversation should be supportive. Remind them that they can handle challenges, and that you are there to solve problems with them. You're doing this together.

In the example of the partner who wants to quit their job, you can discuss in practical terms how both of your lives would be affected by this decision. Where will you need each other's help? How much time will you give to this experiment? How will responsibilities shift? How can you help carry their load to give them time and space to figure out what's next? You can brainstorm ideas for how to support each other. If they're going to be around the house more now, maybe they can handle cooking dinner, giving you more time to get your work done.

The resolution of this conversation should be a set of commitments and agreements. You've assessed how the household and financial responsibilities will change. You've outlined any shifts you'll have to make in how you spend your time and money.

Once you've hashed out the details, put a timeline on this decision. If your partner is quitting their job to reassess their purpose, how long will they take before they start looking for work? If you decide to give them three months, this doesn't mean they have to have everything figured out by then, but that's when you'll revisit the plan and decide what's next.

Celebrate the Small Wins

If our partner went to the gym every day for three months you wouldn't say much, but if they didn't go to the gym for that length of time, you'd point it out. That's generally how we operate. We complain when people are late, but we never thank them for being on time. When someone lands a job, everyone congratulations them, but when someone does the job, nobody congratulates them. When someone quits a job, few people see that as a step toward fulfilling one's purpose, but it often is. Instead of celebrating the obvious wins, watch your partner closely for efforts and successes that nobody else is positioned to notice. Recognizing them helps fuel your partner's drive and satisfaction.

SHOW MINDFUL LOVE

When they do this:	You do this:
Share an idea that you don't like	Encourage them to test it out on a focus group, run it past a mentor, or get real feedback from real people.
Complain about getting distracted	Ask if they want to be accountable to you. You could let them know when they seem distracted or refuse to watch TV with them until they check something off their list. Note—I didn't say you should accuse them of getting distracted. It has to come from them.
Give up	Give them time and space to mourn a setback and continue to share things you think might inspire them. Help them notice how far they've come so they can decide if they want to return to their efforts.
Want to take a financial risk	Set up a meeting with your accountant or a financially savvy friend to have realistic conversations about the consequences of this risk and how it might affect both of you.
Let other responsibilities slide	Things shift when people focus on their purpose. Revisit and reset commitments around the home so everyone's clear on how it will work in this phase and do so regularly.

Two Purposes Collide

When children enter the picture or for any reason you're trying to support and manage a busy household where both partners are trying to pursue their purposes, it can be hard to negotiate time. There's no right option or perfect balance of time spent on purpose, with family, and running a household, but the more deliberate and communicative we are about our strategy, the more satisfied we'll be. Below are four different strategies for how to manage two purposes: you can set your purposes aside temporarily to prioritize earning and spending time with the family while your children are young and the household has financial pressures, you can prioritize one person's purpose, you can take turns prioritizing your purposes, or you can go all in on both partners' purposes.

1. Pursue Your Purposes After Hours

Often our purpose doesn't earn money or support the household. As a couple we need financial stability, and if you can't fulfill your purpose through your job, then you won't be able to give it much time. This is actually where most people start, and it's a healthy place to be. Don't put the burden of financial bills on your developing passion. It doesn't need to carry that weight. Use mornings and evenings to build your passion. Remember something that starts as a pastime can become part-time. And something part-time can become full-time. Starting out slowly and carefully gives you time to see how serious you are about your passion, exploring your options and acquiring skills. Without sacrificing stability, you can put care and effort toward making your purpose central to your life and finding fulfillment through it.

2. Give One Person's Purpose Priority

It's easy to say both partners should prioritize their purposes, but different people's purposes often run on different timelines. Choose this scenario when one person's purpose creates immediate and overwhelming demands on their time and energy, but make sure you mutually decide that their efforts will take precedence while the other partner manages the household. Often this happens when one person's purpose is also financially supporting the household. Even so, don't go all in on one person's purpose without discussing the plan explicitly.

Sometimes one partner will demand that the other sacrifice their dharma. If the demanding partner earns more money, this might even seem like a reasonable position. They are supporting the household, so they think their purpose is more important. They may expect the other partner to pick up the slack at home, and hope or believe that to be a fulfilling purpose for them. But even if they are more financially successful or further along in their career path, their purpose is not more important. Period. Just because you decide to spend a holiday with one partner's family doesn't mean you love that family more. Time is limited and something has to give. While we give one person's purpose priority in terms of time, we must recognize the sacrifice of putting the other partner's purpose on hold.

If you choose to prioritize one person's dharma, you must discuss all the pros and cons and agree that this is best for the household. Set terms that the partner who is making a sacrifice feels comfortable with, such as how long this will go on and how you will check in with each other to make sure that frustration and resentment don't set in.

If your purpose gets priority and your partner takes on a role that isn't their purpose, treat that role with the same respect and accommodation as you would their purpose. When you're living your purpose, you may find yourself busy and less able to support your partner, but remember—you're the one whose purpose is fulfilling you. Purpose comes first, but this doesn't mean you should forget what comes next. You need to figure out how to follow your purpose without neglecting other parts of your life. You should be happy to be there for your partner. Recognize that they might not be as satisfied as you are and compensate. Check in often. Revisit the arrangement you've made. Give them a chance to change their mind and be supportive when the time comes for them to step into their purpose.

If your purpose is taking precedence, you may want your partner to be as enthusiastic about it as you are. This desire for enthusiasm might be insecurity in disguise—when we're insecure we want everyone to validate our choices and tastes.

Meanwhile, if you're the one who put your purpose aside, it's normal to have a number of emotions arise. You might feel competitive with or envious of your partner, you might feel frustrated about your own purpose, you might feel self-doubt. These feelings are normal, and they are tempered by knowing your own purpose. If you don't have time for it right now, look for ways to stay connected to it and keep your passion for it alive. You can turn to all the ways we talk about in this chapter: through books, classes, finding it while supporting your partner, finding it in the job you have to have right now.

If you become impatient and think there might be a way to restructure the household, reopen the dialogue with your partner.

If you feel neglected, first diagnose why your partner seems to be focused on their purpose to the exclusion of the family. Are they immersed in their work? If you understand them and cherish their purpose, then you will see their commitment to it as a positive attribute. You will feel a sense of security knowing that they're focused on something deeply meaningful to them. Is it a personality trait or a choice rather than a necessity? Instead of demanding that they spend more time with you, ask, "Are you okay? Is there anything you're dealing with?" We need to meet them with compassion rather than criticism or complaint. If your partner is unable to spend time with the family because they are wholly focused on making money to support the household, then together you can discuss whether their family actually wants or needs that level of income, or whether the family would rather have their presence instead.

It's all a question of energy or time. If the busier partner can carve time out of their schedule, work together to create meaningful experiences for the whole family. If they don't have time, they can still give energy by being present, loving, and kind when you're together. Chasing a pursuit can be tiring. If they don't have energy for too many activities, you can make staying home together beautiful. Take the time to set the table nicely and light candles at dinner, even if you're eating takeout. Set up a spa day where the family trades massages and other treatments. Create a new holiday or tradition that you'll celebrate every year on the same randomly chosen day. Play a new board game. Google a list of conversation topics (there are also sets of cards that suggest interesting discussions) and have the whole family participate. If your partner isn't willing to do either, you need to communicate about it.

If, on the other hand, your partner is overly busy with their purpose out of an underlying desire to escape the family, nothing will be fixed by forcing them to be with the family. If you can't come to an agreement, use some of the techniques in the following chapter to work through your conflict.

Sometimes partners default to this option because their purposes are on different timelines. When one partner hasn't figured out their purpose, they're often inclined to build their life around the one who has.

My clients Graham and Susanna have been together for twenty years. When he launched a real estate business, she gave up her dream of running a yoga studio and helped him develop the business. He achieved his purpose, the firm is extremely successful, and she continued to work there even after he could afford to hire a replacement. From the outside, their marriage and work together looked like a brilliant partnership. But for fifteen years Susanna had been quietly mourning her unfulfilled dream of a yoga studio, even though she had never taken steps to pursue it.

Serving Graham wasn't Susanna's purpose, nor was growing his company. Most of the time when we end up working on someone else's purpose, it's because we don't know what ours is or we don't know where to start. But it's never too late. Susanna's time wasn't wasted. At any point, she could tap into the skills she had acquired to pursue her own calling, whether it was that yoga studio or something new.

When Graham finally understood how frustrated Susanna was, he encouraged her to open the yoga studio she'd always wanted. He offered to take a year off work to help her get it off the ground. But when she allowed herself to consider what she really wanted to do, she realized that there was a piece of the real estate business she'd fallen in love with. She decided to use the connections and skills she'd acquired to stage houses, preparing them with furniture and art to present them for sale. She worked with the selling agents she already knew, and her business took off quickly.

TRY THIS:

ADJUST A DHARMA IMBALANCE

When your partner's dharma is taking up all the space in the relationship, you follow a similar process to the one I outlined for when your partner is struggling—attend to your own purpose, open conversation without judgment or criticism, make commitments and agreements, and establish a timeline for revisiting the plan.

1. **Focus on your own purpose.** When you're frustrated with your partner's purpose, this is always the first action you should take. This is how you ensure that you aren't making your partner your purpose.
2. **Communicate.** Discuss why you aren't finding time for each other. You should not be competing with your partner's purpose for their time. You want to make room for their purpose, but what you can ask of them is their presence.
3. **Make commitments and agreements.** Together, decide what time each of you will devote to your purpose, and when it will be family time. Set boundaries and commit to them.
4. **Define couple or family activities that make that time more valuable.** For example, instead of watching TV together, find activities that are more interactive. On weekends, this could be something physically active, like a hike or another

←

sport that both of you enjoy. It could be entertaining friends or family or volunteering. On weeknights, when time is at a premium, you could play games, cook together, or listen to or watch something that falls into the "learning" category of one of your purposes and discuss it together. If you have the energy you could plan more activities, like listening to music or a lecture together, or find a new activity that you've never tried before.

5. Establish a timeline for the new plan you put in place. When would you like to touch base again to make sure you're honoring your agreements or to see if you need to make tweaks?

3. Take Turns Prioritizing Your Purposes

If neither of you is willing to sacrifice your purpose, but you can't afford the time or money to pursue both purposes full-time, one person can take a certain amount of time to focus on theirs while the other one keeps the bills paid and/or manages the household. Then, after the term is up, the partners switch roles. In this scenario, if either or both of your purposes is your career, those careers might suffer. You might have to live more simply, but it will likely be worth whatever comforts you have to give up. Just make sure you carve out clear timelines and boundaries and commitments.

Keith and Andrea each had a passion. Andrea wanted to become a naturopath and Keith a competitive triathlete, and each supported the other's dream. Yet when they tried to pursue their passions simultaneously, they found they couldn't balance the time and commitment required to be successful in their chosen careers with the demands of parenting, while also getting enough sleep and making enough money to keep the household running. So, they came up with a compromise—they would take turns. First, Andrea spent three years going through all of the intensive schooling required to complete her training. During this time, Keith became a teacher in their suburban Ohio town. While the pay wasn't great, it got rid of their massive monthly health insurance payment and allowed him to be home with the kids after school and on weekends. Andrea still worked reduced hours, so he wasn't paying the bills on his own; she was mostly able to do her schooling on evenings and weekends.

Once Andrea set up her business and had built up a steady clientele, it was Keith's turn. He kept his job, but Andrea took over with the kids, and he dedicated his nonwork time primarily to training. Now that each is established in their career, they take mini-turns. For example, one year, Keith dialed down his training over the winter months so that Andrea could finish a continuing education course. Once his competitive season ramped up again, Keith was able to dedicate extra time and financial resources to training and race-related travel.

4. Go All In on Both People's Purposes

If both people are somewhat experienced and established, then you can take the opportunity to simultaneously pursue your purposes full-time. Income is an important consideration here. We must have stability to have a good relationship. Jennifer Petriglieri, who studies dual-income couples, says that "in most of the press that you see about dual-career couples, it's presented as a zero-sum game. This means that one person gets more, and the other person gets less. And while some couples do have this 'tit for tat' mindset, successful couples have a mindset that is, rather than thinking about it as 'me vs. you,' [. . .] about a conceptualization of 'we' as the most important piece of the puzzle."

According to Petriglieri, couples who invest themselves in each other then become invested in each other's successes and failures. The desire to see each other succeed then comes more naturally, and the compromises you have to make won't breed resentment.

Going all in on both people's purposes is easy in one sense—both people are putting their purposes first. Both are fulfilled, and both are therefore well positioned to give the other their best self—satisfied and energized. But in this plan, as with the others, you'll have to make sacrifices. You'll have less time together, so you'll have to make your time meaningful. It's important to keep communicating—not about how busy each of you is, but how much you care about what you're doing. Each of you seeing your partner being purposeful will give you respect for each other.

TRY THIS:

DO A TIME TRADE

You and your partner can ease the stress of two busy lives by giving each other the gift of time. Here are some different ways to trade time commitments with your partner.

- Take over a responsibility that's usually your partner's for a period of time or permanently.
- Create an activity that gets yourself (and everyone else) out of their way.
- Cancel evening plans for a whole weekend and both focus on the partner whose purpose needs more time.
- Pick a holiday and make it all about the partner who needs time.

Watching your partner grow and being part of that journey is deeply fulfilling and exciting, as is your own growth. It's not always smooth, but it's a beautiful journey. **When you're a part of each other's growth, you don't grow apart from each other.** You can celebrate the successes together and be there together for disappointments. Of course, with two people prioritizing their own needs, conflict is inevitable. Our next rule will help us find the value in disagreement and how we can bring purpose to our conflicts.

Write a Love Letter to Your Partner

If you want to create a lasting relationship it requires you to dig deep. Take a moment to be open, honest, and vulnerable with your partner, to express what you're often scared to express. Communicate mistakes you've made without beating yourself up over them. Accept responsibility without feeling guilt and shame. Express love without feeling vulnerable and weak.

Dear Partner,

I used to think that love was simple. I thought that one day I'd meet someone who captured my heart, and that would be it. Next stop, happily ever after. But knowing you, and sharing my life and my heart with you, I've learned that love is not the destination, but the journey. And it's not only the journey of us—it's not just our love story, but the story of love itself.

Our relationship isn't just a romance, it's a becoming. Being with you, I have grown so much, and I love seeing all of the ways that you continue to grow as well. And that is one of the things I love the most about being with you—seeing you blossom over this lifetime. In that simple definition of love I used to have, people fell in love only once, and then just stayed that way. But as we both continue to evolve and explore, I find myself falling in love with you over and over again, each time a little differently. Each time more deeply.

I know that I'm not always a perfect partner. I don't always listen or attend to you in the ways you deserve. Sometimes I'm lost in my own thoughts, my own world. Sometimes I'm afraid to be vulnerable—to allow myself to open my heart to you and to be loved fully. Instead, I pick fights or shut down. Thank you for loving me in my wholeness, which includes my imperfection. And thank you for letting me learn to love you in your wholeness, which includes your imperfection. You are one of my greatest teachers, and I am so thankful for you.

I will continue to make mistakes. I will continue to get things wrong. But I will also continue to love you. I am committed to being a team with you—to always being on the same side no matter what we're facing. And to embracing all of what life brings us, the challenges and the triumphs, together.

Love,
Me

Meditation for Compatibility

We often think in passing of the people we love, rarely stopping to give them our full attention. We sometimes even take for granted the love we have for those who are in our lives regularly, or whom we see every day. This meditation brings clarity and focus to our feelings and reminds us just what we love about them.

You can do this meditation alone, or you can do it together with a loved one, and at the end share what came up for you.

Prepare to Meditate

1. Find a comfortable position, whether that's sitting in a chair, sitting upright on a cushion or the floor, or lying down.
2. Close your eyes, if that feels good to you. If not, simply soften your focus.
3. Whether your eyes are open or closed, gently lower your gaze.
4. Take a deep breath in. And breathe out.
5. If you find that your mind is wandering, that's okay. Gently bring it back to a space of calm, balance, and stillness.

Loving Focus Meditation

1. Take a moment to think about someone who is important to you.
2. Visualize them, their face and form, in front of you.
3. See them smiling. Laughing.
4. Take a moment to notice your favorite qualities about them physically.

5. Now, go deeper. Notice and acknowledge your favorite qualities about their mind, their intellect, and their personality. Consider their values.

6. In your mind or out loud, express gratitude to them for all these things that make them who they are.

7. See if you can come up with ten things you love about them.

PART 3

Healing: Learning to Love Through Struggle

||||||||||||||||||||||||||||||||||||||||||||

Vanaprastha is where we reflect on the experience of loving others, discover what blocks our ability to love, and work on forgiveness and healing. In Vanaprastha we learn how to resolve conflict so we can protect our love or know when to let go of love. In the course of overcoming difficulties in relationships or in finding ourselves alone again, we discover the possibility of *bhakti*, a deepening of love.

Win or Lose Together

Conflict is the beginning of consciousness.

—M. ESTHER HARDING

I was in a restaurant having dinner with a friend when the raised voice of a woman at the table next to us caught our attention.

"Put it down," she said. Her date was rapidly typing on his phone. "I said, put it down!" she insisted.

He ignored her for another moment, then finally rested his phone on the table. "You have to give me a break," he retorted. "The constant nagging is driving me crazy."

Their voices fell back to normal volume, and my dinner companion turned to me. I knew he was a few months into a new relationship. He had told me he wanted to be in a "real" relationship, with someone honest who took the time to understand him. Now he said with pride, "Eli and I get along so well. We literally never argue."

Conflict has a bad reputation. It makes us look bad—to ourselves and to other people. We want to think we can be the couple who understands each other deeply *and* never fights. We're special. We're different. But no matter how compatible a couple is, to live in conflict-free bliss isn't love, it's avoidance. It's easy to gloss over disputes for the first few months because the new attraction obscures the cracks in your foundation. But to sustain a conflict-free existence means floating on the surface, where everything looks pretty but we never achieve deep knowledge of each other.

Those who avoid fighting may be calm on the outside, but often they are upset inside. They're afraid to talk about difficult feelings because they or their partner might get angry. They hide how they feel to avoid stirring up trouble. Keeping the peace often comes at the expense of honesty and understanding. And the converse is also true: Love built on honesty and understanding is deep and fulfilling, but not necessarily peaceful. Partners who avoid conflict don't understand each other's priorities, values, or struggles. **Every couple fights—or should.**

Whatever you and your partner fight about, you're probably not alone. According to couples counselors, the top three areas of conflict are money, sex, and how to raise children. Woven among these big topics we find the everyday fights—about what to have for dinner, how to load the dishwasher, something your partner's friends said or did, or whether you were just flirting with that barista. My approach to short-term scuffles and long-term issues is the same, because I believe that often the bigger issues are at the root of the daily conflicts. This is why getting to the core of the issue is part of my approach.

The Bhagavad Gita could be considered the ultimate guide to conflict resolution. It takes place on a battlefield. There are two armies—one good, one evil—about to go to war. A conversation takes place on that battlefield between Arjuna, the leader of the good army, and Krishna, the divine, as Krishna helps guide Arjuna. Krishna, in addressing Arjuna's questions, answers many of those we ourselves face on the smaller battlefields of our relationships.

First, we see that Arjuna is reluctant to fight. This jibes with our idea of being a good person—we think if we do everything right, there should be no fights. This is an understandable aspiration. Avoiding all-out war is always the right thing to do. But we learn in the Bhagavad Gita that, leading up to this moment, Arjuna has already attempted countless negotiations, persuasions, and considerations. This war is the last resort. There will be damage and casualties. Things will be said and done that are painful and irreversible. This is why we should learn how to fight.

We can avoid blowouts, somewhat counterintuitively, by fighting often. If we deal with disagreements as they arise, then we have a better chance to resolve issues before we say things we don't mean and end up feeling worse, without having resolved anything. The first time your partner leaves their dirty socks on the floor, you might be slightly annoyed but throw them in the wash. The second time, you remind them to put their socks away, but it's become a problem. The third time, you might ask them what they could do to change the habit. The fourth time, you might say, "Okay, we need to talk about your sock issue." A small matter like dirty socks becomes a flashpoint because the more time those socks spend on the floor, the more discord they create.

When Krishna, representing all-knowing and goodness, advises Arjuna to go to battle, the divine affirms that even good people must fight sometimes. The enemy—Arjuna's cousins—has been increasingly aggressive. They have poisoned the food of Arjuna and his brothers. Another time, they built them a castle out of wax, which looked beautiful, but they set it on fire when Arjuna and his brothers were inside. Their cousins have been trying to destroy them. The last straw is when they attempt to undress Arjuna's wife in front of a group of people. Ultimately, Arjuna realizes that to let leaders like this take charge will harm the whole world, and he must act against them. Arjuna isn't just fighting over the violation of his wife. He's not fighting to defend his ego or to prove his strength. He is fighting to save future generations. In the same way, we should fight with our partner not out of ego, but because we want to protect and build a beautiful future.

In the Bhagavad Gita, the enemy (and ultimately the loser) is not a person but an ideology. It is darkness, ego, greed, and arrogance. In our relationship conflicts, the same is true. The loser shouldn't be one of us. It should be the flawed ideology or issue and the negativity it provokes between us.

What if we approached a fight as a team? The specter of disagreement builds like a wave in the ocean. As it approaches, it grows taller and more daunting. But instead of turning away from the wave to pretend you don't see it, the two of you face it as it looms over you. Can you keep your heads above water, or will it crash on top of you? The key is understanding that your partner is not the wave. The wave is the issue about which you disagree. If the two of you approach it together, kicking in the same direction, encouraging each other, you can swim through it side by side with a sense of shared victory.

This reframing has changed my life, and it can change yours. When my wife and I see ourselves as a team fighting against the problem, we crush the problem. The desire to win comes from ego, and we want to control our egos. Why would I want to crush my wife? Why do I want to defeat the person I've chosen to spend my life with? My wife is not my opponent—I love her. I don't want her to lose. I don't want to lose either. **Every time one of you loses, you both lose. Every time the problem loses, you both win.**

TRY THIS:

SHIFT AN ARGUMENT TO A SHARED GOAL

Instead of looking at it like you're taking sides *against* one another, frame the conversation as if it's the two of you together taking on the problem. If we come to the table as adversaries, we increase the likelihood we'll fight. So instead, come to the table as a team who take on the problem together.

Here are some examples of how to shift an argument to a shared goal. In the next section I'll explain how you can plan ahead to make your fights as productive as possible.

Argument	Reframe/Shared Goal
"You don't clean up after yourself."	"We should set a routine for daily chores."
"You're always late."	"Can we sit down and talk about how we want to spend our time in the evenings and on weekends?"
"You don't mind spending money on your interests but complain when I spend money on mine."	"Let's set a reasonable monthly budget."
"You don't give the children as much attention as they need from you."	"Let's discuss what we think the children need [maybe with them, depending on their ages] and how we can support that."

Love to Fight and Fight to Love

Fighting, done well, benefits relationships. Long-term relationships don't survive because of great date nights or spectacular holidays. They don't endure because people have good friends (although community certainly contributes to relationship stability). One of the biggest factors in a long-lasting relationship is knowing how to fight.

According to a paper published by the Society for Personality and Social Psychology, when partners can express anger to each other in healthy ways, they build certain qualities and abilities. The qualities—such as compassion, empathy, and patience—help you understand the challenge. The abilities—like communication, listening, and understanding—help you solve equal or greater challenges in the future.

While expressing anger has value, I must add that there is a difference between conflict and abuse. Abuse is stressful, but it is not the positive kind of stress that makes us stronger. Physical abuse, threats, force, control, and manipulation are not love. Nothing productive or positive comes from diminishing another person. If your partner is physically hurting you in any way, that is not acceptable. Beyond that, there are areas where you may have trouble drawing the distinction between conflict and abuse. I hope the following chart is helpful, but if you're in an abusive relationship or aren't sure, I urge you to seek professional help. The National Domestic Violence Hotline is 1-800-799-SAFE (7233).

HOW TO KNOW WHETHER YOU'RE EXPERIENCING CONFLICT OR ABUSE

Topic	How Your Partner Behaves in Conflict About This Topic	How Your Partner Abuses You Over This Topic
Money	Argues with you about your spending habits	Tells you how to spend your money
Family	Criticizes or complains about your family member	Ridicules, humiliates, or alienates your family member
Kids	Argues over what's right for the kids	Threatens you or the kids or uses you or the kids as a threat
Quality time	Complains that you don't spend enough quality time together	Feels ownership over your time and controls whether you spend time with anyone else

Chores	Doesn't think you do enough to help	Tells you what to do
Jealousy	Feels upset about where your attention is going	Accuses you of lying without cause
The little things	Experiences small frustrations that grow over time	Can be set off by anything with an out-of-proportion reaction
Respect	Uses words to elevate their own importance	Uses words to diminish your importance
Sex	Complains about the frequency or style of your sex life	Pressures or forces you to have sex or participate in sexual acts when you're not comfortable or sure

The Root of the Argument

How we approach an argument, big or small, sets the tone for its resolution (or lack thereof). In the Bhagavad Gita, Arjuna approaches the battle with humility. He wants to do what's good and right, to serve and improve life for future generations. Meanwhile, his enemy, Duryodhana, comes from a place of greed, arrogance, and thirst for power. He declines wisdom and insight from Krishna. The results of the battle reflect the warriors' intentions. Arjuna is victorious, and Duryodhana, who had only selfish drives, loses everything.

There are three kinds of arguments, and these are shaped by three "energies of being" described by the Bhagavad Gita. I introduced them in *Think Like a Monk* (and mentioned them briefly in Rule 2): ignorance (*tamas*), passion and impulsivity (*rajas*), and goodness (*sattva*). I use these energies as a way of examining what state of mind we bring to any moment, and they can help us understand the energy we bring to any conflict.

Pointless arguments. A pointless argument arises in the energy of ignorance. It's a thoughtless outburst. You literally don't know what the point is. You have no intention to understand each other or find a solution. Pointless arguments occur in the wrong time and place. They don't resolve anything. We're just lashing out. At best, we recognize them as silly and let them go quickly. At worst, other resentments creep in, and they escalate into outright anger.

Power arguments. Power arguments emerge in the energy of passion. We just want to win for the sake of winning. That is the point of the argument, more than addressing the actual issue at hand. We're focused on our side of the story and try to trap our opponent in their mistakes. We may put on a show of listening to the other side, but we really just want to hear that we're right and get an apology. In the Bhagavad Gita, this is the energy that Duryodhana brings to the war. Ego drives this fight, and our position is "I am right. My way is the only way." Because we're focused on power, the changes we insist on have to do with convincing the person we're arguing against, not resolving the issue.

Productive arguments. In productive arguments, which take place in the energy of goodness, we see the conflict as a hurdle we want to overcome together, and we're open to recognizing each other's side of the story. We want to understand. We know why we're having the argument, and we see resolving it as a healthy step in our relationship. This is the energy that Arjuna has in the Bhagavad Gita. The most important tools in productive arguments are reason, intention, perspective, and love. These aren't techniques, they are spiritual tools. They have to be practiced with the heart and mind aligned. If you go through the motions, but aren't working from your heart, you won't make progress. In productive arguments, we mutually agree on ways we're both going to change our behavior going forward. Both partners are happy with the resolution.

How to Have Productive Arguments

We would all rather have productive arguments than pointless or power arguments, but doing so takes practice. (Part of the reason pointless and power arguments are so common is that they're easier to fall into than productive arguments.) People are often told to take a breath and count to ten when they're angry, but we're never told exactly how we should make use of that breath. In the Bhagavad Gita, we see Arjuna pause and ask for Krishna's wisdom in the middle of a conflict. Think about that! He stops in the middle of a battlefield to talk to God. If Arjuna can manage to shift his attention away from the battle in this very tense moment—the most difficult of conflicts—then we too can learn to pause and bring awareness to the daily skirmishes and the all-out wars we confront in our relationships.

In order for a couple to win together, you must be acting out of love and the desire to be a team with your partner. Remember: If you're operating out of fear and ignorance, there's no goal. If you're operating out of passion, then your ego is leading the argument. We begin to change the energy we bring to arguments when we purify the ego.

Purify the Ego

We can't team up to fight the issue unless we take our egos out of the equation. We know it's a power argument when we enter it with mistaken, ego-driven convictions like: I want to win. I am right. My way is the only way.

Thinking you're right doesn't solve anything. Yet we want our partner to lose unequivocally, declare us the victor, and submit to our demands. If you come to an argument convinced that you are right and your partner is wrong, your tone and your words will make that inflexibility obvious to your partner. You must accept that there is some truth in what your partner is going to share and be open to hearing from them. Your conviction that you are right usually doesn't change your partner's mind. Instead, it tells your partner that you don't care how they feel or what they think. The only outcome you'll accept is for your partner to change themselves and/or their opinion.

It's natural to approach an argument wanting to convince your partner that you are right. Being right validates us. It gives us someone else to blame. It makes us feel secure in our beliefs and assumptions. We don't need to change or take any responsibility. In competitions, the ultimate power environment, it's true that someone loses, and someone wins. The winner gets to be "right" or "better." In politics, the winning candidate's policy dominates. In war, the victors dictate the peace terms. But in a relationship, being right won't solve the issue. Your ego might feel good for a while, but it won't stop the problem from coming up again, and your relationship won't benefit from the resolution. Ego makes you lose even if you win.

Instead, our goal is understanding. We want to connect. We aim not just to resolve our conflicts, but to use the resolutions to grow together. Again, in a relationship conflict, if I win and you lose, then we both lose. And if you win and I lose, then we both lose. The only successful argument is the one in which we both win. We have to not just acknowledge this, but deeply internalize it.

> *I'm right and you're right.*
> *You're wrong and so am I.*
> *These are both win-win scenarios.*

Putting aside our ego to face and overcome obstacles with our partner purifies the ego. Purifying the ego is letting go of the desire to be the focus of attention. With purification, we start to display more understanding, empathy, compassion, trust, and love, and so does the other person.

TRY THIS:

IDENTIFY YOUR EGO AND PASSION IN THE CONFLICT

Figure out if your conflict is pointless (ignorance), power-related (passion), or productive (goodness).

1. Write down why the issue is important to you. What made you angry?

2. Identify your reason for fighting:

> **Am I fighting because I believe my way is best? (ego)**
> **Am I fighting because I think we should do something the "right" way? (ego)**
>
> **Am I fighting because I want the person to change? (passion)**
> **Am I fighting because this situation offends me to the core? (passion)**
> **Am I fighting because I want to feel different? (passion)**
>
> **Am I fighting because I want to improve the situation? (goodness)**
> **Am I fighting because I want us to become closer? (goodness)**

The first step in taking our ego and passion out of the conflict is to acknowledge it, but then realize that being right, being best, being offended, wanting reality to be different—none of these solve problems. To solve together, you have to focus on the intention to improve the situation and get yourselves to a more loving place. Easier said than done. To do this, you must rise to neutrality.

The goal of taking your ego out of the equation is neutrality. When you stop indulging your ego, you become a better neutral observer of the conflict. Neutrality is the ability to separate the issue from your partner. You see that both of you have some role in the issue that has caused the conflict. You can see that you're both struggling. From this perspective, you can set a mutual, team-based goal, like, "Our intention should really be to get along better and be happier together. Do you agree?"

In the beginning of the Bhagavad Gita, speaking from the battlefield, Arjuna tells Krishna what he sees and feels. "Arjuna said: O infallible one, please draw my chariot between the two armies so that I may see those present here, who desire to fight, and with whom I must contend in this great trial of arms. Let me see those who have come here to fight." A subsequent verse reads: "Arjuna said: My dear Kṛṣṇa, seeing my friends and relatives present before me in such a fighting spirit, I feel the limbs of my body quivering and my mouth drying up. My whole body is trembling, my hair is standing on end, my bow Gāṇḍīva is slipping from my hand, and my skin is burning. I am now unable to stand here any longer. I am forgetting myself, and my mind is reeling. I see only causes of misfortune." Arjuna expresses his anxiety and disorientation to Krishna. Krishna acknowledges his feelings, responding with compassion. His eyes are full of tears. He asks, "How have these impurities come upon you? You know the value of life—what is making you feel weak?" Krishna is not judging Arjuna or even instructing him at this point. He has the benefit of being a neutral observer and is first trying to understand him.

We don't have the benefit of Krishna on our battlefields. A therapist has the neutrality to be an ideal moderator, but the reality is that most couples are navigating their issues on their own. Everyone wants the *other* person to be the one to back down and take responsibility, but if neither of you steps up, both of you might end up waiting indefinitely. To resolve a conflict, at least one of you will have to rise to neutrality so you can guide and shape the conversation with an even hand.

You can start a neutral conversation with an apology if it's genuine. This means you've reflected on the situation and accepted your responsibility. If things are heated, your partner may respond to the apology by saying "You *should* be sorry." Taking responsibility means saying, "Yes, I should be, and I am." And not getting defensive. If you can't apologize genuinely at the outset, save it for later. A neutral mediator does not race to solve the problem, but tries to learn about the combatants, and begins to offer observations and insights. We don't have the perspective and wisdom of Krishna or even a therapist, of course, so we must contend with our own state of mind while we try to mediate. If we are engaged in a pointless argument, we're upset, impatient, and don't truly listen. We take on the emotions of the other person, becoming angry if our partner is angry, depressed if our partner is depressed. This escalates the argument, increasing the levels of fear and insecurity for both parties. In a power argument, we can't mediate because we think our way is the only way. We're interested in immediate results rather than the process. Only in a productive argument can mediators focus on hearing each side tell their truth and remaining neutral as details and feelings are expressed.

When we take a neutral role, we remind ourselves that the problem isn't our partner. It is something we don't understand about them and something they don't understand about us. Solving this puzzle will benefit both of us. If you are looking out for yourself and your partner equally, then you can be confident in your actions. If you don't rise to neutrality, the lack of resolution will rankle you both, and you'll return to this place again and again.

Diagnose the Core Problem

Just because we're resolved to have productive arguments doesn't mean they will all start off that way. Sometimes we just explode, but when we do, instead of staying in the argument or letting it go, if we diagnose what went wrong, we have a chance to better understand our partner and reduce the chances of having the same conflict again. Once you're practiced at arguing productively, you may be able to shift to this mode on the spot, but otherwise, you can both step away from the argument, examine your own role in the matter, and prepare to bring that to your partner.

My client Dean had a fight with his girlfriend. They were at a wedding, and she went to get them drinks. Dean watched as a guy at the bar obviously flirted with her. She smiled at him, said something while pointing over at Dean, then returned with the drinks. Dean was upset that she had enjoyed the attention she got from the guy.

"I told her if she was going to flirt like that and disrespect me, then we might as well end it. She said I was getting mad about nothing and was annoyed with me for ruining our night." When Dean and I discussed it further, it became clear that the real reason he felt threatened when someone gave his girlfriend attention was that he felt insecure about their relationship. This was the core of the problem. It wasn't what happened at the bar, but an issue that scene revealed about their relationship. With this knowledge, Dean was able to work on his insecurity rather than falsely accuse his girlfriend and cause more issues in their relationship.

It's hard to diagnose the core issue on the spot. We always think we have a difference of opinion, or the other person did something wrong. Swami Krishnananda, one of the great teachers of the Vedas, explains that there are four types of conflict. Inspired by his model, I developed a similar, but simpler, way of peeling back the layers of an issue in a relationship. First, there are *social conflicts*. These are triggered by external factors that come into your zone and cause you to disagree. Then there are *interpersonal conflicts*, where your complaint is with the other person. And finally there are *inner conflicts*, where the root is an insecurity, expectation, disappointment, or other problem that lies within you. Let's see how these layers work.

A couple is getting married. They can only invite a limited number of people, and each of their mothers has asked to reserve the last two available seats at the dinner for friends of hers. One groom wants to give the seats to his mother's friends, and the other groom wants to accommodate his own mother. Each argues on behalf of their parent— saying how important and close these friends are and why they deserve the seats at the reception. This is a social conflict, brought about by both people wanting to fulfill their mother's expectations.

Then the argument shifts. One person says their family has put more money into the wedding and therefore they should get to decide. The other person says they've worked much harder on the planning, so they should choose. The accusations and arguments now have nothing to do with the parents—this has become a power struggle between the couple. An interpersonal conflict.

But then the couple takes a break. Tempers calm, and they are ready to fight the issue instead of each other. When they return to the issue, they realize that neither of them wanted to let their mothers down. This was, for each of them, an inner conflict. The inner conflict is the one they truly needed to solve. At least one mother was going to be let down. They were arguing with each other instead of confronting their mothers. But then they asked themselves, "Do I often let my mother down, or is this a special circumstance?" "What is another way I could make my mother happy?" "I'm getting married—is it time for me to stop catering to my mother?" Once they got to the root of the problem, they decided to invite two more of their own friends and toasted their mothers at the wedding.

We can use these layers to look at the issue together, get to its core, and address the real problem. Our anger is often misplaced: We start arguing about the laundry, when really we're upset about how our partner spends their time. We argue about how the children should do their homework, when actually what upsets us is that our partner doesn't give us enough attention. We argue about how no one's helping around the house, when really what we're upset about is not feeling understood or heard. The conflict won't go away until we identify and address its true source. We might get someone to fix a behavior—Dean's girlfriend can agree to never smile at another man again—but until they work through the real issue—his insecurity—it won't go away.

Don't waste time arguing about something you don't care about. Instead, find the actual problem.

Know Your Fight Styles

Just as we have different love languages, we have different fight styles. Knowing how each of you processes conflict makes it easier to get a handle on your arguments and helps you stay neutral. Radhi and I have completely different styles of arguing. I want to dive in and talk it out, whereas she wants to collect her thoughts and cool down a bit before we speak. I'm eager to find a resolution, while she wants to take a break, decompress, and think through the issue on her own before reconvening. Understanding this about each other stopped me from feeling hurt when she would go quiet during an argument, and it stopped her from being annoyed when I would want to discuss an issue at length. Identifying your partner's fight style and your own is the first step toward fighting for love.

TRY THIS:

IDENTIFY YOUR PARTNER'S FIGHT STYLE AND YOUR OWN

Look at the three styles below. Which one best describes you?

FIGHT STYLES

VENTING	HIDING	EXPLODING
"We have to find a solution right now!"	"I'm not ready to talk about this."	"It's all your fault!"

1. **Venting.** Some people, like me, want to express their anger and keep hashing it out until a solution is reached. To para-phrase a common saying, there are three sides to every argument: yours, mine, and the truth. There is no objective truth. The fighter who is solution-oriented wants to get to an

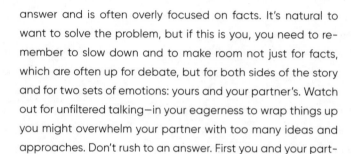

answer and is often overly focused on facts. It's natural to want to solve the problem, but if this is you, you need to remember to slow down and to make room not just for facts, which are often up for debate, but for both sides of the story and for two sets of emotions: yours and your partner's. Watch out for unfiltered talking—in your eagerness to wrap things up you might overwhelm your partner with too many ideas and approaches. Don't rush to an answer. First you and your partner will need to agree about what issue you're up against. Only then can you look for solutions together.

2. **Hiding.** Some people shut down in an argument. The emotions are just too strong, and you need space. You need to process. You either go silent in the middle of the argument or leave the room and need to regroup before continuing. The person who withdraws doesn't want to contemplate solutions in the heat of the moment. They aren't ready to hear them and may grow more annoyed if their partner pushes for a quick resolution. Take the time and space you need, but don't use your silence as a way of doing battle.

3. **Exploding.** Some of us can't control our anger and so erupt with emotion. This response takes a great toll on relationships, and it's a behavior you should make a concerted effort to change. If you fall into this category, you must work on managing your emotions. This might involve bringing in outside resources to help you with anger management. Or you can make a plan with your partner during a time of peace, deciding that the next time you fight, you agree to take a time-out. Figure out what would work best for you: perhaps going for a run, taking a shower, or otherwise letting off steam.

For a quiz revealing your own fight style please visit: www .FightStyles.com.

Once you've identified your fight style, talk to your partner about it. What do they think their own fight style is? Based on your styles, create space for each of you to be angry, and a schedule in which you can deal with it properly.

If one or both of you likes to vent, the other might need more time and space to process. Just because one person isn't ready doesn't mean they don't love the other, and they should reassure their partner of this. Make sure you know each other's process before the next argument so that your different fight styles don't become the reason the fight escalates. Look to develop your self-expression, but make sure you allow yourself the time you need to decompress and think before trying to address the issue. If you both like to vent, this can work well if you make sure you're doing so in an intentional way with the goal of overcoming the issue together.

If one partner needs to retreat, let them go. Withdrawal may feel like a punishment, but that doesn't mean that's the partner's intention. It doesn't mean they don't care. It's an emotional reaction. If you need to withdraw, say so. If one or both of you needs space, plan to talk when you're both ready. Make good use of the extra time this gives you. Instead of allowing yourselves to get even more worked up, remember that you are on the same side, and try to distill the issue to its core, so that when you return to the conversation you can articulate what you and your partner are up against.

If your partner is explosive, encourage them during a peaceful time to work on the behavior (see above). The same is true if you are both explosive. This is a difficult behavior to change, but it isn't a productive way to argue. During an argument, you can simply say, "We're not going to come to a solution when either of us is this upset. Let's talk when we're ready."

Winning Together

When a conflict arises in your relationship, ideally you're able to stop in your tracks, find neutrality, diagnose it, and break down the importance and urgency of the issue. After all this prep work, you are ready to fight the issue together instead of fighting each other. These five steps can help you find PEACE.

1. **P**lace and time
2. **E**xpression
3. **A**nger management
4. **C**ommitment
5. **E**volution

Place and Time

Pick a time and place for resolving your conflict. This may seem unrealistic. After all, fights spring up on impulse. But developing the ability to hold back when an issue arises will change your fights forever. Instead of saying, "How can you keep getting in the shower first when you know I have to be at work earlier?" say, "Hey, I'm feeling frustrated about our morning routine. Can we pick a good time to talk it through?" and schedule it. This skill takes time to master—in the beginning you might have an outburst before you check yourself and remember to put some space between the emotions and the conversation about the issue that called them forth. That's okay. The outburst is your signal to stop yourself next time before you say something you regret.

Conflict doesn't have to be distressing. It doesn't have to leave us with regret. How many times have we had to come back and say, "I didn't mean it"? When we feel mean, we say things we don't mean. We make permanent declarations based on a temporary emotion.

Social work professor Noam Ostrander likes to ask couples, "What does the 5:30 fight look like on weekdays?" As Ostrander told *Time* magazine, "They sort of smile because they know." One of the patterns that Ostrander frequently sees is couples arguing right after they get home from work. Everyone's had a long day; no one knows what's for dinner or has had time to decompress; and suddenly you're arguing over who forgot to pay a bill. Ostrander says the 5:30 fight can often be avoided with a new routine: a quick check-in, maybe a hug and a kiss, then a short separation so each person can transition from work mode. Then, when you've both caught your breath, you can come back together in a more open and relaxed mental and emotional space.

The end of a long workday is usually not the best time for a serious talk, but if you can't put off an issue until an ideal time, another option is to bring time-outs into your fights. If you're in the middle of an argument and you're being reactive, ask for some time to think so that you can share your feelings properly. You can frame the time-out in a way that doesn't make your partner feel like you're walking away. Say, "Look, I'm fighting for the wrong thing right now. I'm sorry about this. I want to have this conversation, but I need ten minutes. I'm not going anywhere. Let me take some time to understand this or cool down, and then let's have a proper discussion." You can also call for a focus on listening, where you both slow down and take turns speaking without judging each other or defending yourselves.

You also may not want to ruin a relaxing weekend the two of you have planned. So explain to your partner that you want to talk about some of the things that you think are affecting the relationship. Tell them you want to do it soon, but when it's best for both of you. You want it to be a time when you're both calm, rather than while the kids are trashing the house or while your partner is trying to respond to a work email. Maybe on a weekend when work pressure is less, maybe after the kids are in bed.

If you and your partner have a recurring issue, consider writing a letter so you have all your facts gathered and don't go off topic. You want to center the talk on what you really care about. You want to focus on what really makes an impact in both of your lives.

Once you've arranged a time, figure out or create a safe space for communication. We use the expression "Let's get it all out on the table." Imagine people just dumping all their baggage out onto a dinner table. Now that you've agreed to address the issue, take the time to *set* the table. Find a quiet space where you can talk.

Don't have it out in the bedroom where you both sleep or at the table where you eat together. These are places where you spend intimate time together, and it's best to hold them sacred. Pick a neutral location where you can discuss things, like the living room or a public library—a space that is going to make you both feel more responsible, committed, focused, and calm rather than a place that calls up other, more negative emotions. Outside, weather permitting, is usually the best choice. Go on a walk or sit in a nearby park.

Try positioning yourselves side by side rather than across from each other. According to cognitive scientist Art Markman, studies show that when we sit next to someone, we literally share their perspective of the world around us, which may help us to feel more empathy for them. In their book *Dimensions of Body Language*, the Westside Toastmasters organization describes sitting next to one another as "the co-operative position" because it "allows for good eye contact and the opportunity for mirroring," where we assume a similar posture or body movements as the other person. Just like repeating some of what the other person says back to them, physical mirroring helps people feel like you're hearing them, and ideally you actually *are* hearing them. Sitting or walking next to someone helps mirroring happen naturally.

TRY THIS:

MAKE AN AGREEMENT FOR YOUR NEXT ARGUMENT

It's easy to forget all our intentions in the heat of the moment. But if you have a plan that you've discussed and signed on to, you can fall back on it when emotions run high. Here are some points to have at the ready. In a calm moment, agree on these with your partner. Then, in your next spat, pause. Use that count of ten to grab this agreement or to pull it up on your phone.

CONFLICT AGREEMENT

We agree to pick a time and place for this conflict instead of having it right now.

We agree that if we come to an agreement, we both win, but if one person wins, we both lose.

Our intention is to (pick as many as you like): find a compromise / understand each other's feelings / address this issue with a solution that will help us avoid this argument in the future / support each other even though we disagree.

A neutral description of the conflict that we agree on is:

We're going to discuss it at this time:

We're going to discuss it in this place:

Before we resolve it, we will each write down what is upsetting the other person.

Here are four possible solutions to the problem or ways we can avoid having this conflict again.

1.

2.

3.

4.

Are we both satisfied with the resolution?

Expression

Now that you've chosen a peaceful time and place, you should choose your words with similar care. Use specific language. Words can't be unsaid; actions can't be undone. Share how you feel, not what you think of the other person. Author Ritu Ghatourey says, "Ten percent of conflict is due to difference of opinion. Ninety percent is due to wrong tone of voice." Channel your inner guru and try to lead gently and calmly without forcing your ideas or desires on the other person.

Don't use extreme words like *always* and *never*, threats like "If you don't change this, I'm leaving you," or attacking words like "This is your fault. You're wrong." These are terms of accusation and escalation. Too often our communication puts the other person on the defensive. We accuse; we don't inspire. Fights often start with the same two words: "You always . . ." This language is a sign that you haven't purified your ego. Make an accusation and bang! you've switched on someone's defensive current. You won't get what you want because of how you're asking for it.

Instead, focus on clarity. Start by saying, "I think our problem is that . . ." or "It's important to me that we . . ." We think we need to establish what is right and wrong about our behavior, but answers don't come from certainty or exaggeration. They come from clarity. We each want to clarify that our partner loves us and that they want to be with us. Each of you should ask and answer the questions:

What's our issue?
What do you need from me right now?

When you enter a discussion calmly, you can use language of request rather than complaint or accusation. Instead of asking, "Why don't you ever clean up after you eat?" you can try, "Do you mind cleaning up after you eat?" Or, "I'm not feeling great. I'm stressed about the way the house looks. Would you mind picking some stuff up?"

Most arguments are you, you, you, you, you, me, me, me, me, me. This is what *you* did to *me*. If all your language is oriented around yourself, you're creating a divide. Your partner will respond with defensive words like "I would never do that. I'm not like that. This is *your* problem." Before you go deep into your individual feelings, establish the intention that unites you. Then you can hear each other's feelings in light of that intention. You might say, "We've been going through a rough patch, and it would be great for us to figure out how we want to handle our chores in the evening." When you start saying *we*, your partner realizes you're not being selfish. It's not just a problem you have with them. It's about both of you. You both have problems and flaws. Acknowledge that and talk about how to address them together. In practice, it can be hard to avoid *I* and *you*, but doing it saves you the far greater discomfort of dealing with someone you've put on the defensive. Here are some useful "we" statements:

> *"We need to work on this."*
> *"We need to change."*
> *"There are things we both need to learn."*
> *"Can we both try this together?"*

Once you've established your intention for the argument, you can start sharing your feelings. When you say "I think," it suggests that you hold a fixed stance, while "I feel" suggests that you're describing your emotional reaction, which can evolve.

"When you do this, I feel this way."

"When you leave the trash out, I feel like our household isn't your priority."

"When you criticize me, I feel unloved."

Don't insult or be defensive. Try being direct and respectful rather than putting your loved one down for their failure to meet your need. You may object that you don't have time for roundabout approaches to your issues; you'd rather be direct. Well, if we don't have time to communicate properly, we'll need to make more time for more conflict.

I don't recommend going straight to your partner and saying, "Oh my God, Jay says we totally do everything wrong." That too will put them on the defensive (and will get me in trouble). Instead, say, "I'd love to talk to you about the way we argue. I know that this could change our relationship." Whenever it comes to communication, set a time and make requests instead of complaints.

TRY THIS:

DISCUSSING COMPLEX ISSUES

We can't resolve complex issues with simple agreements like "I promise to put my socks in the hamper from now on," and "I'll remind you if you leave them on the floor." A big issue may not have a quick fix or easy win and will require more reflection and work to solve. This begins with articulating the issue and thinking about it together. Here are some ways to get you started so you aren't tempted to smooth over the issue with an artificial resolution but leave it open for further understanding and discussion.

"This is what I heard. . . . And here's what I am going to try to do moving forward."

"This point really resonated with me . . . and it helps me see things differently now."

"Now I understand what you actually want. . . . This is how I can respond realistically."

"I am not fully sure what the solution is . . . but I care about you, and I would love for us to revisit this next week to discuss further."

"I am sorry it took me this long to understand. I can see how it affected you. . . . Let's work on this together."

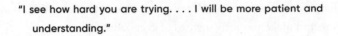

> **"I see how hard you are trying. . . . I will be more patient and understanding."**
>
> Acknowledge what you've learned about each other along the way. At the end of this conversation, you should not promise that you will never do something again, unless you are truly able to make that promise. Instead, commit to what you will try to do.

Anger Management

What if, despite your best efforts, your partner is caught up in anger and ego? They might even deny there's an issue. Well, then you've got to work extra hard if you care about the relationship.

If your partner is resistant, try saying, "Look, I want to have this discussion with you because I believe that we can get to a better place together. I'm not doing this to be right. I'm not doing this for my ego. I'm not doing this to prove you're wrong. I'm not doing this to make you look or feel bad. I'm doing this because I really want us to be in a good place. Let's discuss what kind of relationship we want."

When you explain to your partner what you're trying to do, it raises their awareness. They then have the opportunity to respond, "Okay, I agree with you." And if they can't agree, then at least you have a clearer sense of the relationship's challenges and potential (or lack thereof). Here are some of the attitudes you might confront if your partner isn't on the same page as you.

When you're met with:	Address it by:
Anger/ego	People act out of ego when they feel accused. You haven't successfully achieved neutrality, or they haven't processed it. They still feel like the problem you're bringing up is theirs alone. Schedule a time and return to language that shows you want to work together on this as a team.
Dismissive/belittling	Your partner doesn't understand or refuses to see how much this matters to you. Make sure you've diagnosed the core problem, and then use "we" language when you say, "We're not understanding the real problem here. The real challenge here is [the core issue]." The core issue is something they can't dismiss.
Globalizing/blaming	If your partner is globalizing an issue—applying one instance to the entirety of your interactions or blaming you—take responsibility and apologize. Then find neutrality in order to bring the dialogue back to the intention of the argument and what you want to achieve together. Say, "I understand where these feelings are coming from. Let's focus on one thing at a time."
Shutting down	If your partner shuts down, this isn't the right time or space to resolve the issue. Make sure you know their fight style, and then together set a time and place for the argument.
Giving in/giving up without resolving	Sometimes a partner is so eager to end a conflict that they just agree to do whatever you want, but you don't feel confident that they'll stick to their commitment or that their heart is in it. In this case, use specific language. "This is what we're agreeing to. You're going to be home by six p.m. five days a week, and I'm not going to make weekend plans without checking with you. Can we both agree to this plan?"

You can't resolve an argument by yourself—you both have to be on board. There has to be enthusiasm for the relationship and for keeping it alive. This enthusiasm may not be at the same level as it was in the very beginning, but it settles into an ongoing commitment to making an effort. If your partner refuses to talk about the issue or acknowledge there's a problem, you must decide if you can live with that. But I'll tell you this: If it's important, it's important, and if your partner's not willing to engage about it, turn to Rule 7, where we discuss how to handle intolerable differences.

Commitment

To resolve the issue, you'll need to reach an agreement. This agreement necessarily involves change; otherwise it's likely you'll have the same conflict again. This doesn't mean either partner should make promises like "I'll never do this again," or "This is the last time," or "This will never happen again." We are drawn to these dramatic statements. We want to hear them, and we like to say them, whether because we feel obliged to as a show of our commitment or because such blanket statements are actually easier than the painstaking work of figuring out over time exactly how to adjust and improve the relationship. Conversation is much more likely to get you to a solution than blanket statements.

Sometimes we need outside help to find a solution. Certain topics can be especially complex or challenging to take on by yourselves. If you have trouble reaching resolution on your own, enlist the help of an objective third party to help you work through the issue with your partner. Ideally, it's not a friend or family member—you want someone who is truly objective, such as a therapist or counselor, a mediator, or a trusted spiritual or religious counselor or advisor if they're available to you. It's healthy to get help. And it's worth it.

Keep in mind that the goal of the productive argument isn't to get a specific reaction or a positive response. What you're looking for is a solution to the problem.

Evolution

We grow through conflict by taking responsibility for our part in the issue, and we acknowledge our mistakes by apologizing. Even if you apologized early on, apologizing at the end, when you've found a resolution, provides powerful closure. Of course, if it's done incorrectly, an apology can be as empty as the resolution to "never do it again." As children, we were told "say you're sorry," and those words were presumed to fix the injury. But as adults we need to do more than put a bandage on the problem. In a productive argument, the apology expresses more than regret. Through it, you restate the issue and commit to change. There are three steps to a real apology: acceptance, articulation, and action.

Acceptance. First, the apologizer needs to feel true regret for their behavior or mistake, which involves recognizing how their choices affected the other person's feelings and taking responsibility for the outcome.

Articulation. Next, the apologizer needs to communicate their understanding and regret with clear expression of the challenges and emotions involved. This doesn't mean making a big, lofty statement about how you'll never make the mistake again. Instead, you are expressing the behavioral change that you're going to make in order to ensure it doesn't happen again. You might say, "I recognize that when you're stressed it's not useful for me to remind you of what you still have to do. Instead, I'm going to support you." Or you might say, "I'm sorry that in the beginning of our relationship I belittled you, which made you feel disrespected and unloved and insecure. I'm taking steps to recognize why I do that, and to be more supportive and compassionate in my communication with you. I'm going to try to think before I respond."

Action. Finally, we honor our commitment to avoid making the same mistake again. Following through on this promise of change is the most important outcome of the argument. As I've heard said, "The best apology is changed behavior."

Your partner might take their cue from how meaningful you've made your apology and reciprocate with their own, but if they don't, it might be because they need time. You can set up the opportunity for them to articulate their own apology in their own time by saying, "Does it help to know exactly what I'm sorry for? I'd appreciate your thoughts after you have time to reflect on this."

TRY THIS:

WRITE AN APOLOGY LETTER

Sit down and think about everything you could apologize to your partner for—anything and everything you still feel sorry about. This is not about making yourself feel better or putting yourself down. It's about taking responsibility for your mistakes, making your partner aware that you reflect on how you've affected them, and validating feelings you should have seen but may have missed. It shows them how much you care.

For each mistake, list:

1. The mistake itself

2. How you think it affected them

3. Why you feel sorry

4. How you will fix it or what you intend to do differently going forward

Don't qualify your apology with blame, explanations, or excuses. You already explained yourself when you were working

through the issue. Now your focus is showing that you understand how you hurt your partner. After you've written your note
of apology, give it to your partner. Let them know that you wrote
this without any expectations of what they might do in return;
you just wanted to express your love in a new way, by thinking
seriously about old feelings or mistakes or resentments that may
have never been addressed or resolved.

The Deal-Breaker

Sometimes peace is elusive. An argument feels irreconcilable. Neither
person will budge, and neither of you is happy with the rift in your relationship. If nobody's changing, then you're both going to have to find a
way to make peace with it (or have the same fight over and over again).
Psychiatrists Phillip Lee and Diane Rudolph, a husband-wife team
of relationship experts, say that couples can get in a habit of arguing
without resolution—what they term *argument addiction*—where the
couple is "stuck in a pattern of communication which can send them
on a seemingly endless loop over the same arguments." That doesn't
sound like fun.

Instead of this issue being a zone you either avoid or fight over
repeatedly, this topic might have to be a neutral zone—a space where
you agree to respect each other's opinions and not try to change them.
That's different from just being angry and not talking about an issue. In
some (perhaps many) cases, we can learn to accept these differences.
They don't have to hurt the relationship. For example, your partner
may never be excited about going to that big work party or dancing in a
flash mob with you because they're deeply introverted and prefer quiet
events with opportunities for intimate conversation. That may be okay.
Unsolvable doesn't need to be a discouraging term, but rather may indicate that the issues won't go away because the sources of conflict

won't go away. In such cases, you can negotiate solutions that work for both of you. Find a friend who will go to the party or the mosh pit with you. Or agree to attend in exchange for doing something she loves that doesn't delight you.

There are also difficult topics where you must find a way to agree, like how to manage the family's finances, where to send the kids to school, or what to do if your partner has to be involved with an ex because they have children together. With the tools I've given you and a positive intention, you can likely navigate these arguments. But approaching an issue together and looking for ways to fight it out as a team doesn't guarantee that you'll get the reaction or resolution that you want. When you continue to bump up against a significant, complex issue, and you're far from mutual ground, then you might find yourself confronting a deep rupture in your relationship. This is when our fights lead us to the biggest question we've faced since we first decided to get together: Should we remain together? This is a challenge that we will address in the next rule.

You Don't Break
in a Breakup

*Your task is not to seek for love, but merely to seek and
find all the barriers within yourself that you have built
against it.*

—RUMI

Signs of Trouble

Love doesn't disintegrate overnight. The early days of your relationship were like a freshly painted wall. Smooth, even, ready to be filled
with images of the life that awaited you. The wall underneath may not
have been perfect, but with the fresh coat of paint it looked nice and
solid. But every wall eventually gets scratches—maybe even some from
baggage that arrived on move-in day. Perhaps you've been too busy to
deal with it. Maybe you told yourself it wasn't a problem, but you've
just been saying that to smooth things over. You know the scratches
won't go away until you do something about them, but you can live
with them for a while. Then, over time, more scratches accumulate.
You walk past them every day. If they start to bother you, you might do
some touch-up. Maybe you'll even decide it's time to repaint that wall.

In the same way, flaws emerge in relationships. The hustle of life
generates scratches and nicks that won't go away unless you address
them. Maybe your partner always leaves the gas tank on empty. Maybe
they spend too much time telling you how much their boss annoys
them. Maybe they complain every time you have to visit your parents.

What each person sees as a scratch will be different, but these are small issues. You could touch them up if you wanted to, and that knowledge should give you the confidence to live with them. But you must be willing to accept them as part of the charm of a lived-in house. Every flaw doesn't mean the walls will collapse. If we treat every scratch like an earthquake, we put unnecessary stress on the relationship. In other words, pettiness stretches scratches into cracks.

A crack in a wall suggests a structural problem that needs addressing and shouldn't be ignored for too long. Examples of cracks in a relationship might be that you repeatedly break promises to change a behavior; or you consistently feel uncomfortable around one of their family members but don't feel supported; or you feel like the relationship is on autopilot—you never talk anymore. If there is a crack in the relationship, you can't let this issue go unresolved. We talked about how to work through everyday scratches and cracks in the previous chapter.

Sometimes you look at the wall of your house and you know there's a real problem that can't be solved by a paint job. The building's structure is compromised, and the jagged line that crosses the wall is only a symptom of the major underlying problem. In this case, either the two of you are going to find a way to make repairs, or there's going to be a breakup.

Let's touch on a few examples of major ruptures that need to be addressed one way or another: abuse, infidelity, inertia, disinterest.

Abuse Is a Deal-Breaker

First, I want you to know that you deserve to be safe. If you don't feel safe, whether physically, emotionally, or both, the question isn't whether to go, it's how to leave safely. Abuse is any behavior that one partner uses to control the other, and control has no place in a relationship. The National Domestic Violence Hotline identifies six categories of abuse: physical, emotional and verbal, sexual, financial, digital, and stalking. Physical threats and violence to you, your children, your family, or your pets are the most obvious signs of abuse, but any of the following are common signs of abuse: Your partner interferes with your decision-making—they tell you how you can spend your time, including whether you can work and when you can and can't go out; they tell you what you can and can't wear; they tell you who you can spend time with. They show extreme jealousy and try to control how much time you spend with family and friends. They use hurtful language, looks, and gestures, insulting, demeaning, or threatening you in private or in front of other people. They control money, restricting what you have and what you can spend it on. They control sex, pressuring you to have sex or perform acts you don't like. None of this is partnership. It's ownership.

It can be very difficult and scary to leave relationships where someone is controlling us. When abusive people are stripped of control, they can become dangerous. Yet, if you're in a physically or emotionally abusive relationship, you need to find a safe way out. If you're in this situation, my first recommendation is always, again, to seek professional help. Please contact the National Domestic Violence Hotline: 1-800-799-SAFE (7233).

Fear can be a factor even when it doesn't tip into abuse. You may find that in your relationship you walk on tiptoe because you're scared of provoking your partner. You anticipate a negative reaction from them and find yourself overthinking how you'll respond.

The reaction we're trying to avoid might be straight-up anger, but it can also be derision and criticism. Constructive criticism is valuable when it's coming from a guru with calmness and good intentions. You don't want to have a life full of yes-people. But if your partner demeans you to your face or behind your back, this doesn't help you grow. If your partner is habitually careless or aggressive in their words to you, or vice versa, it takes a measurable toll on your relationship. According to research by psychologists Clifford Notarius and Howard Markman, it takes just one aggressive or passive-aggressive remark to erase twenty acts of kindness.

When your relationship contains fear and criticism, it's hard to feel free to be yourself. You're putting on a performance to make you and the relationship match your partner's requirements. There's a level of performance in many of the roles we play and jobs we have. To greater or lesser degrees, we often call on a slightly controlled, enhanced, or trained version of ourselves to adjust to different circumstances. We can't expect to feel fully ourselves in every situation every day, but with our partner, we shouldn't feel like we're living a lie.

You don't have to instantly bail on the relationship if you realize you're operating out of fear. First, try sharing more of who you truly are. Start to break those illusions. You can say, "Hey, I know I said I like baseball, but really I don't. I'd rather not watch the games with you anymore." In most relationships, something like that probably wouldn't be a huge deal, but another situation could have much higher stakes. Maybe you'll have to say, "I know I said I don't want kids, but I wasn't really being honest. I thought that in time you'd change your mind. The truth is, I really want kids and I'll feel I'm missing out if we don't have them." Or maybe you want to make a significant change in your everyday life— to relocate or pursue a new purpose. If you're deeply invested in the relationship, make a significant effort to express who you truly are. Being judged in the short term is better than being stuck in the wrong situation for the long term. If the only way for you to sustain the relationship is to pretend to be someone you're not, it's time to think about ending it.

Don't view this journey as one you must undertake alone. Loneliness and isolation can keep us from making the tough choice to go. We may fear how our lives might change without that person or that situation. But others have suffered like you, and others are suffering now, and others have left. You may well need help, and there's no shame in recognizing that you're in a bad situation and asking for help and support.

Somewhere inside, my friend Judy knew it was time to leave her husband. She told me, "I have no trouble making decisions at work. I've always prided myself on being clearheaded and sure of myself. But even though we were no longer happy, even though I bore his scorn and disrespect every single day, leaving the father of my children felt somehow beyond me." She hesitated to talk to her friends. "We've been together for twenty-four years. I was embarrassed to admit how long I'd been unhappy and how bad it had gotten. And I feel like sometimes friends just want you to stay together—it makes them feel more stable in their own marriages." Judy ended up turning to an online community of women that she'd joined only recently. "I didn't know them, and none of them were experts, but I was able to present my situation anonymously and as subjectively as I could. Their collective wisdom covered so many different aspects of what I was going through: my need for autonomy, my attachment to the past, my commitment to my wedding vows, my hopes for the future, my fears of being alone, my worries about my children, and my concerns that my husband's reaction might put our family in danger. Among the group, they'd been through it all. I came away almost surprised by how much clarity I had. Plus, they'd given me ways to communicate with my husband that never would have occurred to me with all the emotional buildup of the years, and they connected me with local resources to make sure I was safe." There's no reason to be alone when you make hard decisions and enter the unknown. Seek out supporters or experts, whether it's through on-line forums, books, friends, or organizations. You deserve love and re-spect, and your safety is nonnegotiable.

Infidelity Is a Profound Challenge

One of the most common reasons people end relationships is cheating. According to data from community health centers, of couples where a partner had admitted to cheating, only 15.6 percent of relationships were able to recover. There are all sorts of issues that can lead to one partner betraying the other, and there are whole books on processing it, but there is no question that once trust is broken, only deep work and commitment on both sides can rebuild it.

In *NOT "Just Friends,"* psychologist and infidelity expert Dr. Shirley Glass writes that in the aftermath of cheating, it's natural to want to end the relationship immediately, and that may be the right decision. But it can be hard to tell when emotions are running hot. "Even if you're still not sure whether the [relationship] can be saved," she writes, "you shouldn't make your decision based on the lowest point in your re-lationship. . . . To do the hard work ahead of exploring the meaning of the infidelity, you will need to build a foundation of commitment, caring, and compassionate communication." For the partner who was cheated on, that includes putting your own best foot forward. "You and your partner can work together to create a healing atmosphere that is calm, where information can be shared and where caring begins to bind you together again. [And you] can start making specific repairs to the relationship that will help each of you feel more connected." In one survey of couples who had experienced infidelity, when the person who had cheated was willing to answer their spouse's questions honestly, 72 percent of them said they were able to rebuild trust.

Also, in order to restore trust, the person who was cheated on has to forgive. According to marriage and family therapist Jim Hutt, if the partner who was cheated on continues to punish and scold the other partner, the relationship is doomed. So if you find yourself in a situation where you're punishing the other person, you're also punishing yourself. Nobody expects you to summon instant forgiveness, but recognize that even though the other person broke your trust, you both have to put effort into restoring it.

In some cases, couples say that healing after infidelity has resulted in even more trust than before, so it *is* possible to heal. But it takes total commitment from both partners. And it takes time. Glass notes that in a sample of 350 couples she worked with who experienced infidelity, those who attended at least ten therapy sessions together "had a much better chance of staying together" than those who went to fewer sessions.

If you're the one who cheated—don't leave your relationship for another person. Leave for you. If you betray your partner, you haven't taken the time to understand yourself. The two of you have built something together. If it's fallen apart, then leave. But let the dust settle before you find someone else. If you enter a new relationship while clouds of dust are still swirling around you, that debris will be caught up in the new relationship. You don't want to wind up in another mess with the same issues.

Licensed clinical social worker Robert Taibbi talks about why rebound relationships seem so appealing. "Once the relationship is over, there's a void in your life. . . . [T]here's a loss and grief because the psychological attachment is broken." It's easy to have tunnel vision, Taibbi says, looking only at the bad in the relationship and your partner, and so you think the solution is easy: "Find someone who isn't like that." But of course, you're still the same person you were in your last relationship, so some of the challenges will come along with you. In fact, research by sociologist Annette Lawson shows that just one in ten people who left their marriage for another person actually ended up marrying the person with whom they'd had an affair.

TRY THIS:

CHECK YOUR REASONS FOR LEAVING

Are you truly doing this for you, or have you been dazzled by a shiny new person? Check yourself.

CONSIDERATIONS

1. *Temptation check.* If you hadn't met the new person, would you stay with your current partner? If the answer is yes, then you should focus on resuscitating the relationship.
2. *Reality check.* If a magician tells you how they did a trick, the trick is not as enchanting. A new relationship is full of magic, but it doesn't tell you what's left when the magic fades. Assume the clean slate of your relationship with the new person will develop its own fissures. Are you prepared to work on them as they arise, or will you find yourself with the same frustration and disillusion?
3. *Karma check.* Remember that if you leave for someone else, your new partner might do the same to you. Make sure that if you leave, it's because you genuinely believe there is no future with your partner and that you would rather be alone than with them.

Loss of Interest

Divorce lawyer Joseph E. Cordell says one problem he often sees is a lack of day-to-day communication, where spouses "never shared or discussed the things going on in their lives." That can make your partner feel like they're not a significant part of your life. After you've been married for ten years, you might not be hurrying to the door to greet your partner after work, but, in general, you should think of seeing them as a positive experience. There's something wrong if, when their name pops up as an incoming call, you decline it. It's really important to ask yourself, *Why am I avoiding that call?*

One of the reasons we avoid someone is that we don't want to spend time hearing about their life. We no longer recognize what's interesting about them because we haven't connected for so long. This is hard to admit to ourselves because we like to believe we are caring and constant. In order to fully evaluate this, ask yourself if there are people in your life that you do reach out to, people in your life that you're excited to be around and excited to talk to. This will help you evaluate whether this is a widespread issue for you or whether it's something that relates to this particular relationship. Also notice whether this feeling is ongoing, or whether it's just a phase. You'll know that your feelings toward your partner have permanently changed if you never look forward to seeing them.

Even if you're not avoiding your partner, it's still a bad sign if you feel drained and unenthusiastic when you spend time with them.

Another sign of waning interest is that you don't instantly want to share good or bad news with your partner. Think about who comes to mind when you have good news to share. If your partner isn't in the top three, then this probably means either you don't feel that they're important enough to share it with, or you feel they won't care enough. When we stop sharing intimate information with people it's because we no longer feel an intimate connection with them. Of course, it may be that certain types of good news aren't core to your partner's values—they don't have to be happy for you that you bought a new sweater—but in general you should feel that seeing you happy makes them happy and seeing you sad makes them want to comfort you.

A sure sign that interest has faded is that you no longer feel like you have anything to learn from each other. Marriage and family therapist Marilyn Hough describes a couple in her practice who stopped growing together. Jane was training to become a therapist, and Tom was an engineer and sole provider for the family. He felt Jane's desire to become a therapist was a waste of time. Jane felt unseen by her husband, and Tom felt unsupported in his work. They had stopped growing together, and Hough says that by the time they came to therapy, "the growth gap was just too big to overcome. Too many years had passed without communicating their true feelings and desires." From that point, it wasn't about trying to repair the relationship, but negotiating a conscious and caring breakup.

When one or both partners are no longer putting effort into the relationship, either or both may have fallen out of love. This might well be difficult for the one who lost interest to explain. It is also a hard truth to hear and understand. No relationship is perfect all the time. But when challenges do arise, notice if you're the only one trying to fix them.

Atrophy of Intimacy

Sometimes the primary challenge in a relationship isn't an intolerable disagreement or behavior. Sometimes what we're facing is a matter of disconnection. In the beginning, a relationship is full of sparks. We feel attraction. We feel a positive flow of energy. Then, as time passes, that initial excitement inevitably wanes, and we miss it. We still love our partner, but we question why things aren't what they used to be and whether we should feel as connected as we once did.

A client of mine says she has friends she can talk to for hours, but she doesn't know what to talk to her girlfriend about. She asked me if that meant her girlfriend wasn't "the one." I told her that in the same way a plant needs sun, water, soil, nutrients, and shelter, we need to keep tending our relationship for it to flourish over time. You may say,

well, why don't I just buy a new plant? But if you move on, you'd have
to learn to water that plant every day too.

Nurturing Intimacy

We nurture intimacy in our relationships by learning and growing together. I know a lot of couples who say they have nothing in common.
If they sat together at dinner, they would have nothing to talk about. At
times like this, we tend to default to negativity. We gossip or criticize
or complain about the people we encounter or things we do. As a quote
attributed to Eleanor Roosevelt goes, "Great minds discuss ideas; average minds discuss events; small minds discuss people." When we connect on negative issues, we generate a low vibration—a low energy that
doesn't last long or create satisfaction. When we connect in a neutral
manner over routine matters, like schedules or chores, we generate a
medium vibration that doesn't foster intimacy and love. But when we
experiment together, learning from and through each other, we generate a high vibration that energizes and stimulates our connection.

If you can't generate a high vibration, it might be because you don't
have any new thoughts to share. You aren't spending time developing

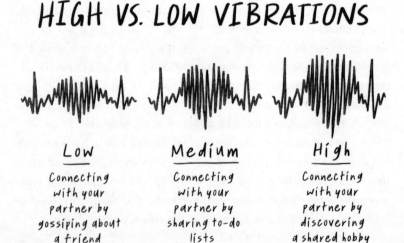

HIGH VS. LOW VIBRATIONS

Low	Medium	High
Connecting with your partner by gossiping about a friend	Connecting with your partner by sharing to-do lists	Connecting with your partner by discovering a shared hobby

yourself; you aren't reading or absorbing new art or ideas. You will never be able to reset or refresh a relationship if you keep doing the same old thing over and over again. Repeating activities may feel comfortable and relaxing, but you don't learn anything new about your partner through familiar routines. On the other hand, if you're growing, you can help your partnership grow. Intimacy develops and thrives when we disclose more, when we try out ideas and let ourselves be vulnerable. This deepens our bond.

You can't order new thoughts and philosophies on Postmates. You open up your world by exploring with your partner. Intimacy is created through shared adventures: entertainment, experiences and experiments, and education, all of which are aimed at the same outcome. A shared experience lets us reflect, share our opinions, and see if we're in agreement. We learn about each other and with each other.

Before the pandemic, Radhi and I used to host events at our home where we'd invite our closest friends to a deep, beautiful meditation. We both place a high value on meditation and spirituality, and those events allowed us to serve our friends together. Radhi would plan the menu and the décor while I did the guest list and the invite, making sure that all the logistics were taken care of. After the event was over and everyone went home, we'd feel joyful and grateful that we had pulled it off together. We may be achieving things in our own personal lives and careers, but our relationships hunger for us to achieve together. Those events helped build our community, and at the same time they gave our relationship purpose.

Entertainment

At the end of a long day, most of us feel like we're too tired to do anything other than curl up in front of the TV. We're often overworked and exhausted and gravitate to entertainment as the easiest way to connect with our partner. If you got into the habit of watching more TV during quarantine, you're not alone. My own guilty pleasure is the real estate show *Selling Sunset*. If you're going to watch TV, there are ways you can get more intimacy out of it. First of all, don't multitask while you're doing it. Stay off your laptop or phone so that you're present with your partner as you watch together. Pick something engaging, and chat about it afterward. We don't have to force our partners to deliver an elaborate critique, but you can make an effort to ask them questions about what they took away from the show to keep you both engaged and connected. Entertainment is only one of three categories I suggest here. I'm not saying you can never do that, but if you use it to fill 100 percent of your spare time together, don't be surprised if you run out of things to talk about! Your brain might appreciate it if you push yourself to get out. A little effort is worth it to deepen intimacy.

Experiences and Experiments

Experiences and experiments require more planning and energy than entertainment, but the rewards are worth it. Afterward, you can share your thoughts and reviews with each other. Experiences don't have to be far-flung, expensive, or wild. This could be a book launch, a magic show, an art show, live music at a bar. You can visit a farmers' market, take a cooking class, go wine-tasting, take a dance class, plan a picnic, go for a hike, drive to see seasonal decorations, or take a walk after dinner. Don't drag the other person to an event that only interests you. Look at the local listings and find something that intrigues both of you and takes you out of your comfort zone. Every one of these activities helps you learn about your partner, feel safe with them, and rekindle intimacy. This gives your relationship the space and resilience to deal with important matters as they arise.

You can also plan a vacation together. Schedule time every week to discuss likes and dislikes, whether you'd rather experience a new city by night or rent an Airbnb in the desert, whether you want to schedule meals and activities in advance or to wing them. A 2000 study commissioned by the U.S. Travel Association (no bias there!) found that couples who traveled together are significantly happier and healthier in their relationships. Eighty-six percent of couples who travel together said that their romance was alive and 63 percent believe that traveling actually inspires romance. And 68 percent of couples believe that traveling together for leisure is *necessary* for a healthy relationship. According to the report, traveling helped people prioritize each other. When you get away together, you're better able to set aside your other obligations and focus on each other.

Every month Radhi and I try to take time away together. It can be a local getaway or just a day trip if that's all you can manage. Traveling together is not just about going to a new place. Being in a place without distractions helps couples go deeper and become closer.

Serving together, doing charity work together, volunteering together—these activities are deeply connected to my time living as a monk. Half of our time as monks was spent in silence, self-awareness, and study, and the other half was spent in service, trying to make a difference in the world. I know couples that have met while volunteering and others who regularly volunteer together, and they all tell me it's such a beautiful experience. Radhi and I consistently serve together, whether it's organizing charity events, feeding the homeless, or gathering a group to learn from an expert.

Like music and sex, the act of service increases our oxytocin levels. It has also been shown to reduce levels of stress and create social connection. It's easy to connect when you're not just trying to help each other or to help others, but to help others together. We gain perspective on real-life issues. We experience gratitude together. We feel a higher purpose together.

A 2017 WalletHub survey found that married couples who volunteer together were more likely to stay together. We don't just bond over movies and TV shows; we bond over beliefs and a shared sense of mission.

Some of the best experiences are experiments—when you and your partner set out to try something new together. You don't just learn something new—you learn about yourself and your partner. The more vulnerable you are when you experiment, the more intimacy you'll feel. A study by psychologist Arthur Aron and colleagues found that couples who spent time together doing new and exciting activities were able to improve their connection and bond.

Seek out adventures that aren't in either of your areas of expertise. You don't want to attempt a sport where one of you has a natural advantage or to play a game that one of you has played for years. To build intimacy, you want to both be novices so that you feel inexperienced and curious together. You both feel similarly uncomfortable. You're both going to learn something new. You're going to need and rely on each other. A challenging hike, a visit to a haunted house, spelunking, roller skating, or (my favorite) an escape room. Intimacy builds as you expose yourselves to each other in a vulnerable moment. Once Radhi and I went to a paint room where they had easels, canvases, brushes, and paints. We were given overalls to wear, and they let us go crazy. It was new and liberating to spray paint wherever we wanted and to create without worrying about the end product. Another time we went to a "rage room" full of bottles, trash cans, old computers, and broken fax machines. We were handed metal pipes and baseball bats and given free rein to break stuff in order to "de-stress." Radhi and I were hesitant. We're not violent people. On our way out we felt more stressed than we had been going in.

Activities like this are a microcosm of the relationship. They don't just help you play a game; they actually teach you about your relationship without having to make it serious. Research shows that play is the mental state in which we learn best, and that play is essential for our mental health. When you attempt a new and challenging activity together in a space where success doesn't matter, you can both let go and learn. Not only do you realize your relationship's weaknesses, but you see your strengths. You get to practice making mistakes together in a situation where the stakes are low. **When you accomplish something new together, you bring that experience to all areas of your life.**

New activities are especially bonding when they take you out of your comfort zone, something daring or challenging, whatever that may be for you—whether it's a bucket list item like skydiving, or jet-skiing, or conquering your fear of heights. Arthur Aron and Don Dutton hired an attractive woman to interview men who had just crossed a very high, somewhat unstable (though not actually dangerous) bridge, along with men who had just crossed a normal, stable bridge. In each case, she asked them some questions, told them if they "wanted to talk further" they could call her, and gave them her number. Of those who had just crossed the shaky bridge, nine of eighteen called her. Of those who had crossed the stable bridge, only two of sixteen called.

Aron and Dutton used the study to point to the "misattribution of arousal" (the men experienced physical arousal, or not, because of the bridge, and it had a halo effect on the woman). But what if the men were simply emboldened by a rush of confidence after having crossed the bridge? In a follow-up study aimed at clarifying the results, the researchers generated physical arousal by telling male participants that as part of the study, they would receive an electrical shock. Some were told this shock would be mild, and some were told it would be painful. Again an attractive woman, ostensibly also a participant, was present. Participants were told that it would take the researcher a few minutes to set up the shock device and were asked to fill out several questionnaires while they waited. One questionnaire assessed their level of attraction to the woman who was participating in the study with them. As it turned out, those who anticipated receiving the painful shock experienced significantly more attraction than those who anticipated only a mild one. This research points to why novel and exciting things—anything that arouses our senses—can help to revive and refresh our interest in our partner. Their takeaway was that "a small amount of stress can spur amorous feelings."

We don't have to fear for our lives, but the novelty and excitement of something new or daring heightens our senses and can create strong feelings of romantic attraction. Dr. Lisa Marie Bobby, founder and clinical director of Growing Self Counseling & Coaching, says, "These shared moments become things to talk about and connect over time and time again." When you've lived through an experience together, it can show you how caring your partner is. If you're about to do something that's slightly daring, and one of you is supporting the other, you may find that the roles reverse. Say you're about to go down a very high water slide. The person who was really confident on the way up might not be the same person who's confident going down. And you start to see how you both support each other. That's a beautiful feeling to experience with your partner in a context like this, because even though the stakes are low, you realize that your partner has that capacity for care. It's also possible that you see that there's no care, no attention, no empathy, no compassion, no support. If that's the case, then you can now see more clearly the void that's hampering your relationship.

Education

The third way to build intimacy is through education. We talked about this option when either or both of you are trying to learn about your purpose. This may require the most time and effort, but it's a great way to support each other's growth. If you share the same interests, you can take a class together. Perhaps you want to take a seminar on real estate or a gardening class. Don't feel like you have to do exactly the same thing. You can each do your own thing, and then share your learning. The point is to expand your own knowledge, so you have something new to bring to the table.

One last way to create intimacy: by expressing gratitude. When we slide into apathy with our partner, we often stop appreciating what they say, do, or achieve. As we've already discussed, you should thank your partner for cooking for you. You should thank your partner for moving the car so that you could leave on time. You should thank your partner for calling to check in. You should thank your partner for putting gas in the car. You should thank your partner for changing the batteries in the smoke alarm. You should thank your partner for going back to the other room to turn out the lights before bed. Why would we not take these opportunities?

The more attention we pay to our partners, the more we appreciate their thoughtfulness and the more likely we are to respond in kind. When they feel appreciated, they are thankful for our thoughtfulness and likely to keep being thoughtful and to reciprocate the appreciation. And so we experience a feedback loop of gratitude where we each have more and more chances to feel love by performing simple tasks for our partners.

Elevate or Separate

If, in spite of our efforts to foster intimacy, our relationship faces one of these four or any other major, structural threat, we have a choice. Love is imperfect, but that doesn't mean we should stay in an unhealthy relationship. Let's look at how to know if you should stay together, work on the issues, and find ways to grow, or if you should break up. There is no right answer; there are only two choices: We can continue with growth—choosing to elevate our relationship. Or we can separate.

There is actually a third option, and it's one that many people choose by default: We can continue as we are. Stagnation is never good—we should always be growing. But one way of growing is to *accept* things as they are. Sometimes we don't feel the way we used to about our partner because we're overworked and overwhelmed with responsibilities and don't have time to nurture our relationship. We might start to imagine there's someone better out there, someone we would never fight with and who would always entertain us, but it's not fair for our partner to have to compete with that fantasy. In this case it makes sense to let go of the fantasy and stay the course.

If your tolerance for managing conflict and stress is low, then it's hard to stay with anyone. Before we give up on a relationship, we should check to make sure we aren't expecting too much from our partner. If a friend was helping you move boxes, and you asked them to carry an extra-large box, they might say, "I'm sorry, but I think it's too heavy for me."

You would not take their refusal to help as a sign that they don't love you. They aren't equipped to give you the help you need. Our partners aren't necessarily equipped to support us in all areas of life. Your partner isn't Target, a one-stop shop for your every need. We talk about the need for a support system, but we never really talk or think about what that system should be.

TRY THIS:

BUILD A SUPPORT SYSTEM

Identify people whom you can turn to for support in key areas of life. You can do this for yourself, but it's also something you can do alongside your partner, so you share an understanding of each other's support system.

Self. Who do you turn to when you experience self-doubt, when you want to discuss your values, when you want to explore your spirituality, or when you want to celebrate your successes?

Financial. Who can best advise you when you have questions about your career and income, and how to make financial decisions?

Mental/emotional. What friends or resources can you turn to for mental health guidance and support?

Health. Who can you go to with questions about your health? Who might be a good person to turn to if you have a health issue that's difficult to deal with either logistically or emotionally?

Relationships. When you have struggles or conflicts with friends, family, colleagues, or your partner, who do you turn to for support and advice?

Identifying your support system together will help you see where you're best at supporting each other, and where you can turn to others without guilt or shame on either side.

Your relationship might have serious cracks that need fixing, but you want a better life together, and you're willing and ready to figure out how to improve it. Perhaps there's an area where you don't fully trust your partner and you want to see if you can build trust. Or maybe you've spent time building intimacy and feel ready to address some of the issues that have been building up over time. You believe progress would benefit your partnership. In this case, you can choose to grow instead of choosing to leave. To elevate instead of separate.

With clients, I've developed a four-step process to help you figure out if an issue is truly intolerable and you should break up, or whether—since you're hoping to elevate—you can find a way to see the issue differently and to eventually accept it. We start by identifying an *intolerable* issue. This is a difference between you and your partner that might be a deal-breaker. This is usually a recurring point of frustration that you think might lead to the end of your relationship. Then we take this issue down a path: from *intolerable* to *tolerable* to *understanding* to *acceptance*. Sometimes we even find our way to

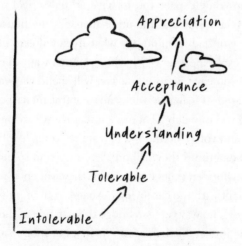

PATH TO ELEVATION

Appreciation

Acceptance

Understanding

Tolerable

Intolerable

appreciation, where we end up admiring our partner for something we once found intolerable.

The journey from intolerance to acceptance is about how patient you can be and how much—with the honesty and commitment of your partner—you can change your perspective. Despite our best efforts, some behaviors or circumstances may remain intolerable at the end of this process, which is how you know you need to separate. Even if your efforts don't pan out, you'll know you tried your best. And if you don't want to bother, then either you'll continue as you are, or you'll decide to separate.

Intolerable

I have a client, Sonia, whose husband, Rohan, insisted on leasing an expensive car instead of paying down their credit card debt. They had two children, and she was concerned not only about their financial situation but that he was modeling irresponsibility and materialism to their kids. This was, for her, an intolerable issue: a rupture that had been forming for some time, and she couldn't imagine continuing to live this way. Other examples might be having a partner whose job requires them to work long hours, and you want a partner who is more present. Perhaps they expect you to have an old-school relationship where one partner works and the other manages the household, and that isn't what you had in mind. Or what if they dream of spending every vacation exploring a new city while you just want to collapse on the beach, and you can't picture how you will spend your leisure time if you stay together. Or maybe they can't control their spending and they're running you into debt. These examples show varying degrees of disagreement, and you're bound to confront ruptures like this in your relationships. Sometimes they will break you up, and sometimes, in a relationship you are determined to protect, they will open your mind.

Like my client with the car-loving husband, your impulse might be to feel that there is no way you can bridge this gap unless the other person changes the intolerable behavior. The first question to ask yourself is: Do you love this person enough to deal with some discomfort as you work through the issue? If the answer is no, there is no way you can live with this issue no matter what, and it's never going to change, then you simply don't care for this person enough to work it out.

Tolerable

My client Sonia was not willing to give up on Rohan. He wasn't irresponsible and materialistic in other ways, and she was willing to make the journey to figure out just what was going on with the car. She wanted to understand why he was so stubborn about this particular issue. The first step on the journey from intolerable to acceptance is when, however begrudgingly, you acknowledge that there *might* be some way of dealing with the issue. You believe the two of you can figure it out somehow, even if you have no idea how. This admission alone shifts the issue from intolerable to tolerable. You're willing to invest time to understand what this person has been through and how this difference between you emerged from what they experienced. They are willing to explain themselves and seek understanding. This is how your capacity for empathy grows.

Understanding

When Sonia opened up the conversation with Rohan about the car, making it clear she was only trying to understand, she learned that when he was young, he took three buses to school, and it was an embarrassment to him. His friends' parents drove them to school in nice cars, and he had vowed that he would never let his kids feel the way he had felt.

Sonia still didn't agree with him, but now she felt compassion for his behavior. It wasn't reckless—it had deep emotional roots. Now she can bring her understanding to the discussions they have about the car. She can help him heal instead of making him feel torn between his need and her dissatisfaction. They haven't solved the issue yet—but they are further on the path.

According to marriage and family therapist Dr. John Gottman, 69 percent of marriage conflicts are about ongoing problems and never get resolved. We tire of the same confrontations, and we give up trying without ever coming to any kind of mutual understanding. Sometimes we give up because we're not invested enough in the relationship to fight for it anymore. Sometimes we stop fighting because we're exhausted by all our fruitless efforts to advocate for our own needs or point of view. And sometimes it seems more important to keep the peace than to solve the problem, so we pretend the issue doesn't exist.

We can get really good at this kind of pretense, but eventually it will come out of hiding, with sometimes catastrophic results. To prevent such catastrophes, we need to face our problems instead of avoiding them. We want the kind of relationship where we know the other person has our back. Where we feel understood. Where we feel like we can talk about anything. We feel like we have to agree for there to be connection, but we can disagree and still connect. In fact, we *need* to disagree in order to connect.

Instead of deciding that our partner's behavior makes no sense, or it means they don't care about us, we now start to study how their past experiences influenced their behavior. Investigate with sincerity, without the threats or criticism that will make your partner shut down. Imagine a couple where the wife always has a "meeting" to attend during events with her husband's family. He opens up a neutral conversation about it. Instead of saying, "You never come to my family dinners, you're the worst!" he asks, "Why don't you come to my family dinners?" He has to be aware that if he asks the question, he may have to accept painful feedback about his family. He resists being triggered. He listens without judging.

She may say, "I'm sorry. I'll try next time," but he knows from the past that this is a false promise. He tries to get to a real answer. She finally admits, "I feel uncomfortable with your family because they always compare me unfavorably to your relatives." He has to be very careful here not to let this turn into an argument about his family's behavior.

Now he says, "I get it—that's not pleasant. But it's important to me that you come. Would it be possible for you to join me sometimes, but not so often that it triggers you?"

She agrees to see his family once a month, and the next month they go to his parents' for dinner. On the way home, in the car, if he hasn't paid attention to her experience, he might say, "That wasn't so bad, was it? It was fun!" But she had a miserable time. She feels misunderstood and explodes. "No! It was the worst experience. I'm never doing it again." But if he's been thoughtful and observant, he says, "Hey, I know that was tough, and I'm grateful that you came with me. Thank you." Through his efforts to understand her, this couple has avoided three arguments: the first when he didn't complain about her behavior but instead asked about it, the second when he didn't take her issues with his family personally, and the third when he listened with care to hear how it went for her. With understanding, the intolerable issue hasn't gone away, but it is no longer intolerable for either partner.

Start conversations about the behavior or issue that troubles you. Ask your partner: "Is this something you enjoy?" "Why do you like it?" "What makes you do it this way?" Ask your partner why they are struggling to make the changes you've asked them to make. Ask questions and take time to hear the answers. These conversations give you the opportunity to understand more deeply instead of judging your partner and taking their behavior personally. Now you're working on it together.

To reach understanding, we not only have to see that there is a reason for the issue, but we have to appreciate that growth is hard. If we're committing to elevating, we have to acknowledge that our partner can't make changes overnight. We have patience as they make their efforts.

Acceptance

When we accept the difference between us, this could mean we come around to the idea that nothing needs to change, but it doesn't have to mean that. Acceptance can also mean that we appreciate the work our partner is doing to make a change, or that we're working on a compromise together, or that we realized we're the ones who have to change.

One client of mine had a partner who confessed that he was addicted to porn. It was something he wanted to overcome, but it had been going on for a long time, and he didn't know how to let it go or whether he could. My client was upset that her boyfriend had hidden his predilection. The first step for her was to recognize and appreciate what it took for her partner to be honest with her. We live in a world where we see keeping secrets as deceitful—a lie that we tell to make ourselves look better than we are. But in reality, we usually keep secrets out of fear and shame. We don't want to lose the other person. We don't want them to lose respect for us. My client and her partner talked openly about the issue, and she learned how he developed his addiction and about his sincere desire to change.

My client had a choice. If she cared enough about the relationship, she could be patient while her partner worked to overcome this challenge. Or she could walk away from the relationship. Could she accept the work her partner was trying to do?

She said, "I understand him. I love him. I want to help him."

"You have to accept the fact that he may never lose this addiction," I said. "But you'll get to know him much better as he tries, and that experience may change both of you." Her understanding of the issue gave her tolerance for the behavior, if it was in concert with ongoing efforts to change it. In accepting our partner, we learn to face hard truths with grace. She was supportive, encouraging, and patient. He went to therapy. He had a few relapses that he was honest about, and over time, this tale had a happy ending. He doesn't have that issue anymore.

As for Sonia and Rohan, Sonia was able to use her new understanding of Rohan to discuss the expense of the luxury car. She said, "You're doing this for the kids, but it's detrimental to them in the long run. Wouldn't we rather save for their college?" She tapped into his psychology. He wanted the kids to have something he didn't have, but they could make it something truly beneficial.

Rohan wasn't willing to give up the car right away, but he agreed to revisit the issue with her at the end of the lease and to make the decision together. Sonia felt that she could work the budget around the remaining year on the lease, and she was willing to be there for him as he let go of this need.

Appreciation

To address an intolerable issue with your partner is one of the greatest challenges love presents. But if you were to find someone "perfect," you would never grow these skills. You would take love for granted. You would miss out on the care, understanding, empathy, and deep appreciation for your partner that you develop in this process. In fact, we may start to see that this issue—the thing we couldn't tolerate—is actually an integral part of the person we love, and maybe part of what makes them lovable. This is the goal of the journey from intolerable to acceptance—we actually get to the heart of why our partner is the way they are.

Sonia was patient with Rohan, and although he couldn't make immediate changes, he was working on it. At the same time, she started to see that he wasn't the only one with stuff to work on. She had her own issues that she was putting on the kids—wanting them to succeed to prove her worth. She needed his patience and grace too.

My client Arden found appreciation in a different way. She was frustrated with her boyfriend because he seemed too attached to his mother. "Whatever she asks him to do, he does. If she wants us to go to their house for Sunday dinner, we go." But when we dug to the root of his behavior, she had to admit, "He's a pleaser. He wants everyone else to be happy all the time. The truth is that I like that he accommodates me in exactly the same way that he accommodates his mother." Love is recognizing that the challenge might be connected to a quality that draws us to our partner. All parts of them are connected, and seeing that connection leads us to appreciation.

The goal isn't to study and track your process through each of these levels with every difference that arises in your relationship. This isn't homework—rather, it's a clarifying question: Do you want to go on this journey with your partner? When differences arise, as they do time and time again in a long-term relationship, are you curious enough to explore and understand why the difference exists between you, how you each arrived at these islands so far apart from each other, and how to build a bridge between them? If you're motivated by commitment to and love for this person, your endurance for this journey will be stronger.

Perfecting Your Breakup

If we decide not to continue as is or to elevate our relationship, then we separate. If you entered a relationship without coming to appreciate solitude, then you might stay in that relationship for too long because you don't want to be single again. If you rely on it to bolster your sense of who you are and what you want, you'll never break up. You think, *I may not be happy or content, but at least I'm not alone.*

Sometimes we justify this inertia by convincing ourselves that our partner will change. You may hope that one day she'll become less ambitious, or he'll give you the attention you deserve, but if you've been waiting a long time, or if you've tried too many times, you need to recognize that they might never change.

Dictionaries define *broken* as having been fractured or damaged, and no longer in one piece or in working order. This might come close to how you feel when you go through a breakup. Research shows that areas activated in the brain when we're in love are the same as those involved in cocaine addiction. So the way your brain experiences a breakup is kind of like the misery of detox. Just as addicts crave a fix, we can literally crave the other person. This happens in part because our brains flood with chemical messengers that are part of our reward and motivation circuitry. Our brain sends urgent signals that we should hurry up and retrieve what's missing. In one study of breakups, participants reported thinking about their exes roughly 85 percent of the time they were awake.

This flood of hormones isn't the brain's only response to a breakup. Areas of the brain that are active in heartbreak are the same as the ones that process physical pain. But as researcher Helen Fisher says, the difference is that while pain from a stubbed toe or a toothache fades, emotions can intensify the sensation of a breakup. We don't get angry with our tooth or feel rejected by the couch we bumped into, but with our exes, we harbor hurt feelings and dashed dreams, which can exacerbate and extend the pain. In this state, our brains can desperately seek oxytocin—the bonding hormone—because it decreases feelings of fear and anxiety. And we're likely to seek that chemical experience from our ex. This can prompt us to do some pretty irrational things. Those folks who thought about their exes 85 percent of their waking hours also exhibited "lack of emotion control . . . occurring regularly for weeks or months. This included inappropriate phoning, writing or emailing, pleading for reconciliation, sobbing for hours, drinking too much, and/ or making dramatic entrances and exits into the rejecter's home, place of work, or social space to express anger, despair, or passionate love."

We must find our way out of this chemical morass, and we begin by remembering this spiritual truth: We may feel empty, lost, broken, and hurt, but the soul is unbreakable. The Bhagavad Gita spends seven verses talking about the indestructibility of the soul. "That which pervades the entire body you should know to be indestructible. No one is able to destroy that imperishable soul. The soul can never be cut to pieces by any weapon, nor burned by fire, nor moistened by water, nor withered by the wind. This individual soul is unbreakable and insoluble, and can be neither burned nor dried. It is everlasting, present everywhere, unchangeable, immovable and eternally the same."

Easy for the Bhagavad Gita to say. It's hard in a breakup to remember that we are still complete even though we've lost someone. This is where all that work you've done pays off. You've taken all the steps to build your ability to be in solitude. You know, intellectually at least, that you don't need a relationship to feel complete. You know your tastes and opinions, your values and goals. And now, in spite of all those hormones telling you otherwise, I want you to recognize that when your relationship crumbles, *you* are not what's breaking. Your soul doesn't end. Your expectations of your partner are breaking. What you thought you were building with them is breaking. What you had together is breaking. That's where the hurt comes from. But you have not lost your purpose. You have not lost yourself. Something *is* breaking, but you are not that something.

You existed before this relationship, and you will outlast it. When you think about your consciousness this way, you start to separate yourself from the pain that you feel in the moment. Acknowledge the pain, but understand where it resides and what has broken. What you created with your partner is being dismantled, but you are not being dismantled. Your life is not falling apart. You are not over. We may not feel this way, but if we believe it then we can take the steps needed to recover from the breakup, learn from it, and use it to bring that love back to all of our relationships. Let's talk about how to handle break-ups, whether you're the one instigating it or your partner is.

Breaking Up with Your Partner

First, set a deadline for the breakup. You've already reached a decision, so why draw it out? Avoiding pain today increases pain tomorrow. Putting it off doesn't benefit either one of you. Carve out a few hours to meet in person.

Be gentle with your partner's emotions. Keep your karma in mind when you end a relationship. Remember: The pain you put out into the world will come back in your direction. So instead of ghosting someone or cheating on them, be honest. Be clear about your reasoning.

It's always difficult to break up with someone. **There are no perfect words to tell someone the relationship is over.** If you're too nice, they may not understand why it isn't working out, and if you tell them why you think you're incompatible, they may not agree with you. You might be scared to be perceived as the villain, to disappoint them or seem mean. You have to accept that what you say probably won't go down well. But you can shape the conversation around the three key elements of a connection: You like their personality, respect their values, and want to help them toward their goals. Try to articulate where you're different. Let them know if you don't think you respect each other's values or think you're the right one to help them toward their goals. This is specific and helpful and gets you away from the overly vague territory of "You don't make me happy anymore" and the painfully specific territory of "I don't like this about you."

Do it face-to-face, look them in the eye, and be truthful. Keep in mind that no matter what you say or how thoughtful you are, your words can't control their response. They can say whatever they want about you to anyone, and they may not accept that you broke up with them for the right reasons and explained those reasons well. All you can do is articulate your decision with love, compassion, and empa-thy, but without sentimentality. Communicate with conviction so they don't try to talk you out of the decision.

This conversation should not last more than one day. Once you've had that conversation, make a clean break. Regardless of who initiated the breakup, take immediate steps to shift your life away from each other. If you have things that belong to each other, return them right away or write them off. Don't use this as an excuse to see your partner again or to try to reconnect with them. Unfollow. Do your best to avoid seeing them on social media or in the real world. Don't continue to exchange phone calls and messages or try to stay friends.

I know plenty of people who manage to be friends with their exes, but I think it's complicated. It can make subsequent partners feel in-secure or give your ex false hope of getting back together. If you really want to give it a try, I suggest you take a long break—a year, perhaps, in which you date other people—to make sure you've truly separated. The less contact you have with your ex, the faster the hole they've left will close up. Especially if you fill it by deepening your other relation-ships. Part of the hole is the friendship and bond you shared with your partner. There may also be a new gap in your community because some of the friends you shared with your ex are no longer available to you, for one reason or another. This is a great time to reinvest. Gather your friend group around you to remind you that your love reaches further than one person. If you have kids, of course you want to go to great lengths to keep things congenial. But don't confuse what's good for you with what's best for the kids. Don't use the kids as an excuse to see your ex. Be honest with yourself, and do what's right for them without sacrificing what's good for you.

Once it's over, it's over. If you broke up with your partner, resist the instinct to be the person who gives them comfort and helps them through this. You just decided you don't want to be in their life and told them so. Being their savior may assuage your guilt. Or you may want to leave them thinking you're amazing. You may even be tempted to keep a little bit of control over them. But let them go in any case. You can communicate your message as gracefully and honestly as you can, but you can't control the consequences of the breakup. Karma means you must accept the reaction you're getting as the natural consequence of your actions.

If Someone Breaks Up with You

If your partner breaks up with you, remember that the person who hurt you can't help you heal. There's no perfect way for them to break up with you, and the expectation that there is one keeps you enmeshed. We want the other person to say they're sorry, to fix us, to admit the mistakes they made and tell us how worthy we are. In some ways, it's odd that we would turn to someone who is the source of pain in our life to help with that pain, but up until very recently we shared intimacy with this person. They may have been our best friend. We told them what happened in our day; we looked to them before anyone else to make plans, solve problems, and process emotions. It's hard to accept that they aren't the person who's going to help us through this much bigger issue—losing someone you're close to—especially since that someone is *them*! How can they stop talking to you when you're counting on them to help you feel better? But it was never that person's job to make you happy. That was and is your job.

So you must set them free. It's fine to ask questions so that you understand their reasoning better, but don't pressure them to stay in the relationship. You don't want to stay with someone who has already checked out. Important as it is to reflect on what went wrong, resist the urge to "help" your ex see the error of their ways. You might feel like they're getting away with bad behavior or they're making a big mistake. Maybe you can see them having a blast all over social media. They've hurt you, and you'd prefer they didn't proceed to have what looks like a great time while you're alone and unhappy. You might want revenge. You might even feel like you *need* revenge to achieve closure. You want to serve up that person's karma. But if you act out of revenge, that will only bring you negative karma. The law of karma states that everyone will receive an equal and opposite reaction to their action. You don't want to be the pain in someone's life. Karma will do what it needs to do. In my coaching practice, a man left his wife of fifteen years to be with a younger woman. When the younger woman ditched him, he was shocked that she had been cheating on him; he had completely forgotten that their relationship started when he was cheating on his wife. Karma doesn't always deliver such obvious and satisfying payback, but actions always have consequences.

Leaving payback to karma allows you to move on and focus on what's important: repairing your ego, building your confidence, and bringing what you learned from this relationship to the next.

Don't wait for an apology. Closure is something you give yourself. Your ex can't give you closure because they don't have the answers. People aren't always aware of their mistakes. They often haven't clarified the situation for themselves. Even if they were to give you a reason, you'd still have questions that they couldn't answer because there is no good answer to the question, "Why didn't you love me the way I wanted you to?" It just doesn't make sense to ask someone else to heal your wound, even if it's their fault. If someone pushed you over and you scraped your knee, you wouldn't wait for them to go get you a bandage. You would take care of yourself. This emotional wound in need of closure is yours to deal with. You can bandage it most effectively yourself.

The human brain is a meaning-making machine, and one of the most powerful ways it makes meaning is through story. When we ruminate about a breakup, part of what we're doing is searching for the story behind it and what we can learn from it. We reject the simple reasons people give us for why they're breaking up with us. Psychologist Guy Winch says, "Heartbreak creates such dramatic emotional pain, our mind tells us the cause must be equally dramatic." We can become conspiracy theorists, creating complicated narratives, when the answer could be comparatively straightforward. A team of researchers asked adults who'd experienced a separation in the previous five months either to write freely about what they were feeling, or engage in directed, narrative storytelling about several aspects of their relationship, including their breakup. Those who constructed a meaningful story around their relationship later showed less psychological distress than those who just wrote down their feelings. We have to remember that these created stories are tools for healing rather than the ultimate truth, but once we have a narrative we can wrap our heads around, it's easier for us to move on. (And we can always revise that story later if other information becomes available.)

TRY THIS:

GIVE YOURSELF CLOSURE

Either in voice notes or in writing, describe the pain your partner caused you. Include everything you'd like to say to them about how they treated you and how it made you feel. The way they spoke to you, the way they treated you, questions, accusations, traumatic events, painful memories. Look at this list as an inventory of all the reasons it was good that you broke up. If you've been dwelling on the best memories, you're not acknowledging the reality of the relationship.

So, write every challenge, every mistake, everything that person said that hit you wrong. Is there anything that your mind is avoiding? Let yourself feel every emotion. You can't heal until you feel. Walking away from something doesn't reduce it. If you don't give an emotion the attention it deserves, it amplifies. In order to truly recognize these emotions, you must articulate them, look for patterns, and explain them to yourself.

Now, next to each action that brought you pain, write down who was responsible for it. Who took the action? Who said things that shouldn't have been said? Who did the things that shouldn't be done? Sometimes the responsibility will lie with you. Realizing that allows you to take ownership, improve, and grow.

You will also become aware of the mistakes your ex made. There may be negative elements that you suppressed while you were in the relationship. We do this because we subconsciously prefer the devil we know. You knew they were going to be rude to you in the morning. You knew they were going to forget your birthday. You knew they weren't going to turn up to dinner on time. You knew they weren't going to call you or message you even though you'd have liked it. You knew what they were going to get wrong, and it was easier to accept that than to be single, in new territory, not knowing how to feel, how to move on, or what pain might come next. We accept less than we deserve in favor of security. We cling to familiar pain.

By writing down everything that went wrong, you can more easily focus on reasons this breakup was good for you. Look for the story that gives you closure. Perhaps you dodged a bullet. Maybe you learned a lesson you never want to repeat. See how this relationship might be nothing more than a step on your path toward better bonds in the future.

Now read what you wrote out loud to an empty room. Your ex isn't there to hear it, but closure will come from the feeling that you shared it and the knowledge that you're writing your own ending to help yourself move forward.

Learn the Karmic Lessons

Often, we want to wall ourselves off from our own emotions after a breakup. The pain sends us into protective mode, where we try to distract ourselves and push memories of the relationship out of our minds.

But think about what it takes for a physical injury to recover. If we experience a torn muscle or a surgical wound, the pain initially makes
us pull back from activities—as it should—so we don't suffer further
injury. Then, as part of healing, the body puts down collagen fibers
at the site of the wound. These fibers are far denser than the original
tissue, creating a mass of scar tissue, which does a good job protecting
the wound. But if we leave the healing wound unattended, the density
of the scar tissue becomes problematic, impairing our movement, increasing pain and the risk of reinjury. And so we approach our recovery
thoughtfully, undergoing some kind of physical therapy to help us mo-
bilize and realign the scar tissue, and then we rebuild strength in our
broken places until we're fully healthy.

The same is true in heartbreak. We can't protect ourselves forever.
We need to work through the pain, understand the injury, build up our
strength, and reenter the world. As Tara Brach, a meditation instructor,
clinical psychologist, and bestselling author, says, "Everything we love
goes. So to be able to grieve that loss, to let go, to have that grief be
absolutely full, is the only way to have our heart be full and open. If
we're not open to losing, we're not open to loving."

Find stillness and space to recognize what has broken and what remains. Reflect deeply on what you can take away from the relationship,
because no matter how much you think you lost, no matter how hurtful
it was, no matter how much pain you suffered (unless it was abuse,
which has no justification), you want to take those lessons forward.

Every ex gives you a gift you may miss out on if you don't take this
step. It could be a piece of advice. It could be a connection they made
for you. Maybe they supported you through a tough time. Maybe you
learned that you really need to be with someone who makes healthy
choices. Maybe you discovered that picking someone who checked off
every box on your list wasn't a good way to see who was standing in
front of you. Honor your ex for the gifts they gave you.

When American Buddhist nun Pema Chödrön looked back on her
marriage, she found something surprising. She says, "I didn't realize
how attached I was to having someone else confirm me as being okay.
It didn't come from inside me, it came from someone else's view of

me." Once she understood that, she knew she no longer wanted to rely on others for her sense of self-esteem. It was a painful realization, but it helped her shift how she related to herself and those around her.

As Chödrön did, I want you to reflect on what you got wrong in the relationship. What were the mistakes you made, and what could you have improved? If you don't learn these lessons, you may find yourself repeating this unsuccessful dynamic for the rest of your life.

TRY THIS:

INSIGHTS

Let's examine the recent past of your relationship to gain some insights that will prepare you for future relationships.

> **Reflect on what you gained**
> **Reflect on what you lost**
> **Reflect on your own shortcomings**
> **Ask yourself: What did I learn about myself in this relationship?**

Wear something cozy, get a mug of tea, sit in front of a fire—do this in a setting and in a way that feels comfortable and supportive, because you might make some uncomfortable real-izations. And that's good. You may feel excited or energized by some things and upset by others, but discomfort often accom-panies healing.

Love can make us blind to others' faults and challenges, and our desire to feel good about ourselves can make us blind to our own missteps. When we love someone, we can overlook their annoying or even destructive habits and behaviors. This exercise helps us look at those things with fresh eyes.

Start by asking yourself: What did I do well in this relationship and what do I not want to repeat? Maybe you found yourself always putting your needs first and not truly listening to your partner. Or maybe you feel like you did a really good job of drawing healthy boundaries, yet your partner couldn't respect them. Again, write it all down.

Now reflect on what you gained from the relationship. Was it advice? Insight? Financial support? Was it help in your toughest times? At one point your partner brought value into your life. No matter how much you think you lost, no matter how hurtful it was, you should honor what they gave you.

Next, reflect on what you lost by being in this relationship. Maybe it's your self-confidence. You may have started to doubt yourself because your partner criticized you. You may have lost time. You may have lost energy. You may have missed out on other people or opportunities while you were devoting yourself to this relationship.

Finally, think about what you got wrong in the relationship. What were the mistakes you made? Did the relationship challenge your ability to stay true to yourself? Did it challenge your ideas about what makes a good partner? You must ask and answer these hard questions because, if you don't process the mistakes they reveal, you're going to repeat them with someone else.

Redefine Your Value

There's an old parable where a boy asked his father the value of his life. The father handed him a shiny red stone and said, "I want you to go ask the baker if he'll buy this from you. When he asks you how much you're selling it for, just hold up two fingers. When you get your answer, bring the stone back home with you."

So the boy went to the baker and showed him the stone. "How much?" asked the baker.

The boy held up two fingers, as instructed by his father.

"I'll buy it for two dollars," said the baker.

The boy went home and told his father the price. His father said, "Now I want you to go to the market and see what the antique dealer offers."

So the boy went to the market and showed the antique dealer the stone.

"That looks like a ruby!" she said. "How much for it?"

The boy held up two fingers.

"Two hundred dollars? It's a lot, but I'll take it," she said.

Next, the boy's father sent him to the jeweler. He held the stone up to the sun and saw how the light refracted through it. He put it under a microscope, and his eyes grew wide. "This is a rare and beautiful ruby," he said. "How much for it?"

The boy held up two fingers.

"Two hundred thousand dollars is a fair price, indeed," said the jeweler. The boy, excited, hurried back to his father to tell him this news. The father smiled and put the ruby in his pocket. "Now, do you know how much your life is worth?" he asked.

This story beautifully illustrates that we have different worth to different people. We are defined by what we accept. Part of what makes a breakup so hard is that this person who once valued us so highly no longer does. We've been devalued, but only by them. This is why we have to set our own worth and find someone who values us for who we are.

Separate the Mind and the Intellect

If we still fear loneliness, the mind plays tricks to keep us entangled. We return to the belief that being alone is not satisfying. Being wanted makes us feel valued, and we attach that value to being with another person rather than recognizing it as the value we carry with us always.

But these are the simple thoughts of the mind, and we need to elevate them. The Bhagavad Gita draws a distinction among the senses, the mind, and the intelligence: "The working senses are superior to dull matter; mind is higher than the senses; intelligence is still higher than the mind." The senses tell you if something hurts physically. The mind thinks in terms of what it likes or doesn't like. And the intelligence asks, "Why don't I want this? What am I learning from it?" So when we break up, the mind tells us that we liked what we had, and we want it back. We miss our ex; we want to know what they're doing on Instagram. We wonder if they're thinking of us. At times like this we might also have self-deprecating thoughts like, *I'm not attractive enough. I'm not strong enough. I wasn't caring enough. I'm not powerful enough.*

You can't stop thinking but you can redirect your thoughts if you don't like them. All of the *I'm not enough* can be put to the side. We train ourselves to redirect our thoughts by asking ourselves questions when we're making a decision.

Mind: I want to go stand outside my ex's apartment and see if his light is on.
Intellect: What's the point of this idea?

Mind: I need to know if he's with someone else.
Intellect: Is this information useful to me?

Mind: Yes, because if he's with someone else I can move on.
Intellect: Do you want your own ability to change to depend on this information?

Mind: No . . . but I still want to see him!
Intellect: What else could you do that would help you move on?

Mind: I could call a friend.

If you have an intrusive thought, ask yourself, do I like this thought? Is this thought useful? Is this thought insightful? Is this thought helping me move forward? This is how we move from the mind's conversation to the intellect's conversation.

> *The mind says reach out to your ex. The intelligence says reach out to your friends.*
>
> *The mind says focus on your ex. The intelligence says focus on yourself.*
>
> *The mind asks, "What will people think?" The intelligence asks, "What do I think?"*

Wait to Date

Christin had been seeing Bradley for a few months when he suggested they go on a running date. She wasn't a runner, but she agreed. Out on the trail, she jogged, walked, and even skipped, gamely making her way forward while he chugged steadily on. Then, at one point, he looked back at her, shot her an annoyed look, and took off down the trail, leaving her behind to find her way back to the car. That was just the latest in a string of red-flag relationships in which men had treated Christin terribly. Finally, much as she wanted to find her future husband and start a family, she decided to take a year off of dating to reset her judgment in men, and to spend time in solitude.

Pretty quickly, when dating was off-limits, men who wanted to date Christin were popping up *everywhere*. Instead of trying to impress them, because each might be her future husband, she was just herself. After all, she couldn't date anyway, so what did she have to lose? Partway through the year, Christin met Nathan, a guy who seemed really nice, but when he asked her out, she explained that she wasn't dating until the following June. Nathan disappeared, and as the months rolled by, she discovered that she was starting to feel more confident, eventually realizing that whatever happened in her love life come June, she would be okay. Then, on June 1, the phone rang. It was Nathan, asking her out again. As it turned out, he *was* her future husband, and they now have two children.

If we spend all our time post-breakup analyzing the breakup, we'll never move on. But we shouldn't move on by hastily jumping into another romantic relationship. This is a great time to start attracting people you actively want to have in your life. Friends who share your interests. Communities where you feel comfortable. Start surrounding yourself with people who fulfill your different needs—someone you like to have deep talks with, someone you like to go dancing with, someone you like to work out with.

Use this time to start new friendships and build existing ones so that you feel whole without a partner. Rediscover solitude. Refocus on your purpose. This is your time to really invest in yourself. This is your time to really get to know yourself. We can lose ourselves in a relationship, so now we have to find ourselves in the heartbreak.

TRY THIS:

CHECKLIST TO SEE IF YOU'RE READY TO DATE AGAIN

☐ Have I learned the lessons my last relationship had to offer that will set me up for a better relationship next time?

    ☐ What do I want to be aware of?
    ☐ What do I want to avoid?
    ☐ What do I want to make sure my next partner understands about me at the outset?

☐ Do I know what I value and what my goals are at this stage of my life? If not, I can take time in solitude to revisit these areas.

$\longrightarrow$

←

- [ ] Do I know what boundaries I want to set for my next partner? I may want to start dating but decide that I don't want to move too fast.
- [ ] Do I want to set physical limits?
- [ ] Do I want to wait to be exclusive?
- [ ] Do I want to be careful not to cancel any commitments for someone like I did last time?

Finally, if you're not sure whether you're ready to date again, just try it. You don't have to be officially dating or not dating. Just see how it feels.

Love's Infinite Expansion

As monks, we learn about *maya*, which means illusion. Part of the *maya* of love is that we can access it only in limited ways, such as only through certain people. We imagine that there's a door guarding love, that to experience deep love and happiness we have to find the one key that opens that door. And that key is another person.

Then you find yourself without a partner. Or you raised your kids and now they're gone. Or you and your partner still feel restless, like there's more purpose to your lives. Imperfect love teaches us. Imperfect love tells us to move on. Imperfect love forces us to break from our expectations, let go of the fantasy, and realize that it's never been just about loving one person or our immediate family.

This epiphany, however disappointing it may be, sets us up for a whole new level of love. UCLA professor Steven Cole says that the best cure for loneliness or disconnection is to combine a sense of mission and purpose in your life with community engagement. Spending time in service marries connection with deep fulfillment, and the result is a boost in health. Prosocial behavior, including volunteering, has also been shown to boost our immune system, combat the physical stress caused by loneliness, and extend our longevity. Sadly, says Cole, these days too many of us have actually dialed back our engagement with others to pursue individual health-enhancing goals, like training for a triathlon, taking yoga classes, or trying to find our "one true love." Those things are all great, but the biggest benefit for all comes when, as Cole describes it, your health is a "means to an end, which is, essentially, to make some meaningful stuff happen, not just for you but for others."

What we thought was the highest love—romantic love—can be expanded. Love creates more love. It is time for you to take a deep breath, to start developing trust in love again, and to prepare to deepen your capacity for love.

No matter where you started or who you loved or how much money you made, you may get to a point of material dissatisfaction. You feel like there must be more. You don't feel fully satisfied. Some people might think of it as a midlife crisis. But this represents a deepening connection to spiritual work. With compassion, empathy, and selflessness you are ready to extend yourself beyond your family and to find your purpose in the greater world.

You're never going to perfect love in this life, and that means you get to practice love every day of your life.

Write a Love Letter to Help You Heal

When a friend is going through a hard time, we comfort and support them, but we are often less patient and sympathetic with ourselves. If we're struggling, we tell ourselves to just get over it. But we would never say that to a friend. Try writing a healing note to yourself as if you were talking to a friend or someone you love.

Dear Brokenhearted One,

I see you. I am here for you. We often think that when we have loved and lost, that we are outcast and alone, but nothing could be further from the truth. In reality, when we experience this hurt and this anguish, we become part of a vast community. The tribe of the heartbroken. There are many of us. And we are strong. And we are tender. Above all, we are healing together.

This healing looks different than you think. Because once your heart is broken, some part of it will always remain so. But this is not a sad thing. It is beautiful, because this brokenness is an aspect of love. Perhaps you feel lonely, but it is an illusion. The pain you feel right now actually connects you more deeply to all of humanity. You may in some way have lost one person, but you have gained the world.

Heartbreak doesn't truly break us, it breaks us open. As Alice Walker once said, "Hearts are there to be broken, and I say that because that seems to be just part of what happens with hearts. I mean, mine has been broken so many times that I have lost count. . . . In fact, I was saying to my therapist not long ago, "You know, my heart by now feels open like a suitcase. It feels like it has just sort of dropped open, you know, like how a big suitcase just falls open. It feels like that.'" The purpose of heartbreak and loss aren't to cut us off from the world, but to open us to it. To keep us from loving small.

The reality is that you are never separated from love. If you want to feel it, simply share it. Love moves through us whether we are receiving it, or giving it. And there are as many opportunities to experience love as there are drops of water in the ocean. We never know what life will bring us, but we can rest in this knowledge—that each and every one of us is, in every moment, surrounded by love.

Love,
Me

Meditation to Heal Through Love

To paraphrase Shakespeare, the course of love does not always run smoothly. Inevitably, life brings hurts and wounds. No matter what we're struggling with, it's important to keep our connection to love—to remember that we are now, as always, worthy to receive love, and we are able to offer love to others.

1. Find a comfortable position, whether that's sitting in a chair, sitting upright on a cushion or on the floor, or lying down.
2. Close your eyes, if that feels good to you. If not, simply soften your focus.
3. Whether your eyes are open or closed, gently lower your gaze.
4. Take a deep breath in. And breathe out.
5. If you find that your mind is wandering, that's okay. Gently bring it back to a space of calm, balance, and stillness.

Meditation to Heal Through Love

1. Bring your full focus to yourself. Notice your breath as it moves in and out of your body.
2. Place a hand gently over your heart and gently breathe into it, feeling the energy of your heart as it beats inside your body.
3. Say to yourself, silently or out loud, "I am worthy of love."
4. Feel your heart beat as you breathe in and out, and say again, "I am worthy of love."
5. Repeat this one more time.
6. Return your attention to your breath.

7. Say to yourself, "I am lovable." As you continue to breathe steadily, repeat this two more times.
8. Return your attention to your breath.
9. Say to yourself, "I am made of love." Keep breathing into your hand, feeling the breath enliven your heart, as you repeat this two more times.

PART 4

Connection: Learning to Love Everyone

||||||||||||||||||||||||||||||||||||||||||||||||

The fourth ashram, Sannyasa, is when we extend our love to each and every person and area of our life. In this stage our love becomes boundless. We realize we can experience love at any time with anyone. We feel karuna, *compassion for all living entities. All of these stages can all be lived simultaneously, but this fourth stage is the highest expression of love.*

Love Again and Again

The river that flows in you also flows in me.

—KABIR DAS

At the ashram, I heard a story in which a teacher asks a student, "If you had one hundred dollars to give, would it be better to give it all to one person or to give one dollar each to one hundred different people?"

The student looks unsure. "If I give it all to one person, it might be enough to change their life. But if I give it to one hundred hungry people, they might be all able to eat something."

"Both of these are true," the teacher says, "but the more people you help, the more you expand your capacity for love." We begin our love lives with the idea that we should give the (metaphorical) one hundred dollars to one person—our partner—or to a few—our family. But in the fourth stage of life we change our approach. We start handing out single dollar bills to many people. The more we can give, the better, but we start small and over time grow our capacity to give love. The way you perfect love is not by waiting to find or have it, but by creating it with everyone, all the time. This is what I've been waiting to tell you— it's the greatest gift that love has to offer.

You probably came to this book wondering how to find or keep love with a partner. We want love in our lives, and we naturally assume it should take the form of romantic love. But it's a misconception that the only love in your life is between you and your partner, your family, and your friends. It's a misconception that life is meant to be a love story between you and one other person. That love is just a stepping-stone. Having a partner isn't the end goal. It's practice for something bigger, something life-changing, a form of love that is even more expansive and rewarding than romantic love. Our partnerships give us a chance to practice for it, but we don't have to fulfill our romantic desires to get there. It's available to all of us, every day, and it is infinite.

In the fourth stage of life, *Sannyasa*, the goal is simply this: to look beyond the self to how we can serve others. To experience love constantly by choosing to give it to others always. To find love in moments of frustration, annoyance, anger, and dismay, when it seems out of reach. To create more loving connections with every person we meet. To feel love for all humanity. Love means noticing that everyone is worthy of love and treating them with the respect and dignity their humanity automatically makes them deserve.

Norwegian philosopher Arne Naess borrowed from Vedic ideas when he described a process of self-realization "where the self to be realized extends further and further beyond the separate ego and includes more and more of the phenomenal world." In other words, when we "widen and deepen" our sense of self, we see our interconnectedness, so serving others serves the self—there is no difference. For those who reach the fourth stage of life, the body, mind, and soul are dedicated to serving the divine and uplifting humanity. *Sannyasis* experience the depths and nuances of love that we can't always find in any one person. We come to appreciate love in different forms. We no longer serve out of a sense of moral duty, but out of an understanding of our oneness with all that is. **We are connected, and when we serve others, we are serving ourselves.**

Science supports this concept. Psychologists refer to the things we do to help others as *prosocial behavior*. Marianna Pogosyan, who specializes in cross-cultural psychology, writes that prosocial behavior helps us feel more connected to others, and this desire for connection is one of our deepest psychological needs.

The *sannyasi* serves as many people as possible. Why limit love to one person or one family? Why experience love only with a few people?

When we expand our radius of love, we have the opportunity to experience love every day, at every moment.

When you think this way, love stretches its arms wider and wider. If a parent loves their children, they love the other children who surround them at school because they care about the community their own children experience. And if you care about the community, then you care about the school itself. And if you care about the school, then you care about the ground where it sits. This is why, if you love your kids, you should want to better their world and the world at large. Loving those around us teaches us to love each living entity, and loving everyone teaches us to love the world around us—the place they call home. And if we love the environment, then we love its creator, the divine, a power beyond ourselves. When Kabir Das, the fifteenth-century Indian poet and saint, wrote, "The river that flows in you also flows in me," he was suggesting that we're connected to all humanity through our actions, words, behaviors, and breath. We impact one another in all we do. We saw this during the pandemic, when it was important to take care of one another, to protect one another, to look beyond our loved ones to consider the whole community.

Anne Frank said, "No one has ever become poor by giving." By gradually broadening our concept of love, we begin to see new ways to access it. Love is available whenever you want to feel it by giving it to others.

Giving love solves a human need that is even greater than romantic love: I need to be of service. There is no greater ecstasy than that. I like the Chinese proverb that advises, "If you want happiness for an hour, take a nap. If you want happiness for a day, go fishing. If you want happiness for a year, inherit a fortune. If you want happiness for a lifetime, help someone else." The joy we feel from serving others has been labeled the "helper's high" or "giver's glow," defined by scientists as a feeling, following selfless service to others, of elation, exhilaration, and increased energy, then a period of calm and serenity. Researcher Allan Luks, author of *The Healing Power of Doing Good*, looked at data from more than three thousand people who had volunteered and

EXPECTING LOVE VS. EXPRESSING LOVE

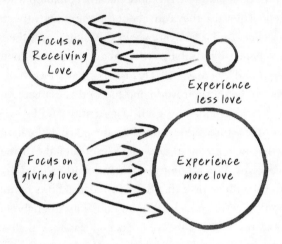

noted that helper's high not only endured for several weeks of service, it came back when people simply recalled their service. And helper's high doesn't just feel good in our brains; it's accompanied by lower levels of stress hormones and improved immune system function.

Instead of expecting love, we have to find ways of expressing love. We've been taught to believe that the only way you can experience love is when you receive it, but the Vedas say you can feel love anytime you want simply by connecting with the love that is always within you. In the Vedic point of view, we don't need to find love, build love, or create love. We are wired to love and be loving. The Vedas say the soul is *sat, chit, ananda*: eternal, full of knowledge, full of bliss. This is our loving core. As we experience the world, this core is covered by layers of ego, envy, pride, jealousy, lust, and illusion that get in the way of our ability to love. We have to work to remove these layers and return to our most loving selves. This is how the Vedas would see even the most evil and dangerous members of society. The love at their core is utterly obscured by layers of impurity. We all have impurities, but in most of us they are small and relatively harmless, whereas a leader whose loving core is fully covered can use their scale and influence for the destruction of life. A *sannyasi* is able to look at each person's behavior and actions and see them as opportunities to respond with love, no matter how inaccessible that core of love is. They do this, of course, without risking life and limb, without lending support to the corrupt leader's cause.

How to Give Love

In the fourth stage of life, we come to a point where we're not just looking for love in one person anymore. This may be because we find ourselves without a partner. Or we may be happy with our partner and feeling like we now have enough love to expand it. **You've been a student of love, and now you're a steward of love.** The Bhagavad Gita talks about the principles of *śreyas* and *preyas*, which roughly translates to what we seek, and what we ought to seek. If we have the capacity and opportunity to look beyond our own needs, then we should do so. You have been striving to fulfill your own purpose. Perhaps you have been striving to fulfill the goals of a partner and children. Now you can set the goal of service. If you have a partner, you deepen your love for each other by doing this together. Embarking on these efforts prematurely leads to arguments and misunderstandings. By the time you start thinking about ways to serve others together—your community, the world— you need to deeply understand each other's strengths and weaknesses. Once we understand that in ourselves and others, collaboration comes more easily, and we can extend that compassion to everyone.

Being a *sannyasi* is hard work. Without practice, we are not necessarily ready for this infinite expansion of love. It can easily slip into the desire to feed one's ego by people pleasing. And the further we get in time and space from those we know and love, the harder it is to feel love. Jamil Zaki, a Stanford professor of psychology and director of the Stanford Social Neuroscience Laboratory, writes, "Empathy is also ancient, tuned to a time when we lived in small groups of hunter-gatherers. Much as we did back then, we still find it easier to care for people who look or think like us, who are familiar, and who are right in front of us." Zaki is describing why we as a global community struggle to address climate change. He says, "People feel strong empathy after hearing about one victim of a disaster—whose face we can see and whose cries we can hear—but hearing about hundreds or thousands of victims leaves us unmoved. Such 'compassion collapse' stymies climate action."

Yet, as Rumi says, "I, you, he, she, we—/ in the garden of mystic lovers, / these are not true distinctions." Although it's not hard to imagine a peaceful world full of love, it may not be obvious how we can make it so this afternoon, and tomorrow, and every day. Rumi suggests that we are not as separate from others as we think we are. Distinctions exist, but, with practice, we can broaden our spectrum of love from the personal to the professional to the community to the planet. The Bhagavad Gita puts it simply: "The humble sage, by virtue of true knowledge, sees with equal vision a learned and gentle brahmana, a cow, an elephant, a dog."

Love Those Closest to You

We first expand our circle of love to those who are easiest to love. We can show love to our friends and family not just through what we say or do. Behind those acts are four key qualities.

1. *Understanding.* All of us want to be understood. To love your nearest and dearest is to try to understand who they are and what they are trying to achieve. We do this by listening and asking questions rather than pushing our ideas and agendas.
2. *Belief.* Our friends and family want us to believe in them. This means believing that they have the potential to achieve their dreams. When someone you love shares an idea, give positive feedback. Be supportive and encouraging.
3. *Acceptance.* Our friends and family want to be accepted and loved just the way they are, for who they are, with all their flaws and differences. We don't project our expectations of what they should do or how they should act onto them.

4. *Appreciation*. We give love through appreciating the little
   and big things our friends and family do, the struggles
   they face, the efforts and changes they make, the energy
   they bring to the relationship. We think that merely being
   present is showing enough appreciation, but I can't think
   of anyone who doesn't want to be told with specificity and
   sincerity what they have done well.

A Radius of Respect

Sometimes there are challenges in loving those who are closest to us.
The person doesn't respond in a positive way. They're difficult to deal
with, but we still care for them and want to continue to love them.
When someone is toxic, we can love them from a radius of respect.

The psychologist Russell Barkley said, "The children who need the
most love will always ask for it in the most unloving ways." It's hard to
accept that someone does something hurtful because they're seeking
love. We don't accept abuse, but we understand that a person causes
pain because they're in pain. They're trying to offload their pain onto
you. Like a child who might scream, cry, shout, or throw a tantrum in
order to get attention, the behaviors we see in others are misdirected
pleas for love. It's not uncommon to have a friend or family member whom you consider to be difficult or toxic. Spending time with
them, you face a negative environment where your ideas are shunned,
your voice isn't heard, or where you feel rejected or neglected. If you
find yourself in a situation like this, it can be easy to turn from loving
thoughts to negative, hurtful, hateful thoughts. Don't feel guilty or bad
for this. It's natural to feel upset if someone is treating you unfairly.
Our difficult loved ones are in our lives to teach us tolerance. Meet
people with love even when they don't meet you with love. A *sannyasi*
offers love to everyone the same way a doctor tries to heal people on
both sides of a fight, no matter who started it. Don't compromise your
values, and don't accept abuse, but stretch your capacity to give love.

When we encounter someone whom we find difficult to be around,
the first step toward loving them is to understand what, if anything, our

reaction to them reveals about ourselves. Is it our own insecurity? Is it our ego? Is it fear? If you're waiting and wishing for your friends or family to agree with you, cheer you on, and encourage every idea you have and every decision you make, that's a lot to ask. For better and worse, they can't help but project their limited viewpoint, with all their own doubts and fears, onto you. When their response to you upsets or worries you, consider whether part of your reaction comes from your own lack of confidence about the decision you're making. Instead of spending energy trying to gain their confidence, focus on building your own in solitude. When you accept who you are and what you want, you're less likely to be triggered by someone else's opinion of you or perception of your ideas.

When we broaden our scope of love, we're not excluding people for what they do or how they act (unless they are abusive). We love them because we want to be loving people. If you like a clean house, you keep it clean whether you have guests or not—it makes it a more pleasant place for you to live. The same is true when you create a loving environment in your heart. You do it for yourself, no matter who receives or returns it. You don't mess your house up if someone messy comes in. You don't fill your heart with hate because someone hateful enters your radius. You want to live in a house of love.

That said, we can't love everyone from the same vantage point. We may try to love certain people up close, but find that every time we leave them, we complain about their negativity, bitterness, and energy. It's better to stand at the distance where we can still respect and support them than to be too close and have our resentment grow. If you have a difficult family member that you want to keep in your life, this might mean you love them best when you see them once a year. It might mean keeping all contact to phone calls rather than in-person visits. Deal with them for whatever amount of time you can handle. The distance protects you from feeling used and allows you to be a well-wisher from afar until you're ready to love them up close. It gives you the space and opportunity to develop strength and confidence in solitude. And, potentially, in the long run, you'll be able to return with compassion to help them on their journey.

One way of giving love to a difficult person is to find other sources of love for them. Sometimes we think we are their sole source of love—and maybe that's the situation that has evolved—but this dependence isn't beneficial for either person. We may not have time, inclination, ability, or even patience to take on a difficult person as a full-time project. That's okay. We don't have to be saviors. Loving such a person can, and perhaps should, mean pivoting away from the one-on-one love that we've been focusing on till now. We might not be the best or only person to love them. After all, we want them to be surrounded by love, and we want them, too, to have the opportunity to spread more love.

TRY THIS:

HELP A DIFFICULT FAMILY MEMBER FIND LOVE IN THEIR COMMUNITY

If it's hard to love a friend or family member up close, you can include them in your circle of love by helping them find other sources of love. Find them new friends. Introduce them to like-minded people. Ask your friends if they have contacts who live in the same area and might get along with the person.

Find them services. Connect them with a spiritual community, local gym, or arrange for a service that helps with a chore they can't or don't like to do.

Help them pursue their interests. We can help a lonely parent start a book club or plan a poker tournament.

Arrange for a family event on neutral ground. Being in public tends to ease tensions and improve everyone's behavior. If visiting at home is too intense, try meeting at a restaurant or at a public place where you both feel comfortable.

←

> Write them a letter of appreciation. Share any fond memo-
> ries you have with them, let them know what you admire about
> them, and let them know any positive ways in which they've
> made a difference in your life.

If you make efforts like the ones in this TRY THIS, but still can't find ways to love them, don't force yourself to do it. Sometimes the best thing you can do for a once-important friend or family member is to step away from them. Sometimes that's all you can do. This can be difficult. We feel uncertain about giving up on someone who is or has been important to us. Part of what makes this hard is that we know, instinctively, that the Vedas are right. There is goodness in this person's soul, obscured as it is by the layers of bad experiences, negative emotions, even trauma. It is easier to create the distance we need if we let go with love. Just as you wouldn't judge someone for the clothes they wear, don't judge them for the external. **Try to love someone for the spark in them, not what surrounds them.**

A Conscious Commitment of Time

Giving love to our friends and family requires time, but we're all so busy and distracted that we can have trouble finding the time. The solution to this problem is organization. British anthropologist Robin Dunbar hypothesized that brains can only handle a certain sized social group, and after looking at historical, anthropological, and current data, he and his colleagues determined that number to be about 150. An article on BBC.com adds, "According to the theory, the tightest circle has just five people—loved ones. That's followed by successive layers of 15 (good friends), 50 (friends), 150 (meaningful contacts), 500 (acquaintances) and 1500 (people you can recognize). People migrate in and out of these layers, but the idea is that space has to be carved out for any new entrants."

Though these numbers are just averages, if you categorize your personal contacts this way, you can be much more deliberate about how to divide your time among them. Instead of passively giving your presence to anyone who reaches out to you, you can consciously decide whom you want to see and how often.

TRY THIS:

STRUCTURE YOUR LIST OF LOVED ONES

Make a list of your larger circle of friends and family. (Using your social media lists of friends or followers is one way to start. Facebook and Instagram allow you to categorize your friends to what level of online information they receive.) Now do the same thing in real life. Organize this list into close friends and family, good friends and family, meaningful contacts, and acquaintances. Decide how much time you can give to each category. Maybe you'll decide that you want to check in or make plans with close friends and family once a week and good friends once a month. Perhaps you want to make an effort to touch base with meaningful contacts every quarter and acquaintances once a year. This breakdown enables you to be conscious about how you want to divide your time and helps you communicate this to your circle—you can say, "I'd love to make sure we have lunch once a month." Though it would be odd to tell your meaningful contacts that you've assigned them a quarterly frequency, having it in your head that you see them every season, perhaps around holidays, will keep you in touch and aware of what's going on in their life.

If you have trouble making friends, or you've recently moved and are starting fresh, this list can remind you of the people you cherish. Are there distant family members or acquaintances you want to build into closer relationships? Having a working list of those who interest you and who you care about will help you build a network.

Appreciate Your Colleagues

It's not uncommon to spend more time with our colleagues than with our family. Our workplace is as much a community as any other we inhabit. The person in the mailroom, the IT savior, the guard downstairs, the marketing guru, and the colleagues we're actually close to— these are the main people we see every day, working at our sides or in a little box on our Zoom screen, but it's not intuitive to show love for them, nor is it clear how to do it. We feel inhibited from loving our colleagues because of the formality of a professional environment. Love in the work world looks different. It's not deep. It's often not emotional. You may not share a level of trust that allows you to be very personal or vulnerable. In fact, connecting on a personal level may not be appropriate or suitable to your work culture. We overcome this by finding ways to inject appreciation and warmth into an office environment.

We love our juniors, peers, and seniors in different ways. We love our **juniors** through guidance and mentorship, not control and ownership. Serving cake for every birthday isn't the only way to show love in the office. We connect them to knowledge and wisdom that gives them access to personal growth. When we can, we provide mentorship or access to ideas and insights that aren't available in their day-to-day work life. Can you bring in a guest lecturer or share a TED Talk on meditation or organize a charity run that colleagues can do together?

We look for new and creative ways to show our appreciation for juniors' dedication to their work. Blueboard is a company that takes the idea of appreciating employees to heart. One of the founders, Kevin Yip, says he got the idea for the company when his boss thanked him for working on a project seven days a week, for twelve- to fifteen-hour days, by putting an American Express gift card on his desk. Blueboard enables employers to show their appreciation for employees through all kinds of experiences, like going to a zero-gravity float tank, learning about cheese from a cheese monger, seeing the Northern Lights, or using heavy machinery to have an "extreme sandbox adventure."

When we recognize what someone did, we appreciate who they are. According to Work.com, nearly half of employees said they would switch jobs just to feel more appreciated.

We love our **peers** through support, encouragement, collaboration, cooperation, and appreciation. The loving qualities we bring to work echo those we bring to our friends and family, but they shift slightly to reflect the need to be professional and productive.

TRY THIS:

BRING LOVE TO WORK

1. *Understanding.* You don't need to understand who they are and what they want to the extent you do with your closest friends and family, but take interest in their personal lives and follow up on the highs and lows, especially taking care when they have good reason to be distracted from work and

$\longrightarrow$

need extra support from you. Check in with colleagues if their mood shifts. Follow up on challenges you know they're facing. If they're going through a rough period, see if there's a way you can support them by taking on more work or otherwise finding ways to lighten their load.

Notice the effort they put into their work, when they do a good job, and how they improve, and celebrate their success.

2. *Connection.* Whether online or in person, start your day or a meeting by checking in with your colleague. Try to get a read on how their day is going. Follow up on personal issues that they've shared with you. Humanize the experience instead of diving right into an agenda.

3. *Appreciation.* Every day choose one person from your professional life to send a brief message, by voice mail, text, or email, commending them or thanking them specifically for something they did at work.

Make these efforts because you want to bring more love into the world without expecting or demanding reciprocation from your coworkers.

We love our **seniors** by following through on what we've signed up to do, being respectful, and holding on to our boundaries. We actively accept guidance instead of resenting it.

The Crocodile and the Monkey

There's a Zen story about a monkey who sees a banana that he wants across a river. The crocodile, observing the monkey's desire, offers to carry him across the river. The monkey readily jumps on his back and the crocodile begins to swim across. In the middle of the river, however, he stops and says, "Stupid monkey, now you're stuck on my back in the middle of the river, and I'm about to eat you."

The monkey smartens up quickly and says, "Well, crocodile, I'd love for you to eat me, but I left my heart on the other riverbank, and that's the tastiest part of me. It's juicy and rich, a real delicacy. I wouldn't want you to have a less satisfying meal."

The crocodile says, "Oh, that does sound tasty. All right then, I'll swim to the other bank so you can bring me your heart."

They arrive at the far bank, and the monkey runs off, saving his own life.

The point of this story is that when you're dealing with crocodiles, you should leave your heart at home. You can't always be vulnerable. Sometimes it will be used against you.

If you love unconditionally in a professional context, it may take people off guard. They're used to being motivated by fear or results but not love. It's an alien experience, and people may not respond well to it. We think of love as reciprocal, but *sannyasis* love without reciprocation. We must hold on to our loving hearts, the essence of who we are, even in a workplace full of crocodiles. We try to be compassionate to those who have hurt us. We give the best energy we can under the circumstances and get on with our lives. At the same time, we make sure that we ourselves are not the crocodile because what we become at work bleeds into who we are at home. If you can't be the *sannyasi* you want to be at work, make sure that you strive to give love in your personal life.

Be Proactive in Your Community

When we look to expand our love beyond our workplace, we reach out to the communities we're part of: neighborhood groups, school committees, religious institutions, book clubs, and other interest groups. We show love in our communities by noticing a need and working to fulfill it. This might be starting a neighborhood watch, or helping solve an infrastructure issue, or organizing ways for neighbors to meet and socialize. If this is done for power, authority, or control, it will leave us feeling empty. But if we make these efforts from a position of love, compassion, and empathy, they will fulfill us.

As you scale your love, you will encounter dissent. The more people you serve, the more will disagree with you. If you're on a neighborhood watch group, there might be one or two people who don't like your ideas. If you're on the city council, as you do an increasing amount of work in the community, more people will dislike or disagree with you. If you're the president of the United States, nearly half the country will be against you. If you find yourself dealing with more conflicting opinions, recognize that they're proportionate to the journey you're on.

Inspire Strangers

We encounter strangers on the street with a certain level of caution, and rightly so. We have no idea if they are receptive to love or how to show love without making them uncomfortable. Yet we see people who are not related to us every day, whenever we leave our houses. Many of us spend the majority of our time by far in the presence of people who don't even know our names: The bus driver. A cashier. A waiter. The person behind us in line.

The easiest (and safest) way for us to give love to the people who cross our path is to smile. Thanks to our survival circuitry, our brains are constantly scanning for cues as to whether we're welcome in our surroundings. Scientists say that when we smile at someone, it signals social connection, putting them more at ease.

Purdue University researchers wanted to investigate the extent to which a split-second interaction with a stranger can impact us. A research assistant walked a busy path on campus and, as they passed strangers, either made eye contact with them, made eye contact and smiled, or looked right through them, as if they didn't exist. Then, just a few steps later, the unknowing study subjects were stopped by another researcher, this one asking if they'd mind taking a brief survey. Those who were ignored reported feeling more social disconnection than those who had received some form of positive acknowledgment. The researchers concluded that being obviously ignored, even by strangers, can have a negative impact on us.

The reason might be purely chemical—that when we're ignored, we're missing the positive impact of smiles. Smiling releases dopamine, serotonin, and endorphins, the feel-good neurotransmitters, which lift our mood. And countless studies back up what most of us have known our whole lives—smiling is contagious. So if you smile and someone returns it, you're both benefiting from your feel-good hormones.

If we truly care about the strangers around us, their lives can be transformed. According to the Bureau of Labor Statistics, roughly 70 percent of service doesn't involve a formal organization but entails people engaging locally on their own initiative. Think of the Little Free Libraries and Little Free Pantries people create in their communities to distribute books and food. Countless anonymous donors stop by to restock the reading material or food in these mini-libraries and food banks.

Then there are the folks who see a need and simply take matters into their own hands. On a cold November night in New York City, a homeless man walked barefoot down the sidewalk on his heels, trying to protect his toes from the freezing ground. New York City police officer Lawrence DiPrimo saw the man, whom he engaged in conversation. As they chatted, DiPrimo found out the man's shoe size, then disappeared briefly. When he returned, he presented the man with a pair of weatherproof boots he had just purchased. We wouldn't know of this story except that a passerby happened to notice what was happening and snapped a photo of DiPrimo kneeling next to the man, helping him lace up the boots. And when the clerk at the shoe store had learned why DiPrimo was buying the boots, he had offered his employee discount to lower the price. That's love.

Give Resources to Organizations

Organizations can seem impersonal, and so are the ways we're encouraged to love them—primarily by giving money, sometimes by giving time or skills. The more emotionally connected you are to a cause, the more passion you'll be able to bring to your efforts on its behalf.

Leanne Lauricella had a bustling career as a corporate event planner in New York, throwing fancy affairs for wealthy clients. One day a coworker mentioned "factory farming." Leanne had no idea what the term meant, but that evening, she googled it, and was horrified by what she found. On the spot, Leanne decided to stop eating animals. She also started learning more about animal agriculture, including visiting farms, where she fell in love with the animals—especially with goats. Leanne was surprised and delighted to discover how playful, intelligent, and engaged goats are when they're treated well. She just couldn't get goats out of her mind, so she rescued two—Jax and Opie, named after characters from the TV show *Sons of Anarchy*. Leanne started an Instagram account she jokingly titled "Goats of Anarchy," where she could share Jax and Opie's exploits. People loved engaging with them, and Leanne enjoyed caring for them, so much so that she adopted more goats, including several with special medical needs. Eventually Leanne quit her job, and today, Goats of Anarchy is a registered charity on a thirty-acre property that more than 250 animals call home. Leanne and her helpers care for the goats, and they provide educational programs—and lots of smiles—for the public.

Connect with Earth

It's hard to show love to Earth because it's so big. We can't fix or even see every element of nature. We're not trained to believe that Earth is our home or responsibility. We think it will take care of itself, or that taking care of it is the government's job.

We make Earth smaller by finding ways to connect with it. On a trip to Halaiʻi Volcanoes National Park, Radhi and I were shown circular petroglyphs that Native Hawaiians carved into the rocks hundreds of years ago. Our guide told us that when babies were born, their elders would carve these circles and place the umbilical cord there so that the child was connected to the earth forever. This connection is not only good for nature. Nature has love to give us too.

Native Americans and other Indigenous cultures have countless practices to honor nature, including songs and dances dedicated to water, earth, wind, and fire. Yogis practice *Surya Namaskar*, or sun salutations. Ancient Celts and other peoples gathered for festivals to celebrate the cycles of the seasons. Jungian analyst Erich Neumann wrote, "Opposition between light and darkness has informed the spiritual world of all peoples and molded it into shape."

Modern science shows that our biology is regulated by nature. Samer Hattar, who heads the Section on Light and Circadian Rhythms at the National Institute of Mental Health, says that light impacts us beyond just helping us see—it actually regulates many of our body's functions. Neurons in our eyes set our body clocks based on information from the sun's rising and setting, and everything from our sleep-wake cycle to our metabolism and our mood is influenced by sunlight. (Artificial light affects us, as well, but our bodies function best when we're exposed to the bright light of the sun.) As neuroscientist Andrew Huberman says, we can actually experience a kind of "light hunger" when we don't get enough sunlight. We already connect with Earth in more ways than we know—learning that inspires us to take care of our planet.

Make your way outward through the circles of love, starting in your comfort zone with those you know best and getting further and further from those you know personally. We serve in ignorance when we don't

COMFORT ZONES OF LOVE

The Earth
Organizations
Strangers
Community
Colleagues
Friends
Family

want to be left out. We serve out of passion when we want credit for what we've done, or we want the recipient to owe us a debt. We serve in goodness when we don't want recognition or an outcome—we just want to show pure love.

When you started reading this book, maybe you were hoping love would show up at your doorstep, sweep you off your feet, and carry you away. Maybe you felt willing to do anything to find love. We think love has to be obtained, earned, achieved, and received. We look for it in the form of attention and compliments and people acknowledging us. But actually the greatest way to experience love is to give it.

What if, when you enter a room, you ask yourself, how can I love everyone here today? You tell yourself, *I'm just going to give love.* This is an amazing way to start your day and to guide you through it. If someone gives off a negative or unwelcoming vibe, try going up to them and asking them a question about something they care about. It's that simple. Give love.

I began this book by talking about how when we love a flower, we water it every day. Now you are the one doing the planting—planting seeds for others, giving fruits to others, providing shade for others. **You can seek love your whole life and never find it, or you can give love your whole life and experience joy.** Experience it, practice it, and create it instead of waiting for it to find you. The more you do this, the more you will experience the depths of love from different people throughout every single day for the rest of your life.

Write a Love Letter
to The World

Once I was walking on a beach in south India with one of my teachers. We were in a fishing community, and many fish had been brought up to the beach in nets, but there were thousands of other fish that for some reason were stranded on the beach, slowly dying. One by one, my teacher began to throw fish back into the sea in hope that they would survive. There were so many fish on the beach, I knew we wouldn't be able to save them all. I asked him what the point was in saving them.

"It's only one fish to you," my teacher said, "But to that fish, it is everything."

My teacher was enacting in real life a message from a Zen story that I would later come across, about a teacher throwing starfish back into the sea.

The news today is overwhelming. We see widespread pain and suffering and wonder what difference we can make, but I like to believe that if we send positive wishes and good energy out to anyone who needs them, they will reach someone and mean something to them. We underestimate what helping one person could do. Writing a love letter to the world reminds you to operate this way in all your interactions of the day.

Dear World,

For so much of my life, I have viewed love as caring for those who care for me. Starting with my first years, I experienced love as something I received and returned. But that experience of love, while beautiful, is limited.

It restricts my experience of love to those I know, those who engage with me in a certain way. I want to experience more love. A bigger love. One not confined to my own backyard, but one that reaches out beyond the borders of my own world into the whole world, to all of humanity. Love beyond biology or reciprocity. Beyond even acquaintance. Because as I now understand, I do not need to know you to love you. Or, rather, in some way I do know you, because of our shared humanity. We are all here together in this place, with our struggles and our triumphs, doing our best. What connects us all to one another is our connection to love. I know that sometimes it's hard to see that, divided as we are by our different opinions, values, and beliefs. But underneath it all, every single one of us has one powerful thing in common—we all want to experience love.

And that's what I share with you now. No matter who you are, no matter what you've done or haven't done in your life, I offer you love. I promise you are worthy of receiving it. Please know that no matter what you're going through, someone loves you. Without reservation. Without judgment. Fully and completely.

Love,
Me

Meditation to Connect

This meditation focuses on noticing and sharing love in all its forms. It can help you feel more deeply connected to love and to the world around you.

1. Find a comfortable position, whether that's sitting in a chair, sitting upright on a cushion or on the floor, or lying down.
2. Close your eyes, if that feels good to you. If not, simply soften your focus.
3. Whether your eyes are open or closed, gently lower your gaze.
4. Take a deep breath in. And breathe out.
5. If you find that your mind is wandering, that's okay. Gently bring it back to a space of calm, balance, and stillness.

Sharing Love Meditation

1. Take a deep breath. And breathe out.
2. Take a moment to think about all the love you have received in your life.
3. Think about all the love you have expressed and shared with others.
4. Now, feel all the love within you, from every source, including yourself. Bring your awareness to all the love you have chosen to have within you. Notice it in your heart. Feel it cascading across your body, enlivening your feet, legs, arms, chest, and head.
5. Feel the love getting stronger, and more powerful. Notice it radiating from your heart space.

6. Now, see this love going out to the people you know and
    care for.
7. See it reaching out to every person who you know is strug-
    gling.
8. Now, feel it projected to people you've never met, and the
    strangers you see every day.
9. Now, feel the love within you extending even beyond that,
    reaching every person in the entire world.

Acknowledgments

The teachings of the Vedas and the Bhagavad Gita have affected my life, relationships, and career in the deepest way. This book is my humble attempt to interpret and translate them into a form that is relevant and practical so that you can create purposeful, meaningful, and powerful relationships in your life. I want to express my gratitude for the relationships that helped this book come to life.

I'd like to thank my agent James Levine for living so many of these principles and reassuring me of their validity through his fifty-five-year marriage. He and his wife recently marked the sixtieth anniversary of their first date. What an inspiration! I'd like to thank my editor Eamon Dolan, who drew from his own deep, loving relationship when pushing me to write a better book for all of you. To my collaborator Hilary Liftin for never giving up, always being adaptable (qualities that she no doubt brings to her twenty-years-and-counting marriage), and her incredible ability to now teach and live these lessons. Kelly Madrone and her wife were best friends before they were married and fell in love because they knew each so well—which explains why she brought such incredible research and insight to this book. To Jordan Goodman, who somehow, while keeping my schedule on track, always with a smile, is newly engaged and claims that she followed every rule in this book (but given how busy I've kept her, I can't confirm that she's actually read it). To Nicole Berg for all the creative discussions, dedication to the cover and illustrations, and support. While she was planning her own wedding, she was helping to plan this book. What an achievement! To Rodrigo and Anna Corral for the cover design and illustrations—a married team who have found that trust grows in even the smallest tasks and words, and this attention to detail is evident in their work. To Oli Malcolm at HarperCollins UK, who has been married eight years and says his wife is the brains of the operation. He is extremely patient—though maybe his wife should get the credit?

To all my clients who allowed me into their lives so that I could understand human emotion deeper. So that I could implement these ideas in reality. So that I could see transformation and genuine connection.

Author's Note

In this book I have drawn from the wisdom of many religions, cultures, inspirational leaders, and scientists. And I have done my very best in each instance to attribute quotes and ideas to their original sources; these efforts are reflected here. In some cases, I have come across wonderful quotes or ideas that I've found attributed to multiple different sources, widely so with no specified source, or attributed to ancient texts where I could not locate the original verse. In these cases, I have, with the help of a researcher, tried to give the reader as much useful information as I could regarding the source of the material. Additionally, in this book I have shared the true stories of my clients and friends, but I have changed their names and other identifying details to protect their privacy.

Notes

Introduction

1 **"What is the difference between like and love?":** Terence M. Dorn, *Quotes: The Famous and Not So Famous* (Conneaut Lake, PA: Page Publishing Inc., 2021).

2 **Psychologist Tim Lomas, a lecturer:** Tim Lomas, "How I Discovered There Are (at Least) 14 Different Kinds of Love by Analysing the World's Languages," The Conversation, February 13, 2018, https://theconversation.com/how-i-discovered-there-are-at-least-14-different-kinds-of-love-by-analysing-the-worlds-languages-91509.

2 **The ancient Greeks said there were seven basic types:** Neel Burton, "These Are the 7 Types of Love," *Psychology Today*, June 15, 2016, https://www.psychologytoday.com/au/blog/hide-and-seek/201606/these-are-the-7-types-love.

3 **An analysis of Chinese literature:** "Love: Love Across Cultures," Marriage and Family Encyclopedia, accessed May 9, 2022, https://family.jrank.org/pages/1086/Love-Love-Across-Cultures.html.

3 **In the Tamil language:** Chrystal Hooi, "Languages of Love: Expressing Love in Different Cultures," *Jala* blog, February 10, 2020, https://jala.net/blog/story/30/languages-of-love-expressing-love-in-different-cultures.

3 **In Japanese, the term *koi no yokan*:** Hooi, "Languages of Love."

3 ***kokuhaku* describes a declaration of loving commitment:** Marian Joyce Gavino, "The 'Pure' Intentions of Kokuhaku," Pop Japan, February 13, 2018, https://pop-japan.com/culture/the-pure-intentions-of-kokuhaku/.

3 **In India's Boro language, *onsra* describes:** Hooi, "Languages of Love."

3 **If we look at the Billboard Top 50 Love Songs of All Time:** Fred Bronson, "Top 50 Love Songs of All Time," *Billboard*, February 9, 2022,

https://www.billboard.com/lists/top-50-love-songs-of-all-time/this-guys-in -love-with-you-herb-alpert-hot-100-peak-no-1-for-four-weeks-1968/.

5 **The Vedas describe four stages of life:** S. Radhakrishnan, "The Hindu Dharma," *International Journal of Ethics* 33, no. 1 (October 1922): 8–21, https://doi.org/10.1086/intejethi.33.1.2377174.

5 **If you look up *ashram* in a dictionary:** "Ashram," Yogapedia, February 11, 2018, https://www.yogapedia.com/definition/4960/ashram.

10 **On the wedding site The Knot, 97 percent of proposal stories:** Ashley Fetters, "'He Said Yes!' Despite Changing Norms, It's Still Exceedingly Rare for Women to Propose in Heterosexual Couples," *Atlantic*, July 20, 2019, https://www.theatlantic.com/family/archive/2019/07 /women-proposing-to-men/594214/.

10 **Eighty percent of brides receive a diamond engagement ring:** Alexandra Macon, "7 Ways Engagement-Ring Buying Is Changing," *Vogue*, April 12, 2019, https://www.vogue.com/article/how-engagement -ring-buying-is-changing.

10 **According to a survey in *Brides* magazine:** "This Is What American Weddings Look Like Today," *Brides*, August 15, 2021, https://www.brides .com/gallery/american-wedding-study.

10 **The nuclear family is still the most common:** D'vera Cohn and Jeffrey S. Passel, "A Record 64 Million Americans Live in Multigenerational Households," Pew Research Center, April 5, 2018, https://www .pewresearch.org/fact-tank/2018/04/05/a-record-64-million-americans -live-in-multigenerational-households/.

10 **Seventy-two percent of Americans live in or near:** "What Percentage of Americans Currently Live in the Town or City Where They Grew Up?" PR Newswire, November 5, 2019, https://www.prnewswire .com/news-releases/what-percentage-of-americans-currently-live-in-the -town-or-city-where-they-grew-up-300952249.html.

10 **the number of people who say they'd *like* a nonexclusive partnership:** Jamie Ballard, "A Quarter of Americans Are Interested in Having an Open Relationship," YouGovAmerica, April 26, 2021, https:// today.yougov.com/topics/lifestyle/articles-reports/2021/04/26/open-rela tionships-gender-sexuality-poll.

10 **only about 4 to 5 percent of Americans:** Jason Silverstein and Jessica Kegu, "'Things Are Opening Up': Non-Monogamy Is More Common Than You'd Think," CBS News, October 27, 2019, https://www.cbs news.com/news/polyamory-relationships-how-common-is-non-monogamy -cbsn-originals/.

PART 1
SOLITUDE: LEARNING TO LOVE YOURSELF

13 *atma prema*, **self-love:** Richard Schiffman, "Ancient India's 5 Words for Love (And Why Knowing Them Can Heighten Your Happiness," *YES!*, August 14, 2014, https://www.yesmagazine.org/health-happiness /2014/08/14/ancient-india-s-five-words-for-love.

Rule 1: Let Yourself Be Alone

15 **"I wish I could show you":** "Poems by Hafiz," The Poetry Place, August 13, 2014, https://thepoetryplace.wordpress.com/2014/08/13/poems -by-hafiz/.

15 **Researchers at the University of Toronto:** Stephanie S. Spielmann, Geoff MacDonald, Jessica A. Maxwell, Samantha Joel, Diana Peragine, Amy Muise, and Emily A. Impett, "Settling for Less Out of Fear of Being Single," *Journal of Personality and Social Psychology* 105, no. 6 (December 2013): 1049–1073, https://doi: 10.1037/a0034628.

17 **Steven Glasberg, a throwaway cameo in *Superbad*:** *Superbad*, directed by Greg Mottola, Columbia Pictures/Apatow Productions, 2007.

17 **like Tom Hanks in *Cast Away*:** *Cast Away*, directed by Robert Zemeckis, Twentieth Century Fox/DreamWorks Pictures/ImageMovers, 2000.

21 **"Language has created":** Paul Tillich, *The Eternal Now* (New York: Scribner, 1963).

21 **In one study, researchers gave more than five hundred visitors:** Martin Tröndle, Stephanie Wintzerith, Roland Wäspe, and Wolfgang Tschacher, "A Museum for the Twenty-first Century: The Influence of 'Sociality' on Art Reception in Museum Space," *Museum Management and Curatorship* 27, no. 5 (February 2012): 461–486, https://doi.org/10.1 080/09647775.2012.737615.

21 **In *Flow: The Psychology of Optimal Experience*:** Mihaly Csikszentmihalyi, *Flow: The Psychology of Optimal Experience* (New York: Harper Perennial Modern Classics, 2008), 273.

21 **His research found that young people were less likely:** Mihaly Csikszentmihalyi, *Creativity: Flow and the Psychology of Discovery and Invention* (New York: HarperCollins, 1996).

28 **Oxford Languages dictionary defines *confidence*:** "Confidence," Lexico, accessed June 23, 2022, https://www.lexico.com/en/definition /confidence.

32 **Research shows that not only does high self-esteem:** Hamid Reza Alavi and Mohammad Reza Askaripur, "The Relationship Between Self-Esteem and Job Satisfaction of Personnel in Government Organizations," *Public Personnel Management* 32, no. 4 (December 2003): 591–600, https://doi.org/ 10.1177/009102600303200409.

32 **better physical and psychological health:** Ho Cheung William Li, Siu Ling Polly Chan, Oi Kwan Joyce Chung, and Miu Ling Maureen Chui, "Relationships Among Mental Health, Self-Esteem, and Physical Health in Chinese Adolescents: An Exploratory Study," *Journal of Health Psychology* 15, no. 1 (January 11, 2010): 96–106, https://doi.org/10.1177/13 59105309342601.

32 **it also predicts better and more satisfying romantic relationships:** Ruth Yasemin Erol and Ulrich Orth, "Self-Esteem and the Quality of Romantic Relationships," *European Psychologist* 21, no. 4 (October 2016): 274–83, https://doi.org/10.1027/1016-9040/a000259.

32 **Frida Kahlo said, "I paint self-portraits":** "Become an Instant Expert in the Art of Self-Portraiture," Arts Society, October 1, 2020, https://theartssociety.org/arts-news-features/become-instant-expert-art-self-port raiture-0.

33 **Krishna says, "The senses are so strong and impetuous, O Arjuna":** Verse 2.60 from C. Bhaktivedanta Swami Prabhuppada, *Bhagavad-gita As It Is* (Bhaktivedanta Book Trust International), https://apps .apple.com/us/app/bhagavad-gita-as-it-is/id1080562426.

33 **"As a strong wind sweeps away a boat on the water":** Verse 2.67 from Prabhuppada, *Bhagavad-gita As It Is.*

34 **Buddhist teacher Rigdzin Shikpo writes:** Rigdzin Shikpo, *Never Turn Away: The Buddhist Path Beyond Hope and Fear* (Somerville, MA: Wisdom, 2007), 116.

36 **Neuroscientist Lisa Feldman Barrett writes:** Lisa Feldman Barrett, *7½ Lessons About the Brain* (New York: Houghton Mifflin Harcourt, 2020), 84–85, 93.

Rule 2: Don't Ignore Your Karma

38 **"Do not be led by others":** "Vedic Culture," Hinduscriptures.com, accessed October 3, 2022, https://www.hinduscriptures.in/vedic-lifestyle /reasoning-customs/why-should-we-perform-panchamahayajnas.

39 *Samskara* **is the Sanskrit word for impression:** "Samskara," Yogapedia, July 31, 2020, https://www.yogapedia.com/definition/5748/samskara.

39   **The Karmic Cycle:** Verses 3.19, 3.27 from Prabhuppada, *Bhaga-vad-gita As It Is.*

44   **In the *New York Times'* "Modern Love" column:** Coco Mellors, "An Anxious Person Tries to Be Chill: Spoiler: It Doesn't Work (Until She Stops Trying)," *New York Times*, September 10, 2021, https://www.nytimes.com/2021/09/10/style/modern-love-an-anxious-person-tries-to-be-chill.html.

44   *Matha Pitha Guru Deivam* **is a Sanskrit phrase:** "The True Meaning of Matha, Pitha, Guru, Deivam," VJAI.com, accessed May 11, 2022, https://vjai.com/post/138149920/the-true-meaning-of-matha-pitha-guru-deivam.

44   **It's a basic Freudian principle:** "The Freudian Theory of Personality," Journal Psyche, accessed June 21, 2022, http://journalpsyche.org/the-freudian-theory-of-personality/.

45   **In their book, *A General Theory of Love*:** Thomas Lewis, Fari Amini, and Richard Lannon, *A General Theory of Love* (New York: Vintage, 2007).

50   **Snow White sings "Someday my prince will come":** *Snow White and the Seven Dwarfs*, directed by William Cottrell, David Hand, and Wilfred Jackson, Walt Disney Animation Studios, 1938.

51   **In *Forrest Gump*, Tom Hanks:** *Forrest Gump*, directed by Robert Zemeckis, Paramount Pictures/The Steve Tisch Company/Wendy Finerman Productions, 1994.

51   **But in his book *Face Value*:** Alexander Todorov, *Face Value: The Irresistible Influence of First Impressions* (Princeton, NJ: Princeton University Press, 2017); Daisy Dunne, "Why Your First Impressions of Other People Are Often WRONG: We Judge Others Instantly Based on Their Facial Expressions and Appearance, but This Rarely Matches Up to Their True Personality," *Daily Mail*, June 13, 2017, https://www.dailymail.co.uk/sciencetech/article-4599198/First-impressions-people-WRONG.html.

51   **a group of psychologists at the University of Pennsylvania:** Greg Lester, "Just in Time for Valentine's Day: Falling in Love in Three Minutes or Less," *Penn Today*, February 11, 2005, https://penntoday.upenn.edu/news/just-time-valentines-day-falling-love-three-minutes-or-less.

51   **psychologists from Yale University:** Lawrence E. Williams and John A. Bargh, "Experiencing Physical Warmth Promotes Interpersonal Warmth," *Science* 322, no. 5901 (October 24, 2008): 606–607, https://www.science.org/doi/10.1126/science.1162548.

51   **the *context effect* refers to how the atmosphere:** Andrew M. Colman, *A Dictionary of Psychology*, 4th ed. (Oxford: Oxford University Press, 2015).

52 **In *500 Days of Summer*:** *500 Days of Summer*, directed by Marc Webb, Fox Searchlight Pictures/Watermark/Dune Entertainment III, 2009.

52 **before World War II only 10 percent of engagement rings:** "The History of the Engagement Ring," Estate Diamond Jewelry, October 10, 2018, https://www.estatediamondjewelry.com/the-history-of-the-engagement-ring/.

52 **In 1977, an ad for De Beers jewelers:** "De Beers' Most Famous Ad Campaign Marked the Entire Diamond Industry," The Eye of Jewelry, April 22, 2020, https://theeyeofjewelry.com/de-beers/de-beers-jewelry/de-beers-most-famous-ad-campaign-marked-the-entire-diamond-industry/.

53 **"No maiden in the land fits the shoe":** Emily Yahr, "Yes, Wearing That Cinderella Dress 'Was Like Torture' for Star Lily James," *Washington Post*, March 16, 2015, https://www.washingtonpost.com/news/arts-and-entertainment/wp/2015/03/16/yes-wearing-that-cinderella-dress-was-like-torture-for-star-lily-james/.

53 **"You had me at hello":** *Jerry Maguire*, directed by Cameron Crowe, TriStar Pictures/Gracie Films, 1996.

53 **"I wish I knew how to quit you":** *Brokeback Mountain*, directed by Ang Lee, Focus Features/River Road Entertainment/Alberta Film Entertainment, 2006.

53 **"To me, you are perfect":** *Love Actually*, directed by Richard Curtis, Universal Pictures/StudioCanal/Working Title Films, 2003.

53 **"As you wish":** *The Princess Bride*, directed by Rob Reiner, Act III Communications/Buttercup Films Ltd./The Princess Bride Ltd., 1987.

53 **"You want the moon?":** *It's a Wonderful Life*, directed by Frank Capra, Liberty Films (II), 1947.

53 **"I'm also just a girl":** *Notting Hill*, directed by Roger Michell, Polygram Filmed Entertainment/Working Title Films/Bookshop Productions, 1999.

54 **In 2015, the artist Rora Blue:** The Unsent Project, accessed May 12, 2022, https://theunsentproject.com/.

54 **doesn't develop fully until we're about twenty-five years old:** "Understanding the Teen Brain," University of Rochester Medical Center Health Encyclopedia, accessed May 12, 2022, https://www.urmc.rochester.edu/encyclopedia/content.aspx?ContentTypeID=1&ContentID=3051.

54 **As brain expert Daniel Amen describes it:** Daniel Amen, *The Brain in Love: 12 Lessons to Enhance Your Love Life* (New York: Harmony, 2009), 27.

54 **Vedic teachings say that there are three levels of intelligence:** Verse 14.19 from C. Bhaktivedanta Swami Prabhuppada, *Bhagavad-gita As It Is* (The Bhaktivedanta Book Trust International, Inc.), https://apps.apple.com/us/app/bhagavad-gita-as-it-is/id1080562426.

55 **In the movie *I Know What You Did Last Summer*:** *I Know What You*

Did Last Summer, directed by Jim Gillespie, Mandalay Entertainment/ Original Film/Summer Knowledge LLC, 1997.

55 **from Rochester in *Jane Eyre*:** Charlotte Brontë, *Jane Eyre* (New York: Norton, 2016).

55 **Heathcliff in *Wuthering Heights*:** Emily Brontë, *Wuthering Heights* (New York: Norton, 2019).

55 **Edward in *Twilight*:** Stephenie Meyer, *Twilight* (New York: Little, Brown, 2005).

56 **anthropologist Helen Fisher:** Helen Fisher, *Why Him? Why Her? Finding Real Love by Understanding Your Personality Type* (New York: Henry Holt, 2009), 208.

59 **oxytocin is related to feelings of being in love:** Amen, *The Brain in Love,* 65.

59 **sex causes men's oxytocin levels to spike more than 500 percent:** Amen, *The Brain in Love*, 65.

59 **neuroscientist Robert Froemke says that oxytocin:** Alexandra Owens, "Tell Me All I Need to Know About Oxytocin," Psycom, accessed May 12, 2022, https://www.psycom.net/oxytocin.

60 **temporary blocking effect on negative memories:** Amen, *The Brain in Love,* 65.

60 **John and Julie Gottman:** "John & Julie Gottman ON: Dating, Finding the Perfect Partner, & Maintaining a Healthy Relationship," interview by Jay Shetty, *On Purpose*, Apple Podcasts, September 28, 2020, https:// podcasts.apple.com/us/podcast/john-julie-gottman-on-dating-finding -perfect-partner/id1450994021?i=1000492786092.

60 **The Bhagavad Gita talks about six opulences:** Verse 10.1 from C. Bhaktivedanta Swami Prabhuppada, *Bhagavad-gita As It Is* (Bhaktive- danta Book Trust International), https://apps.apple.com/us/app/bhagavad -gita-as-it-is/id1080562426; "Bhagavad Gita Chapter 10, Text 01," Bhaga- vad Gita Class, accessed May 12, 2022, https://bhagavadgitaclass.com /bhagavad-gita-chapter-10-text-01/.

60 **In Beyoncé's song "Halo":** Beyoncé, "Halo," *I Am . . . Sasha Fierce*, Columbia Records, January 20, 2009.

60 **the *halo effect* is a type of cognitive bias:** Ayesh Perera, "Why the Halo Effect Affects How We Perceive Others," Simply Psychology, March 22, 2021, https://www.simplypsychology.org/halo-effect.html.

61 **The *Bhagavad Gita* says that divine love of God:** Pramahansa Yogananda, "Practising the Presence of God," Pramahansa Yogananda, accessed August 11, 2022, http://yogananda.com.au/gita/gita0630.html.

61 ***Energy of ignorance:*** Verse 14.5 from Prabhuppada, *Bhagavad-gita As It Is.*

62 ***Energy of passion:*** Verse 14.5, Prabhuppada.

62 ***Energy of goodness:*** Verse 14.5, Prabhuppada.

63 **One study showed that 53 percent of online daters:** Greg Hodge, "The Ugly Truth of Online Dating: Top 10 Lies Told by Internet Daters," HuffPost, October 10, 2012, https://www.huffpost.com/entry/online-dating-lies_b_1930053; Opinion Matters, "Little White Lies," BeautifulPeople.com, accessed May 12, 2022, https://beautifulpeoplecdn.s3.amazonaws.com/studies/usa_studies.pdf.

64 **Or, as Russell Brand puts it:** Emily Wallin, "40 Inspirational Russell Brand Quotes on Success," Wealthy Gorilla, March 20, 2022, https://wealthygorilla.com/russell-brand-quotes/.

69 **One of the translators of the Bhagavad Gita, Eknath Easwaran:** Eknath Easwaran, *Words to Live By: Daily Inspiration for Spiritual Living.* (Tomales, CA: Nilgiri Press, 2010).

PART TWO
COMPATIBILITY: LEARNING TO LOVE OTHERS

75 **kama/maitri—loving others:** "Kama," Yogapedia, accessed May 12, 2022, https://www.yogapedia.com/definition/5303/kama; "Maitri," Yogapedia, July 23, 2020, https://www.yogapedia.com/definition/5580/maitri.

Rule 3: Define Love Before You Think It, Feel It, or Say It

77 **Writer Samantha Taylor says:** Kelsey Borresen, "8 Priceless Stories of People Saying 'I Love You' for the First Time," HuffPost, September 28, 2018, https://www.huffpost.com/entry/saying-i-love-you-for-the-first-time_n_5bad19b8e4b09d41eb9f6f5a.

78 **A survey showed that men are quicker:** Martha De Lacy, "When WILL He Say 'I Love You?' Men Take 88 Days to Say Those Three Words—But Girls Make Their Man Wait a Lot Longer," *Daily Mail,* March 7, 2013, https://www.dailymail.co.uk/femail/article-2289562/I-love-Men-88-days-say-girlfriend-women-134-days-say-boyfriend.html.

79 **Bhakti describes the journey of falling in love:** "Chapter 25—The Nine Stages of Bhakti Yoga," Hare Krishna Temple, accessed May 12, 2022, https://www.harekrishnatemple.com/chapter25.html.

81 **Researchers describe what we call love:** Helen Fisher, "Lust,

Attraction, and Attachment in Mammalian Reproduction," *Human Nature* 9, no. 1 (1998): 23–52, https://doi.org/10.1007/s12110-998-1010-5.

81 **The brain chemicals involved in lust differ:** Jade Poole, "The Stages of Love," MyMed.com, accessed May 12, 2022, https://www.mymed.com/health-wellness/interesting-health-info/chemistry-or-cupid-the-science-behind-falling-in-love-explored/the-stages-of-love.

82 **Professor Matthias Mehl at the University of Arizona:** Matthias R. Mehl, Simine Vazire, Shannon E. Holleran, and C. Shelby Clark, "Eavesdropping on Happiness: Well-being Is Related to Having Less Small Talk and More Substantive Conversations," *Psychological Science* 21, no. 4 (April 1, 2010): 539–541, https://doi.org/10.1177/0956797610362675.

83 **Social scientists say that vulnerability:** Marlena Ahearn, "Can You Really Train Your Brain to Fall in Love?" Bustle, October 19, 2016, https://www.bustle.com/articles/190270-can-you-really-train-your-brain-to-fall-in-love-the-science-behind-building-intimacy-in.

88 **Psychologist Lisa Firestone says:** Lisa Firestone, "Are You Expecting Too Much from Your Partner? These 7 Ways We Over-Rely on Our Partner Can Seriously Hurt Our Relationship," PsychAlive, accessed May 13, 2022, https://www.psychalive.org/are-you-expecting-too-much-from-your-partner/.

88 **"what one [team of researchers] called 'relationshopping'":** Rebecca D. Heino, Nicole B. Ellison, and Jennifer L. Gibbs, "Relationshopping: Investigating the Market Metaphor in Online Dating," *Journal of Social and Personal Relationships* 27, no. 4 (June 9, 2010): 427–447, https://doi.org/10.1177/0265407510361614.

88 **John Cacioppo, a neuroscientist who researched love:** Florence Williams, *Heartbreak: A Personal and Scientific Journey.* (New York: Norton, 2022), 112.

90 **A small survey conducted by High-Touch Communications:** "Response-Time Expectations in the Internet Age: How Long Is Too Long?" High-Touch Communications Inc., accessed June 21, 2022, https://blog.htc.ca/2022/05/18/response-time-expectations-in-the-internet-age-how-long-is-too-long/.

90 **Clinical psychologist Seth Meyers advises new couples:** Seth Meyers, "How Much Should New Couples See Each Other? To Protect the Longevity of a Relationship, Couples Should Use Caution," *Psychology Today*, November 29, 2017, https://www.psychologytoday.com/us/blog/insight-is-2020/201711/how-much-should-new-couples-see-each-other.

Rule 4: Your Partner Is Your Guru

100 **"Love does not consist of gazing at each other":** Antoine de Saint-Exupéry, *Airman's Odyssey* (New York: Harcourt Brace, 1984).

101 **Psychology researcher Jeremy Dean:** Jeremy Dean, "How to See Yourself Through Others' Eyes," Psych Central, June 1, 2010, https://psychcentral.com/blog/how-to-see-yourself-through-others-eyes#1.

104 **Researchers Arthur and Elaine Aron developed "self-expansion theory":** Arthur Aron and Elaine Aron, *Love and the Expansion of Self: Understanding Attraction and Satisfaction* (London: Taylor & Francis, 1986).

108 **In *The Guru and Disciple Book*:** Kripamoya das, *The Guru and Disciple Book* (Belgium: Deshika Books, 2015).

108 ***Dambha asuyadhi muktam*:** Kripamoya das, *The Guru and Disciple Book*.

108 **Zen master Shunryu Suzuki was set to visit:** Sean Murphy, *One Bird, One Stone: 108 Contemporary Zen Stories* (Newburyport, MA: Hampton Roads, 2013), 67.

109 **In the Marvel movie *Doctor Strange*:** *Doctor Strange*, directed by Scott Derrickson, Marvel Studios/Walt Disney Pictures, 2016.

109 ***sthira dhiyam*:** Kripamoya das, *The Guru and Disciple Book*.

110 **St. Francis said, "It is no use walking anywhere":** Jamie Arpin-Ricci, "Preach the Gospel at All Times? St. Francis Recognized That the Gospel Was All Consuming, the Work of God to Restore All of Creation Unto Himself for His Glory," HuffPost, August 31, 2012, https://www.huffpost.com/entry/preach-the-gospel-at-all-times-st-francis_b_162 7781.

110 ***Dayalum*:** Kripamoya das, *The Guru and Disciple Book*.

110 **There is a story in Bhakti scripture:** "Ramayana Story: Little Squirrel Who Helped Lord Rama!" Bhagavatam-katha, accessed May 14, 2022, http://www.bhagavatam-katha.com/ramayana-story-little-squirrel -who-helped-lord-rama/.

111 **When Sokei-an Shigetsu Sasaki:** Murphy, *One Bird, One Stone*, 13.

112 ***dirgha bandhum*:** Kripamoya das, *The Guru and Disciple Book*.

114 ***satya vacam*:** Kripamoya das, *The Guru and Disciple Book*.

115 **Researchers have identified critical feedback:** Matt Beck, "The Right Way to Give Feedback," Campus Rec, June 27, 2019, https://campus recmag.com/the-right-way-to-give-feedback/; Carol Dweck, *Mindset: The New Psychology of Success* (New York: Ballantine Books, 2006).

115 **Carol Dweck describes in her book *Mindset*:** Dweck, *Mindset,* 6.

117 ***tattva bodha abhilasi*:** Kripamoya das, *The Guru and Disciple Book* (Belgium: Deshika Books, 2015).

117 **The Buddhist term *shoshin*:** Christian Jarrett, "How to Foster 'Shoshin': It's Easy for the Mind to Become Closed to New Ideas: Cultivating a Beginner's Mind Helps Us Rediscover the Joy of Learning," Psyche, accessed May 14, 2022, https://psyche.co/guides/how-to-cultivate-shoshin-or-a-beginners-mind; Shunryu Suzuki, *Zen Mind, Beginner's Mind*, 50th Anniversary Edition (Boulder, CO: Shambhala, 2020).

118 ***tyakta mana*:** Kripamoya das, *The Guru and Disciple Book.*

119 ***danta*:** Kripamoya das, *The Guru and Disciple Book.*

119 **Stephen Covey:** Stephen Covey, *The 7 Habits of Highly Effective People*, 30th Anniversary Edition (New York: Simon & Schuster, 2020).

122 ***krita-vid-sisya*:** Kripamoya das, *The Guru and Disciple Book.*

123 **Studies have found that couples start to adopt:** Nicole Weaver, "5 Ways You Become More Like Your Partner Over Time (Even If You Don't Realize It)," Your Tango, May 6, 2021, https://www.yourtango.com/2015275766/5-ways-couples-become-more-alike-when-in-love.

123 **In the Vedic scriptures, this is described as:** David Bruce Hughes, "Sri Vedanta-Sutra: The Confidential Conclusions of the Vedas," Esoteric Teaching Seminars, accessed August 11, 2022, https://www.google.com/books/edition/śrī_Vedānta_sūtra_Adhyāya_2/gfHRFz6lU2kC?hl=en&gbpv=1&dq=Vedic+%22scriptures%22+meaning&pg=PA117&printsec=frontcover.

Rule 5: Purpose Comes First

125 **"The meaning of life is to find your gift":** David Viscott, *Finding Your Strength in Difficult Times: A Book of Meditations* (Indianapolis, IN: Contemporary Books, 1993).

125 ***dharma*:** "Dharma," Yogapedia, April 23, 2020, https://www.yogapedia.com/definition/4967/dharma.

126 ***artha*:** "Artha," Yogapedia, October 9, 2018, https://www.yogapedia.com/definition/5385/artha.

126 ***kama*:** "Kama," Yogapedia, accessed May 12, 2022, https://www.yogapedia.com/definition/5303/kama.

126 ***moksha*:** "Moksha," Yogapedia, April 23, 2020, https://www.yogapedia.com/definition/5318/moksha.

127 **The Vedas were intentional about the order:** "Dharma, Artha, Kama,

and Moksha: The Four Great Goals of Life," David Frawley (Pandit Vamadeva Shastri), Sivananda, accessed May 16, 2022, https://articles .sivananda.org/vedic-sciences/dharma-artha-kama-and-moksha-the-four -great-goals-of-life/; David Frawley, *The Art and Science of Vedic Counseling* (Twin Lakes, WI: Lotus Press, 2016).

127 **Researchers from the University of California, Los Angeles, and the University of North Carolina:** Barbara L. Fredrickson, Karen M. Grewen, Kimberly A. Coffey, Sara B. Algoe, Ann M. Firestine, Jesusa M. G. Arevalo, Jeffrey Ma, and Steven W. Cole, "A Functional Genomic Perspective of Human Well-Being," *Proceedings of the National Academy of Sciences* 110, no. 33 (July 2013): 13684–13689, https://doi .org/10.1073/pnas.1305419110.

127 **Anthony Burrow, a professor of human development:** Anthony L. Burrow and Nicolette Rainone, "How Many *Likes* Did I Get? Purpose Moderates Links Between Positive Social Media Feedback and Self-Esteem," *Journal of Experimental Social Psychology* 69 (March 2017): 232–36, https://doi.org/10.1016/j.jesp.2016.09.005.

128 **As Burrow says, "We are confronted with":** Jackie Swift, "The Benefits of Having a Sense of Purpose: People with a Strong Sense of Purpose Tend to Weather Life's Ups and Downs Better: Anthony Burrow Investigates the Psychology Behind This Phenomenon," Cornell Research, accessed May 16, 2022, https://research.cornell.edu/news-features/bene fits-having-sense-purpose.

128 **There's a story attributed to the Buddha about two acrobats:** Thich Nhat Hanh, *How to Fight* (Berkeley, CA: Parallax Press, 2017), 87–88.

129 **As marriage and family therapist Kathleen Dahlen deVos:** Kelsey Borresen, "6 Ways the Happiest Couples Change Over Time: Long, Happy Relationships Don't Happen by Accident: They Take Work and a Willingness to Evolve," HuffPost, March 29, 2019, https://www.huff post.com/entry/ways-happiest-couple-change-over-time_l_5c9d037de4b 00837f6bbe3e2.

131 **Sal Khan went to business school:** Sal Khan, "Khan Academy: Sal Khan," interview by Guy Raz, *How I Built This*, podcast, NPR, September 21, 2020, https://www.npr.org/2020/09/18/914394221/khan-academy -sal-khan.

136 **Pulitzer Prize–winning journalist Brigid Schulte:** Brigid Schulte, "Brigid Schulte: Why Time Is a Feminist Issue," *Sydney Morning Herald*, March 10, 2015, https://www.smh.com.au/lifestyle/health-and-wellness /brigid-schulte-why-time-is-a-feminist-issue-20150309-13zimc.html.

141   **Lewis Hamilton:** "F1 Records Drivers," F1 Fansite, accessed June 22, 2022. https://www.f1-fansite.com/f1-results/f1-records-drivers/.

141   **To be a top driver, in season, Hamilton:** HAO, "Lewis Hamilton: Daily Routine," Balance the Grind, April 9, 2022, https://balancethegrind .co/daily-routines/lewis-hamilton-daily-routine/; Lewis Hamilton, "Optimize Your Body for Performance," MasterClass, accessed June 22, 2022, https://www.masterclass.com/classes/lewis-hamilton-teaches-a-winning -mindset/chapters/optimize-your-body-for-performance.

144   **in the traditional Vedic wedding ceremony:** "Seven Steps (Seven Pheras) of Hindu Wedding Ceremony Explained," Vedic Tribe, November 17, 2020, https://vedictribe.com/bhartiya-rights-rituals/seven-steps -seven-pheras-of-hindu-wedding-ceremony-explained/.

144   **An article in the *New York Times* says:** Claire Cain Miller, "The Motherhood Penalty vs. the Fatherhood Bonus," *New York Times*, September 6, 2014, https://www.nytimes.com/2014/09/07/upshot/a-child-helps-your -career-if-youre-a-man.html.

147   **Inspired as Sal Khan was:** Khan, "Khan Academy."

148   **"If you want to live":** A. P. French, *Einstein: A Centenary Volume* (Cambridge, MA: Harvard University Press, 1980), 32.

158   **Jennifer Petriglieri:** Jeremy Brown, "How to Balance Two Careers in a Marriage Without Losing Yourselves: It's Possible: You Just Have to Follow These Rules," Fatherly, January 2, 2019, https://www.fatherly.com/love -money/marriage-advice-two-career-household/.

PART THREE: HEALING: LEARNING TO
LOVE THROUGH STRUGGLE

Rule 6: Win or Lose Together

167   **"Conflict is the beginning of consciousness":** "M. Esther Harding Quotes," Citatis, accessed May 17, 2022, https://citatis.com/a229/12e75/.

171   **a paper published by the Society for Personality and Social Psychology:** Society for Personality and Social Psychology, "Sometimes Expressing Anger Can Help a Relationship in the Long-Term," ScienceDaily, August 2, 2012, www.sciencedaily.com/releases/2012/08/120802133649.htm; James McNulty and V. Michelle Russell, "Forgive and Forget, or Forgive and Regret? Whether Forgiveness Leads to Less or More Offending Depends on Offender Agreeableness," *Personality and Social Psychology Bulletin* 42, no. 5 (March 30, 2016): 616–631, https://doi.org/10.1177/0146167216637841.

173   **three "energies of being":** Verse 14.5–9 from the Bhagavad Gita, introduction and translation by Eknath Easwaran (Tomales, CA: Nilgiri Press, 2007), 224–225.

178   **"Arjuna said: 'O infallible one'":** Verses 1.21, 28–30, from C. Bhaktivedanta Swami Prabhuppada, *Bhagavad-gita As It Is* (Bhaktivedanta Book Trust International), https://apps.apple.com/us/app/bhagavad-gita-as-it-is /id1080562426.

180   **Swami Krishnananda:** Sri Swami Krishnananda, "The Gospel of the Bhagavadgita—Resolution of the Fourfold Conflict," Divine Life Society, accessed May 17, 2022, https://www.dlshq.org/religions/the-gospel -of-the-bhagavadgita-resolution-of-the-fourfold-conflict/.

185   **Social work professor Noam Ostrander:** Carly Breit, "This Is the Best Way to Fight with Your Partner, According to Psychologists," *Time*, September 24, 2018, https://time.com/5402188/how-to-fight-healthy-partner/.

187   **cognitive scientist Art Markman:** Art Markman, "Seeing Things from Another's Perspective Creates Empathy: Should You Literally Try to See the World from Someone Else's Perspective?" *Psychology Today*, June 6, 2017, https://www.psychologytoday.com/us/blog/ulterior-motives /201706/seeing-things-anothers-perspective-creates-empathy.

187   **In their book *Dimensions of Body Language*:** *Dimensions of Body Language*, "Chapter 17: Maximize the Impact of Seating Formations," Westside Toastmasters, accessed May 17, 2022, https://westsidetoastmasters .com/resources/book_of_body_language/chap17.html.

189   **Author Ritu Ghatourey says:** "Ritu Ghatourey Quotes," Goodreads, accessed May 17, 2022, https://www.goodreads.com/quotes/10327953 -ten-per-cent-of-conflict-is-due-to-difference-of.

197   **Psychiatrists Phillip Lee and Diane Rudolph:** Phillip Lee and Diane Rudolph, *Argument Addiction: Even When You Win, You Lose— Identify the True Cause of Arguments and Fix It for Good.* (Bracey, VA: Lisa Hagan Books, 2019).

Rule 7: You Don't Break in a Breakup

199   **"Your task is not to seek for love":** "Rumi Quotes," Goodreads, accessed September 5, 2022, https://www.goodreads.com/quotes/9726-your -task-is-not-to-seek-for-love-but-merely.

200   **The National Domestic Violence Hotline identifies six categories:** "Types of Abuse," National Domestic Violence Hotline, accessed May 18, 2022, https://www.thehotline.org/resources/types-of-abuse/.

201 **research by psychologists Clifford Notarius and Howard Markman:** Clifford Notarius and Howard Markman, *We Can Work It Out: How to Solve Conflicts, Save Your Marriage, and Strengthen Your Love for Each Other* (New York: TarcherPerigee, 1994).

203 **According to data from community health centers:** "Admitting to Cheating: Exploring How Honest People Are About Their Infidelity," Health Testing Centers, accessed May 18, 2022, https://www.healthtest ingcenters.com/research-guides/admitting-cheating/.

203 **psychologist and infidelity expert Dr. Shirley Glass:** Shirley P. Glass, with Jean Coppock Staeheli, *NOT "Just Friends": Rebuilding Trust and Recovering Your Sanity After Infidelity* (New York: Free Press, 2003), 162–163.

204 **In one survey of couples who had experienced infidelity:** Glass, *NOT "Just Friends,"* 192.

204 **marriage and family therapist Jim Hutt:** Jim Hutt, "Infidelity Recovery—Consequences of Punishing the Cheater," Emotional Affair Journey, accessed May 18, 2022, https://www.emotionalaffair.org/infidelity -recovery-consequences-of-punishing-the-cheater/.

204 **Glass notes that in a sample of 350 couples:** Glass, *NOT "Just Friends,"* 5, 133.

204 **Licensed clinical social worker Robert Taibbi:** Robert Taibbi, "The Appeal and the Risks of Rebound Relationships: When Every Partner Is 'The One,' Until the Next One," *Psychology Today,* November 14, 2014, https://www.psychologytoday.com/us/blog/fixing-families/201411 /the-appeal-and-the-risks-rebound-relationships.

205 **sociologist Annette Lawson:** Annette Lawson, *Adultery: An Analysis of Love and Betrayal* (New York: Basic Books, 1988).

206 **Divorce lawyer Joseph E. Cordell:** K. Aleisha Fetters, "The Vast Majority of Divorces Are Due to Inertia—and 7 More Marriage Insights from Divorce Lawyers," *Prevention,* February 10, 2015, https://www.pre vention.com/sex/relationships/a20448701/marriage-tips-from-divorce -lawyers/.

207 **Marriage and family therapist Marilyn Hough:** "Growing Together Separately," Relationship Specialists, accessed June 22, 2022, https:// www.relationshipspecialists.com/media/growing-together-separately/.

208 **a quote attributed to Eleanor Roosevelt:** "Great Minds Discuss Ideas; Average Minds Discuss Events; Small Minds Discuss People," Quote Investigator, accessed May 18, 2022, https://quoteinvestigator .com/2014/11/18/great-minds/.

210 **A 2000 study commissioned by the U.S. Travel Association:** "Travel Strengthens Relationships and Ignites Romance," U.S. Travel Association, February 5, 2013, https://www.ustravel.org/research/travel-strengthens-relationships-and-ignites-romance.

211 **A 2017 WalletHub survey found that married couples:** Melissa Matthews, "How to Be Happy: Volunteer and Stay Married, New U.S. Study Shows," Yahoo! News, September 12, 2017, https://www.yahoo.com/news/happy-volunteer-stay-married-u-121002566.html?guccounter=1.

211 **A study by psychologist Arthur Aron and colleagues:** Charlotte Reissman, Arthur Aron, and Merlynn Bergen, "Shared Activities and Marital Satisfaction: Causal Direction and Self-Expansion Versus Boredom," *Journal of Social and Personal Relationships* 10 (May 1, 1993): 243–254.

212 **Research shows that play is the mental state:** Andrew Huberman, "The Power of Play," *Huberman Lab*, podcast, Scicomm Media, February 7, 2022, https://hubermanlab.com/using-play-to-rewire-and-improve-your-brain/.

212 **hired an attractive woman:** Arthur P. Aron and Donald G. Dutton, "Some Evidence for Heightened Sexual Attraction Under Conditions of High Anxiety," *Journal of Personality and Social Psychology* 30, no. 4 (1974): 510–517.

213 **Dr. Lisa Marie Bobby:** Lisa Marie Bobby, Growingself.com.

219 **marriage and family therapist Dr. John Gottman:** "Marriage and Couples," Gottman Institute, accessed May 18, 2022, https://www.gottman.com/about/research/couples/.

224 **Research shows that areas activated in the brain:** Helen E. Fisher, Lucy L. Brown, Arthur Aron, Greg Strong, and Debra Mashek, "Reward, Addiction, and Emotion Regulation Systems Associated with Rejection in Love," *Journal of Neurophysiology* 104, no. 1 (July 1, 2010): 51–60.

224 **In one study of breakups, participants reported:** Fisher et al., "Reward, Addiction, and Emotion Regulation Systems Associated with Rejection in Love."

224 **But as researcher Helen Fisher says:** Florence Williams, *Heartbreak: A Personal and Scientific Journey* (New York: Norton, 2022), 36–37.

224 **In this state, our brains can desperately seek oxytocin:** "Oxytocin Bonding in Relationships—Dr. C. Sue Carter, Ph.D.—320," interview by Jayson Gaddis, *The Relationship School Podcast*, Relationship School, December 8, 2020, https://relationshipschool.com/podcast/oxytocin-bonding-in-relationships-dr-c-sue-carter-ph-d-320/.

225   **Those folks who thought about their exes:** Fisher et al., "Reward, Addiction, and Emotion Regulation Systems Associated with Rejection in Love."

225   **The Bhagavad Gita spends seven verses:** Verses 2.17, 23-24 from C. Bhaktivedanta Swami Prabhuppada, *Bhagavad-gita As It Is*. (The Bhaktivedanta Book Trust International, Inc.). https://apps.apple.com/us/app /bhagavad-gita-as-it-is/id1080562426.

229   **"Heartbreak creates":** Guy Winch, "How to Fix a Broken Heart," TED2017, April 2017, https://www.ted.com/talks/guy_winch_how_to_fi x_a_broken_heart.

229   **adults who'd experienced a separation:** Kyle J. Bourassa, Atina Manvelian, Adriel Boals, Matthias R. Mehl, and David A. Sbarra, "Tell Me a Story: The Creation of Narrative as a Mechanism of Psychological Recovery Following Marital Separation," *Journal of Social and Clinical Psychology* 36, no. 5 (May 24, 2017): 359–379, https://doi.org/10.1521 /jscp.2017.36.5.359.

232   **If we experience a torn muscle:** Brett Sears, "Scar Tissue Massage and Management," Verywell Health, April 19, 2022, https://www.very wellhealth.com/scar-tissue-massage-and-management-2696639.

232   **Tara Brach:** Mark Matousek, "Releasing the Barriers to Love: An Interview with Tara Brach," *Psychology Today*, November 24, 2015, https:// www.psychologytoday.com/us/blog/ethical-wisdom/201511/releasing -the-barriers-love-interview-tara-brach.

232   **Pema Chödrön:** Lisa Capretto, "What Buddhist Teacher Pema Chödrön Learned After a 'Traumatizing' Divorce," HuffPost, May 6, 2015, https:// www.huffpost.com/entry/pema-chodron-divorce-lesson_n_7216638.

236   **The Bhagavad Gita draws a distinction:** Verse 3.42 from C. Bhaktivedanta Swami Prabhuppada, *Bhagavad-gita As It Is* (Bhaktivedanta Book Trust International), https://apps.apple.com/us/app/bhagavad-gita -as-it-is/id1080562426.

237   **Christin had been seeing Bradley:** Christin Ross, "Christin Ross at Story District's Sucker for Love," Story District, February 14, 2020, https://www.youtube.com/watch?v=8ClCLIs3h5Q&list=PLDGn_6N 3BeYprjF0ExwvVvWU6ndzshh3d.

239   *maya,* **which means illusion:** "Maya," Yogapedia, October 21, 2018, https://www.yogapedia.com/definition/4986/maya.

239   **UCLA professor Steven Cole:** Williams, *Heartbreak*, 222–223.

241   **As Alice Walker once said:** "Shambhala Sun: A Wind Through the Heart; A Conversation with Alice Walker and Sharon Salzberg on Loving

Kindness in a Painful World," Alice Walker Pages, August 23, 1998, http://math.buffalo.edu/~sww/walker/wind-thru-heart.html.

PART FOUR: CONNECTION: LEARNING TO LOVE EVERYONE

245   *karuna*, **compassion for all living entities:** "Karuna," Yogapedia, April 10, 2016, https://www.yogapedia.com/definition/5305/karuna.

Rule 8: Love Again and Again

245   **"The river that flows in you also flows in me":** "Kabir," Poet Seers, accessed May 18, 2022, https://www.poetseers.org/the-poetseers/kabir/.

248   **Norwegian philosopher Arne Naess:** Joanna Macy, *World as Lover, World as Self: Courage for Global Justice and Ecological Renewal* (Berkeley, CA: Parallax Press, 2007), 156.

248   *Sannyasis* **experience the depths:** "Sannyasin," Yogapedia, August 5, 2018, https://www.yogapedia.com/definition/5348/sannyasin.

248   **Marianna Pogosyan:** Marianna Pogosyan, "In Helping Others, You Help Yourself," *Psychology Today*, May 30, 2018, https://www.psychologytoday.com/us/blog/between-cultures/201805/in-helping-others-you-help-yourself.

249   **"No one has ever become poor":** "Anne Frank," Goodreads, accessed May 18, 2022, https://www.goodreads.com/quotes/81804-no-one-has-ever-become-poor-by-giving.

249   **Researcher Allan Luks:** Larry Dossey, "The Helper's High," *Explore* 14, no. 6 (November 2018): 393–399, https://doi.org/10.1016/j.explore.2018.10.003; Allan Luks with Peggy Payne, *The Healing Power of Doing Good: The Health and Spiritual Benefits of Helping Others* (New York: Fawcett, 1992).

250   **The Vedas say the soul is** *sat, chit, ananda***:** "Sat-Chit-Ananda," Yogapedia, April 10, 2019, https://www.yogapedia.com/definition/5838/sat-chit-ananda.

251   **the principles of** *shreyas* **and** *preyas***:** Sampadananda Mishra, "Two Paths: Shreyas and Preyas," Bhagavad Gita, March 14, 2018, http://bhagavadgita.org.in/Blogs/5ab0b9b75369ed21c4c74c01.

251   **Jamil Zaki:** Jamil Zaki, "Caring About Tomorrow: Why Haven't We Stopped Climate Change? We're Not Wired to Empathize with Our Descendents," *Washington Post*, August 22, 2019, https://www.washingtonpost.com/outlook/2019/08/22/caring-about-tomorrow/.

252   **"I, you, he, she, we":** "Rumi Quotes," Goodreads, accessed May 18, 2022, https://www.goodreads.com/author/quotes/875661.Rumi?page=8.

252   **The Bhagavad Gita puts it simply:** Verse 5.18 from C. Bhaktivedanta Swami Prabhuppada, *Bhagavad-gita As It Is* (Bhaktivedanta Book
Trust International), https://apps.apple.com/us/app/bhagavad-gita-as-it-is
/id1080562426.

252   **"The humble sage":** Verse 5.18 from C. Bhaktivedanta Swami Prabhuppada, *Bhagavad-gita As It Is*. (The Bhaktivedanta Book Trust International, Inc.). https://apps.apple.com/us/app/bhagavad-gita-as-it-is
/id1080562426.

253   **"The children who need the most love":** "Russell A. Barkley Quotes,"
Goodreads, accessed May 18, 2022, https://www.goodreads.com/quotes
/1061120-the-children-who-need-love-the-most-will-always-ask.

256   **Robin Dunbar:** "Dunbar's Number: Why We Can Only Maintain 150
Relationships," BBC, accessed May 18, 2022, https://www.bbc.com/future
/article/20191001-dunbars-number-why-we-can-only-maintain-150-rela-
tionships.

259   **Blueboard:** Kevin Yip, "Recognizing Value: Blueboard's COO Explains
Why Companies Send Employees Skydiving," interview by Sean Ellis and
Ethan Garr, *The Breakout Growth Podcast*, Breakout Growth, February 22,
2022, https://breakoutgrowth.net/2022/02/22/podcast-recognizing-value
-blueboards-coo-explains-why-companies-send-employees-skydiving/;
Kevin Yip and Taylor Smith, "Kevin Yip & Taylor Smith—Cofounders of
Blueboard—the Other Side of Success Equals Sacrifice," interview by
Matt Gottesman, H&DF Magazine, April 12, 2022, https://hdfmagazine
.com/podcast/ep-37-kevin-yip-taylor-smith-co-founders-blueboard-the
-other-side-success-equals-sacrifice/.

259   **According to Work.com, nearly half of employees:** Kristin Long,
"Infographic: 49 Percent of Employees Would Change Jobs to Feel More
Appreciated," Ragan, April 23, 2013, https://www.ragan.com/infographic
-49-percent-of-employees-would-change-jobs-to-feel-more-appreciated/.

262   **Purdue University researchers wanted to investigate:** Stephanie
Pappas, "Why You Should Smile at Strangers," Live Science, May 25, 2012,
https://www.livescience.com/20578-social-connection-smile-strangers
.html; Neil Wagner, "The Need to Feel Connected," *Atlantic*, February 13, 2012,
https://www.theatlantic.com/health/archive/2012/02/the-need-to-feel
-connected/252924/; "Being Ignored Hurts, Even by a Stranger," Association for Psychological Science, January 24, 2012, https://www.psychologi-
calscience.org/news/releases/being-ignored-hurts-even-by-a-stranger.html.

263   **Smiling releases dopamine, serotonin, and endorphins:** Ron-
ald E. Riggio, "There's Magic in Your Smile," *Psychology Today*, June 25,

2012, https://www.psychologytoday.com/us/blog/cutting-edge-leadership/201206/there-s-magic-in-your-smile.

263   **smiling is contagious:** "Why Smiles (and Frowns) Are Contagious," Science News, February 11, 2016, https://www.sciencedaily.com/releases/2016/02/160211140428.htm.

263   **According to the Bureau of Labor Statistics, roughly 70 percent:** "Volunteering Facts & Statistics," Trvst, June 11, 2021, https://www.trvst.world/charity-civil-society/volunteering-facts-statistics/#cmf-SimpleFootnoteLink1; "Volunteering in the United States—2015," Bureau of Labor Statistics, February 25, 2016, https://www.bls.gov/news.release/pdf/volun.pdf.

263   **On a cold November night in New York City:** Dave Anderson, "A Short Story of Great Selflessness in 500 Words," Anderson Leadership Solutions, March 27, 2018, http://www.andersonleadershipsolutions.com/short-story-great-selflessness-500-words/; "Family of Man Who Was Pictured Being Given Boots by NYPD Cop Say They Didn't Know He Was Homeless," *Daily Mail*, December 2, 2012, https://www.dailymail.co.uk/news/article-2241823/Lawrence-DePrimo-Family-man-pictured-given-boots-NYPD-cop-say-didnt-know-homeless.html.

264   **Leanne Lauricella:** "Our Story," Goats of Anarchy, accessed June 22, 2022, https://www.goatsofanarchy.org/about.

264   **Native Americans and other Indigenous cultures:** Gertrude Prokosch Kurath, "Native American Dance," Britannica, accessed May 19, 2022, https://www.britannica.com/art/Native-American-dance/Regional-dance-styles.

265   **Yogis practice *Surya Namaskar*, or sun salutations:** Richard Rosen, "Sun Salutation Poses: The Tradition of Surya Namaskar," *Yoga Journal*, August 28, 2007, https://www.yogajournal.com/poses/here-comes-the-sun/.

265   **Ancient Celts and other peoples gathered for festivals:** McKenzie Perkins, "Irish Mythology: Festival and Holidays," ThoughtCo, December 29, 2019, https://www.thoughtco.com/irish-mythology-festival-and-holidays-4779917.

265   **Jungian analyst Erich Neumann:** Rosen, "Sun Salutation Poses."

265   **Samer Hattar:** "Dr. Samer Hattar—Timing Light, Food, & Exercise for Better Sleep, Energy, and Mood," interview by Andrew Huberman, *Huberman Lab*, podcast, Scicomm Media, October 25, 2021, https://hubermanlab.com/dr-samer-hattar-timing-light-food-exercise-for-better-sleep-energy-mood/

265   **As neuroscientist Andrew Huberman says:** "Dr. Samer Hattar."

Next Steps

GENIUS COACHING

This book was crafted from countless hours of research, writing, editing, and love. I pour my whole self and heart into everything I do. And the purpose at the center of all my work, no matter the type of project or medium, always remains the same. My wish is to help others grow in any way they can through truth, science, and intention.

With that said, I gratefully invite you to join Genius.

Genius is my global coaching community that meets weekly for live workshops and meditations. We understand that transformational change begins within and that real growth requires nurturing our whole selves—mentally, physically, emotionally, and spiritually.

When you are a member, I'll guide you through weekly live sessions based on practical wisdom and the latest research surrounding personal development and well-being. You'll also be able to revisit any workshop or meditation in the full collection on the Genius App. I cover everything from relationships to career, health, spirituality, and personal development.

My Genius methodology is simple yet powerful. When coaching, consistency, and community are combined, everything in your life improves from the inside out. This time we carve out together each week serves as a safe space where we can quiet our minds, meditate, and release stress and anxiety, and focus on what matters most—learning the ways in which we can improve both ourselves and the world.

What's more, you may also attend monthly in-person meetups with your fellow Genius members in over 150 countries worldwide to make new friends and connect with like-minded people.

For more information, please go to www.jayshettygenius.com today.

JAY SHETTY CERTIFICATION SCHOOL

If the rules and concepts in this book resonate with you on a deep level and you feel called to be a greater source of guidance in the world, I invite you to consider becoming a life coach through Jay Shetty Certification School.

With a vision to impact one billion lives, I founded this school in 2020 to train the next generation of coaches. This is a fully accredited institution striving to make the world a better place through a purposeful curriculum that honors traditional coaching theories, industry competencies, Eastern philosophy, and Vedic wisdom.

We train our students to become specialized coaches in a variety of niches— relationship coaches, business coaches, life coaches. Whatever change you wish to make in the world, we can help you achieve it.

Your certification journey will consist of guided study, supervised peer coaching, and group sessions that provide you with the tools and techniques necessary for professional client sessions. Beyond this, you'll learn how to build a thriving professional practice and market both yourself and your business. All Jay Shetty Certified Coaches are listed in a global database where clients can browse and choose coaches.

More than anything, I wanted this school to be accessible to all. You may study online from anywhere in the world, at your own pace and in your own time.

Jay Shetty Certification School is an official member of the Association for Coaching and EMCC Global.

For more information, please visit www.jayshettycoaching.com today.

Index

abuse, 124, 200–203, 232, 253
  conflict vs., 172–73
acceptance:
  of friends and family, 252
  on path to elevation, 217, 221–22
advice, 4–5
  accepting of, 117–18
Amen, Daniel, 54, 59
Amini, Fari, 45
amygdala, 54
anger management, 183, 192
apologies, 178–79, 193, 195–97,
  229
appreciation:
  for friends and family, 253, 256
  in path to elevation, 218, 223
  for work colleagues, 258–60, 260,
  261
argument addiction, 197
arguments, see conflict
Arjuna, 33, 168, 169, 173, 174, 175,
  178
Aron, Arthur, 104, 211, 212, 213
Aron, Elaine, 104
arousal, "misattribution of," 213
artha (work and finance), 126, 127

ashrams, 3, 8–9, 17, 46, 100–101,
  108–9, 117, 247
  definition of, 5–6
  see also Brahmacharya; Grhastha;
  Sannyasa; Vanaprastha
Atharva Veda, 38
attachment, 80, 81
  see also bonding; connection
attraction, 1, 7, 33, 34–35, 63, 98, 207
  first impressions and, 51
  "frustration," 56
  as phase one of love, 81–88, 167
  six opulences and, 60, 61, 62–64, 65
attractiveness stereotype, 60

Barkley, Russell, 253
Barrett, Lisa Feldman, 36
BBC.com, 256
Beyoncé, 60
Bhagavad Gita, 33, 60, 61, 69, 168,
  169, 173, 174, 175, 178, 225,
  236, 251, 252
Bhakti scripture, 82, 110
  stages of love in, 79–80
blowout fights, 169, 179, 221
Blue, Rora, 54

Blueboard, 259
Bobby, Lisa Marie, 213
Bollywood movies, 52
bonding, 90, 212
    oxytocin and, 59–60
    see also connection; intimacy
boundaries, setting of, 90
Brach, Tara, 232
Brahmacharya (first ashram:
    preparing for love), 6, 8, 13–73,
    106
    karma and learning from past
        mistakes in, see karma,
        relationship
    solitude in, see solitude
brain, 45
    breakups and responses in,
        224–25, 229
    and capacity to handle limited
        sized social groups, 256
    "frustration attraction" and, 56
    oxytocin and, 59–60, 224
    self-control and, 54
    service to others and, 250
    smiling and, 262, 263
    three drives of love in, 81
Brand, Russell, 64
breakups, 4, 7, 8, 35, 38, 199,
    224–40
    abusive partners and, 124, 201,
        202
    brain's responses to, 224–25, 229
    closure after, 229, 230–31
    dating after, 237–39
    declining intimacy as cause of,
        207–8
    and determining if issue is deal-
        breaker, 197–98, 215, 217–19,
        224

fear of, 202–3
    healing after, 9, 225–26, 227, 228,
        229–32, 235–37, 241–42
    infidelity and, 203–5
    initiating of, 226–28
    learning from, 231, 232–34, 236
    loss of interest as cause in, 206–7
    love letter to self after, 241–42
    redirecting negative thoughts after,
        235–37
    revenge impulse in, 228–29
    support systems in, 227, 238
Brides, 10
Brokeback Mountain (film), 53
Buddha, 111, 128
Buddhism, Buddhists, 34, 100, 108,
    111, 117, 232, 260, 267
Buddhist Society of America, 111
Bureau of Labor Statistics, 144, 263
Burrow, Anthony, 127, 128

Cacioppo, John, 88
California, University of, at Los
    Angeles, 127
Cambridge Buddhist Association,
    108
caregivers, in relationships, 57, 58
Cast Away (film), 17
Celts, ancient, 265
The Chase (dating type), 56
cheating, 203–5, 226, 229
Chen, Nathan, 118
Chödrön, Pema, 232–33
Cinderella (film), 53
closure, after breakups, 229, 230–31
coaches, coaching, 31
    Genius, 295–96
    life, 296
Cole, Steven, 239–40

commitment, 3, 8, 78, 99
conversations on, 92–93
dating partners with no interest in,
2, 44, 59, 60
to resolving conflict, 194, 195
communication, 79, 114–15, 197,
203
apologies and, 178–79, 193, 195–97
in conflict resolution, 170–71,
178–79, 186, 189–92, 193, 195,
202, 219, 220, 221, 222
of constructive criticism, 115–16
declarations of love in, 3, 8, 77–78,
79
deep conversations in, 82–83, 84,
85–87, 208, 209
in initiating breakups, 226–27
lack of, as leading to breakups,
206–7
listening and responding effectively
in, 119–21
love letter to partner and, 161–62
nurturing intimacy with, 208, 209
in pursuit of purpose, 138,
143–44, 146, 148, 149–50, 152,
153, 154, 155, 156–57, 159
on relationship pace and
commitment, 92–93
community, 249, 252
helping difficult family members
find love in, 255–56
service to others in, 125, 126, 211,
239–40, 249–50, 261–62, 263,
265
as support system in personal
growth, 31
workplace as, 258
compassion, 6, 16, 44, 214, 227,
240, 245, 262

for partner, 110, 114, 171, 176, 219
for strangers, 251–52
for those who have hurt you, 254,
261
compatibility, 75
confronting differences and
disappointments in, 93–95
deep conversations and, 82–83, 84,
85–87
false expectations and, 88–89
goals and, 87–88, 89
learning and growing with partners
in, see partners, partnership,
learning and growing with
meditation for, 163–64
personalities and, 83–85, 87
pursuit of purpose and, see purpose
setting rhythms and routines and,
89–92
three-date rule in determining of,
83–88
trust and, 95–98
values and, 85–87, 89
confidence, 47, 59, 109
solitude in gaining of, 22, 28–32,
254
conflict, 7, 8, 25, 47, 49, 155, 160,
165, 167–98, 199–200, 215
abuse vs., 172–73
apologies in, 178–79, 193, 195–97
benefits of fighting and, 169, 171,
220
blowout fights in, 169, 179, 221
choosing words carefully in,
189–92, 193
determining if issue is deal-breaker
in, 197–98, 215, 217–19, 224
diagnosing of core problem in,
179–81, 193

conflict (*cont.*)
   discussing complex issues in,
      191–92, 194, 198, 202
   fighting styles in, 181–84, 193
   infidelity and, 203–5
   path from intolerable issue to
      appreciation in resolving of,
      216–23
   picking time and place for, 185–88,
      193
   purifying of ego in, 175–79
   resolving of, as a team, 169–71,
      175, 178, 184–94, 198
   in service to others, 262
   in struggle and growth phase,
      93–95, 104
   third-party mediators in resolving
      of, 178, 179, 194, 204
   three layers of, 180–81
   three types of arguments in,
      173–74, 175, 177, 179; *see also*
      productive arguments
   see also breakups
connection, 37, 38, 81, 89, 226
   attraction opulences in inhibiting
      of, 63
   through conflict resolution, 176, 220
   deep conversations in forging of,
      82–83, 84, 85–87, 208, 209
   with Earth, 264–65
   meditation for, 269–71
   service to others and, 248, 249, 251
   social, 126, 127
   with spirit, 126, 127
   with strangers, 262–63
   with work colleagues, 260
   see also bonding; compatibility;
      intimacy
constructive criticism, 115–16, 201

context effect, 51
controlling, of partners:
   by abusive partners, 201
   imposed timelines as form of, 114
   supporting vs., 108–9, 114, 148
Cordell, Joseph E., 206
Covey, Stephen, 119
critical feedback, 115
criticism, 115–16, 117, 123, 149–50,
   201
Csikszentmihalyi, Mihaly, 21–22

daily trust, 97–98
Dalai Lama, 100
dambha asuyadhi muktam, 108
danta, 119
dating:
   after breakups, 237–39
   online, 5, 63, 64, 88
dayalum, 110
deal-breakers, 197–98
   abuse as, 124, 200–3
   determining if issue is, 198, 215,
      217–19, 224
Dean, Jeremy, 101
De Beers, 52
decision-making:
   abusive partners interfering with,
      201
   energies and, 61–62
   karma and, 38–39, 40, 41–42, 44,
      55, 56, 61–62
   oxytocin and, 59–60
   solitude in creating space between
      sensory stimulation and, 33–34,
      35
   values and, 23, 25, 96
   in whether to leave relationship,
      202, 203, 205, 215, 217–19

deep conversations, 82–83, 84, 85–87, 208, 209
dependency, 35, 36, 37, 45, 58, 129
dependents, in relationship roles, 58–59
Desika, Vedanta, 108
desire, 34–35, 60, 79
  see also attraction
deVos, Kathleen Dahlen, 129
Dharamsala, 100
dharma (purpose), see purpose
Dimensions of Body Language (Westside Toastmasters organization), 187
dining alone, 20
DiPrimo, Lawrence, 263
dirgha bandhum, 112
discomfort, in solitude, 22, 25–28
divine, 79, 80, 169, 248, 249
Doctor Strange (film), 109
dopamine, 81
dreams, as phase two of love, 88–93
Dunbar, Robin, 256
Duryodhana, 173, 174
Dutton, Don, 212, 213
Dweck, Carol, 115

Earth, connecting with, 264–65
Easwaran, Eknath, 69
ego, 9, 44, 57, 101, 102, 108, 118, 124, 248, 250, 251, 254
  in conflict, 169, 170, 174, 175–79, 192, 193
  purifying of, 175–79
  repairing of, 229
egocentric bias, 101
Einstein, Albert, 148
emotional abuse, 124, 200, 201
emotional trust, 96

empathy, 6, 16, 110, 171, 176, 187, 214, 219, 223, 227, 240, 262
  for strangers, 251–52
engagement rings, 9, 10, 52
eudaimonia, 127
expectations, 9, 17, 42, 78, 88, 90, 102, 110
  conflict and, 180
  false, 88–89
  parental, 48–49
experiences, shared and new, in nurturing intimacy, 210–14
experiments:
  in nurturing intimacy, 210, 211–14
  in pursuit of purpose, 131, 138–39, 140, 145, 146–47
exploding, as fighting style, 183, 184, 185

Face Value (Todorov), 51
fairy-tale love, 10–11, 80
false expectations, 88–89
false motivation, 149
false promises, 220
F-boys, F-girls (dating types), 59–60
feedback loops, 122
fights, fighting, see conflict
fight styles, 181–84, 193
Firestone, Lisa, 88
first dates, 83–85
first impressions, 51
first loves, 54, 65–66
Fisher, Helen, 56, 224
500 Days of Summer (film), 52
fixed mindset, 115
fixers, in relationship roles, 57, 58–59
Flow: The Psychology of Optimal Experience (Csikszentmihalyi), 21–22

Formula One, 141–42
Forrest Gump (film), 51
four pursuits, in Vedas, 126–27
Francis, St., 110
Frank, Anne, 249
Froemke, Robert, 59
"frustration attraction," 56

General Theory of Love, A (Lewis,
    Amini, and Lannon), 45
Genius coaching, 295–96
Ghatourey, Ritu, 189
ghosting, 4, 77, 226
giving love, 247–66
    connecting with Earth and, 264–65
    conscious commitment of time in,
        256–58
    donating resources to organizations
        and, 263–64
    service to others in, 248, 249–50,
        261–62, 263, 265
    to closest friends and family,
        252–58
    to strangers, 262–64
    to toxic and difficult loved ones,
        253–56, 266
    to work colleagues, 258–60, 261
Glass, Shirley, 203–4
goals, 7, 22, 32, 83, 124, 129, 225, 226
    compatibility and, 87–88, 89
    in personal growth, 28–32
    shifting arguments to shared,
        170–71
    supporting of partner's, 110–12,
        114, 123
    see also purpose
Goats of Anarchy, 264
goodness (*sattva*), energy of, 62, 173,
    174, 177

Gottman, John, 60, 219–20
Gottman, Julie, 60
gratitude, 97, 98, 211
    expressing of, 122–23, 214
Greeks, ancient, types of love
    defined by, 2–3
Grhastha (second ashram: practicing
    love), 6–7, 8, 75–164
    defining love and compatibility in,
        see compatibility; love, defining
        of
    learning and growing with partner
        in, *see* partners, partnership,
        growing and learning with
    purpose and, *see* purpose
Growing Self Counseling &
    Coaching, 213
growth, 99, 124, 160
    goals in personal, 28–32
    as phase three of love, 93–95, 104
    in relationships, *see* partners,
        partnership, growing and
        learning with
    through struggle, 93–95, 104,
        140–41
Guru and Disciple Book, The
    (Kripamoya das), 108
gurus, 44, 100–101, 103, 104, 108–9,
    110, 111, 112, 114, 115, 117,
    124
    becoming effective, for partners,
        108–16
    partners as, 117–23

Hafiz, 15
Halai'i Volcanoes National Park, 264
halo effect, 60
Hamilton, Lewis, 141–42
Hanks, Tom, 17, 51

Hanuman (monkey god), 110
Harding, M. Esther, 167
Hattar, Samer, 265
healing, 7, 8, 44, 66, 165
    after breakups, 9, 225–26, 227,
        229, 229–32, 235–37, 241–42
    after infidelity, 204, 205
    love letter to self in, 241–42
    meditation for, 243–44
Healing Power of Doing Good, The
    (Luks), 249–50
hedonia, 127
"helper's high," 249, 250
hiding, as fighting style, 183, 184
High-Touch Communications Inc., 90
hiking alone, 20
Hinduism, 3, 44, 79, 125
    see also Vedas
Hindu monks, 3, 4, 5, 17, 46, 94,
        101, 102, 103, 108–9, 211, 239
Hough, Marilyn, 207
Huberman, Andrew, 265
HuffPost, 129
humility, 118–19, 173
Hutt, Jim, 204

ignorance (tamas), energy of, 61–62,
        173, 174, 175, 177
I Know What You Did Last Summer
    (film), 55
impressions (samskaras), 39, 40–42,
        69
    context effect and, 51
    first loves in, 54, 65–66
    halo effect and, 60
    parental gifts and gaps in, 44–50,
        65, 66
    popular media in planting of,
        50–53, 65

unearthing of, 42–44
unreliability of first, 51
infatuation, 54
infidelity, 203–5, 226, 229
inner conflicts, 180, 181
insecurity, 15, 16, 21, 40, 43, 66, 68,
        154, 254
    conflict resulting from, 179, 180, 181
Instagram, 82, 236, 257, 264
intelligence, three levels of, 54
interpersonal conflicts, 180–81
intimacy, 228
    loss of, 207–8
    nurturing of, 9, 208–15
    see also connection
intolerable issues, 217–19, 221, 223
It's a Wonderful Life (film), 53

James, Lily, 53
Jay Shetty Certification School, 296
Jerry Maguire (film), 53
judging, judgment, 65, 237
    avoiding, with partners, 102, 110,
        115, 124, 148, 149–50, 220
    difficult people and, 256
    oxytocin as affecting, 59–60
    see also decision-making

Kabir Das, 247, 249
Kahlo, Frida, 32
kama (pleasure and connection), 75,
        126, 127
kama/maitri (loving others), 75
karma, 226, 228–29
    definition of, 38–39
    intertwining of, 123–24
karma, relationship, 38–69, 229
    attracting what you use to impress
        in, 62–65

karma, relationship (*cont.*)
  breakups in learning how to
    change, 231–34
  cycle of, 39–44, 54–55
  first giving self what you want to
    receive and, 65–68
  five dating "types" and lessons in,
    55–61
  impressions in, *see* impressions
  parental gifts and gaps in
    influencing of, 44–50, 65, 66
  reflecting and learning from past
    in, 61–62
karuna (compassion), *see* compassion
Khan, Sal, 131, 147
Khan Academy, 131, 147
The Knot (wedding site), 10
Kripamoya das, 108, 109, 112, 114,
  117, 118, 119, 122
Krishna, 33, 168, 169, 173, 175,
  178, 179
Krishnananda Swami, 180
krita-vid-sisya (grateful for knowledge),
  122

Lannon, Richard, 45
Lauricella, Leanne, 264
Lawson, Annette, 205
learning:
  from breakups, 231, 232–34, 236
  helping partner in, 145–46, 157
  in pursuit of purpose, 131, 132–36,
    137, 139, 140, 157
  see also partners, partnership,
    learning and growing with
Lee, Phillip, 197
letters:
  of apology, 196–97
  of appreciation, 256

  to help you heal, 241–42
  to partner, 161–62
  in resolving conflict, 186
  to world, 267–68
  to yourself, 70–71
Lewis, Thomas, 45
life coaches, 296
Little Free Libraries, 263
Little Free Pantries, 263
Lomas, Tim, 2–3
loneliness, 9, 62, 239, 240
  fear of, 15–17, 202, 203, 235
  path to solitude from, 21–32, 69
Lord Ram, 110
love:
  advice on, 4–5
  ancient Greeks on types of, 2–3
  compatibility in, *see* compatibility
  declarations of, 3, 8, 77–78, 79
  defining of, 7, 77–99
  expansion of, 7, 8, 240; *see also*
    giving love
  four ashrams of, 5–9; *see also*
    Brahmacharya; Grhastha;
    Sannyasa; Vanaprastha
  in popular media, 3, 9, 10–11, 34,
    42, 50–53, 55, 60
love, four phases of, 79–98
  attraction, 81–88, 167
  dreams, 88–93
  struggle and growth, 93–95, 104
  trust, 95–98
love letters:
  to help you heal, 241–42
  to partner, 161–62
  to world, 267–68
  to yourself, 70–71
love stories, 2, 10, 51
loving core, 250–51

Luks, Allan, 249–50
lust, 2, 81, 250
Mahabharata, 33
Markman, Art, 187
Markman, Howard, 201
marriage proposals, 9–10, 11, 52
Match.com, 56
Matha Pitha Guru Deivam, 44, 45
maya (illusion), 239
media:
  impressions formed from, 50–53,
    65
  love as portrayed in, 3, 9, 10–11,
    34, 42, 50–53, 55, 60
meditation retreats, 17
meditations, 209, 295
  for compatibility, 163–64
  for connection, 269–70
  for healing, 243–44
  for solitude, 72–73
  younger-self, 42–44
Mehl, Matthias, 82
Mellors, Coco, 44
memories, childhood, 48
mental abuse, 124
mental trust, 96
mentors, 80
  giving love to colleagues by acting
    as, 258–59
  in pursuing purpose, 134–35, 140,
    146, 151
Meyers, Seth, 90–91
Mindset (Dweck), 115
"misattribution of arousal," 213
mistakes:
  acknowledging of, 161–62,
    178–79, 195, 196
  learning from, 6, *see also* karma,
    relationship

modeling, of relationships, 41, 45,
    47, 49, 66
"Modern Love" column, 44
moksha (connecting with spirit), 126,
    127
monks, 3, 4, 5, 17, 46, 94, 101, 102,
    103, 108–9, 111, 211, 239
movies, 17
  going alone to, 20
  love in, 3, 9, 10–11, 34, 42, 50–53, 65

Naess, Arne, 248
National Domestic Violence Hotline,
    172, 200, 201
National Institutes of Health, NIMH,
    Section on Light and Circadian
    Rhythms at, 265
Native Americans, 264
Native Hawaiians, 264
Neem Karoli Baba, 100
Neumann, Erich, 265
New York Times, 44, 88, 136, 144
norepinephrine, 81
North Carolina, University of, 127
Notarius, Clifford, 201
NOT "Just Friends" (Glass), 203–4

online dating, 5, 63, 64, 88
opulences, 60, 61, 62–64, 65, 88, 127
Opulent One (dating type), 60–61
organizations, giving resources to,
    263–64
Ostrander, Noam, 185
Overwhelmed (Schulte), 136
oxytocin, 59–60, 211, 224

parental gifts and gaps, 44–50, 65, 66
  filling your own, 67–68
  identifying of, 48–50

partners, partnership:
  assessing potential for, 105–7
  avoiding criticism, judgment, or
    abuse in, 114–16, 123, 124
  becoming a better guru in, 108–16
  becoming a better student in,
    117–24
  in conflict resolution, 176, 178,
    195, 223
  identifying learning styles in,
    112–14
  learning and growing with, 7, 59,
    100–24, 160, 207, 211, 214
  listening and responding effectively
    in, 119–21
  maintaining sense of self in,
    123–24, 129
  nurturing intimacy by, 208–9
  open-mind and curiosity in,
    117–18
  practicing humility in, 118–19
  pursuit of purpose in, see purpose
  setting a good example in, 109–10,
    122
  showing appreciation in, 122–23
  supporting of goals in, 110–12,
    114, 123
passion, 2, 3, 81
  energy of, 62, 173, 174, 175, 177
  purpose as, see purpose
patience, 6, 16, 58, 102, 114, 171, 218
  with partner's struggles, 148–50,
    222, 223
  solitude in learning of, 34, 35, 37
Pennsylvania, University of, 51
personalities, 22, 32, 51, 83, 124
  compatibility and, 83–85, 87
Petriglieri, Jennifer, 158
Pew Research Center, 144

physical abuse, 124, 172, 200, 201
physical trust, 96
Pogosyan, Marianna, 248
pointless arguments, 174, 175, 177,
  179
possessiveness, 40
power arguments, 174, 175, 177, 179
prefrontal cortex, 54
presence, in solitude, 22
productive arguments, 174, 175–94
  authentic apologies in, 178–79,
    195–97
  choosing words carefully in,
    189–92
  diagnosing of core problem in,
    179–81, 193
  identifying fighting styles in,
    181–84, 193
  picking time and place for, 185–88,
    193
  purifying of ego in, 175–79
The Project (dating type), 56–57
prosocial behavior, 248
Psychology Today, 90
Purdue University, 262
purpose (dharma), 125–60, 209, 211,
    214, 225, 238, 239, 251
  adjusting imbalance in, 156–57
  benefits of having sense of,
    127–28, 129
  celebrating successes in, 141–42,
    150–51
  communication with partner in
    pursuit of, 138, 143–44, 146,
    148, 149–50, 152, 153, 154,
    155, 156–57, 159
  engaging partner in your pursuit
    of, 137, 138, 139, 140, 141,
    143–44

facing challenges in, 140–41,
148–50
finding time for, 136–38
focusing on the process in, 142
giving partner time and space for,
147–48, 151
performing of, 131, 140
pursuing and prioritizing of your
own, 127–29, 131–44
strategies for managing colliding
pursuits of, 152–59
supporting partner in their pursuit
of, 141, 144–51
purpose (*dharma*), pyramid of,
131–42, 144–45
experimenting in, 131, 138–39,
140, 145, 146–47
learning in, 131, 132–36, 137,
139, 140, 145–46, 157
struggle in, 131, 140–41, 148–50
thriving in, 131, 140
winning in, 131, 141–42, 150–51

Radhanath Swami, 101, 108
Radhi (author's wife), 9–10, 11, 46,
52, 64, 90, 94, 103, 109, 114,
145, 181–82, 209, 211, 212, 264
radius of respect, 253, 254, 256
rajas (passion and impulsivity),
energy of, 173, 174, 175, 177
see also passion
Ramakrishna, 100
Rebel (dating type), 55–56
rebound relationships, 204–5
red flags, 90, 237
relationship roles, 57–59
resentment, 57, 128–29, 130, 153,
158, 174, 254, 260
respect, radius of, 253, 254, 256

revenge, 228–29
rhythms and routines, setting of,
89–92
Rigdzin Shikpo, 34–35
Roosevelt, Eleanor, 208
Rudolph, Diane, 197
Rumi, 199, 252

Saint-Expuréry, Antoine de, 100
samskaras, see impressions
Sannyasa (fourth ashram: perfecting
love), 7, 8, 245–66
expansion and giving of love in, *see*
giving love
Sanskrit language, 3, 5, 44, 108
sattva (goodness), energy of, 62, 173,
174, 177
satya vacam, 114
Schulte, Brigid, 136, 137
second dates, 85–87
self, sense of, 248
maintaining of, 123–24, 129
self-awareness, 106, 107, 211
love letter to self as tool of, 70–71
solitude in gaining of, 23–25,
26–27, 28, 32–34, 35, 37, 129
self-control, 34–35, 37, 54, 102
self-disclosure, 83, 86
self-doubt, 9, 43, 154, 216, 234
self-esteem, 28, 32, 47, 48, 233
sense of purpose and, 128
see also confidence
"self-expansion theory," 104
self-gratitude, meditation for, 72–73
self-love, 3, 13, 16, 37, 47, 103
meditation for, 72–73
self-reflection, 94, 101
after breakups, 232–33
see also solitude

self-regulation, 35–37

serotonin, 81

service, to others, 125, 126, 211, 239–40, 261–62, 263, 266
  connection to humanity through, 248, 249
  happiness through, 249–50
  see also volunteering

settling, in relationships, 15, 16

7 Habits of Highly Effective People, The (Covey), 119

sex, 63, 90
  abuse vs. conflict in, 173, 201
  judgment affected by, 59–60

Shakespeare, William, 243

Shaku, Soyen, 111

shoshin ("beginner's mind"), 117

small talk, 82, 84

smiling, 262–63

social conflicts, 180

social media, 24, 63, 82, 127–28, 227, 228, 236, 257

Society for Personality and Social Psychology, 171

Sokei-an Shigetsu Sasaki, 111

solitude, 6, 8, 13, 69, 101, 106, 107, 124, 129, 224, 225, 237, 238
  baseline audit of, 17, 18–20
  benefits and rewards of, 21–22, 32–37
  confidence and personal growth in, 28–32, 254
  discomfort in, 22, 25–28
  learning self-regulation and whole self in, 35–37
  making use of time alone in, 26–27, 28
  mastering the senses in, 33, 35
  meditation for, 72–73

path from loneliness to, 21–32, 69
  self-awareness gained in, 23–25, 26–27, 28, 32–34, 37, 129
  self-control and patience learned in, 34–35, 37

solo audits, 18–20

songs, love, 3, 10–11, 50, 52, 53, 60

Sons of Anarchy (TV show), 264

spare time worksheet, 137–38

speed dating, 51

sthira dhiyam, 109

strangers, giving love to, 262–64

struggle, 168
  in growth phase of love, 93–95, 104
  in pursuit of purpose, 131, 140–41, 148–50
  see also conflict

sunlight, mood influenced by, 265

sun salutations (*Surya Namaskar*), 265

Superbad (film), 17

supporters, in relationship roles, 58–59

support systems, 31, 106, 215
  in breakups, 227, 238
  building of, 216
  online communities as, 202–3
  parents as, 49–50

Surya Namaskar (sun salutations), 265

Suzuki, Shunryu, 108, 117

Taibbi, Robert, 204–5

tamas (ignorance), energy of, 61–62, 173, 174, 175, 177

tattva bodha abhilasi ("eagerness to learn"), 117

Taylor, Samantha, 77–78

therapy, therapists, 36, 178, 179, 194, 204, 207, 222

Think Like a Monk (Shetty), 33, 173
three-date rule, 85–88
thriving, in performing your purpose, 131, 140
Tillich, Paul, 21
Time, 185
time-outs, in fights, 186
time trades, 159
time-use surveys, 136–38
Todorov, Alexander, 51
tolerable issues, 217, 219, 222
Toronto, University of, 15
transformation, three c's of, 31
travel, 24, 26–27, 210–11
trust, 83, 99, 103, 109, 176, 217, 258
  building of, 82–83, 84
  infidelity and, 203, 204
  oxytocin and, 59–60
  as phase four of love, 95–98

understanding:
  for friends and family, 252
  on path to elevation, 217, 219–21, 222, 223
  for work colleagues, 259–60
Urban Dictionary, 17
U.S. Travel Association, 210–11

validation, seeking of, 45–46, 50, 59, 154, 176
values, 7, 9, 22, 34, 78, 83, 96, 103, 110, 124, 127, 136, 137, 168, 225, 226
  compatibility and, 85–87, 89
  getting to know your own, 23–25, 32
Vanaprastha (third ashram: protecting love), 7, 8, 165–244
  resolving conflict in, *see* conflict

Vedas, 3–4, 5, 33, 38, 123, 180, 248, 250, 256
  four ashrams of, 5–9, 100; *see also* Brahmacharya; Grhastha; Sannyasa; Vanaprastha
  four pursuits of, 126–27
  three levels of intelligence in, 54
Vedic weddings, 144
venting, as fighting style, 182–83, 184
verbal abuse, 200, 201
Viscott, David, 125
volunteering, 27, 125, 211, 239–40, 249–50
  see also service, to others
vulnerability, 44, 149, 162, 258, 261
  connection and intimacy fostered by, 82–83, 84, 86, 209, 211–12

WalletHub, 211
Washington Post, 53
weddings, 10, 144
Westside Toastmasters organization, 187
Why Him? Why Her? (Fisher), 56
Winch, Guy, 229
work colleagues, appreciation for, 258–60, 261
Work.com, 259

Yale University, 51
Yip, Kevin, 259
yogis, 265
younger-self meditation, 42–44

Zaki, Jamil, 251–52
Zen Buddhism, 100, 108, 111, 117, 260, 267